Anger Management
FOR
DUMMIES®

Anger Management FOR DUMMIES®

By Gillian Bloxham and W. Doyle Gentry, PhD

WILEY

A John Wiley and Sons, Ltd, Publication

Anger Management For Dummies®

Published by
John Wiley & Sons, Ltd
The Atrium
Southern Gate
Chichester
West Sussex
PO19 8SQ
England

Email (for orders and customer service enquires): cs-books@wiley.co.uk

Visit our Home Page on www.wiley.com

Copyright © 2010 John Wiley & Sons, Ltd, Chichester, West Sussex, England

Published by John Wiley & Sons, Ltd, Chichester, West Sussex

For general information on our other products and services, please contact our Customer Care Department within the US at 877-762-2974, outside the US at 317-572-3993, or fax 317-572-4002.

For technical support, please visit www.wiley.com/techsupport.

Wiley also publishes its books in a variety of electronic formats. Some content that appears in print may not be available in electronic books.

British Library Cataloguing in Publication Data: A catalogue record for this book is available from the British Library

ISBN: 978-0-470-68216-6

Printed and bound in Great Britain by Bell and Bain Ltd, Glasgow

10 9 8 7 6 5 4 3 2 1

WILEY

About the Authors

Gillian Bloxham is a Chartered Clinical Psychologist and Associate Fellow of the British Psychological Society. In her career, Gill has worked with adults and adolescents in GP practices, NHS clinics and hospital units, and also within the criminal justice system and secure mental health services. Her interests in anger management, self-harm and risk management arise from working with adults with complex psychological difficulties, including those with interpersonal difficulties and those surviving childhood trauma. Gill has also been involved in developing and delivering training and workshops for many years, delivering psychological topics intended to be accessible to everyone.

W. Doyle Gentry, PhD, is a clinical psychologist and Director of the Institute for Anger-Free Living in Lynchburg, Virginia. He is a Fellow in the American Psychological Association and was the Founding Editor of the *Journal of Behavioral Medicine*. In Dr Gentry's four-decade career as a scientist-practitioner, he has authored over 100 publications, including eight books, and is a pioneer in the fields of health psychology, behavioural medicine and anger management. He has previously served on the faculty of Duke University Medical Center and the University of Texas Medical Branch, Galveston. Gentry has conducted training seminars for lay and professional audiences throughout the United States, Canada and Europe. He has also served as a consultant to major industry, where he specialises in conflict management, team building and health promotion.

Dedication

From Gill: This book is for Nige Coles, warrior and true friend. Anger is an energy.

Authors' Acknowledgments

From Gill: My warm thanks to Jill Patel, currently Director at Hillingdon Mind.

My thanks are also due to the many people who have shared their struggles with anger with me, and to Elaine, Mark and Neil for their steadfast support.

From W. Doyle Gentry: I would like to thank a number of 'teammates' who made writing this book both possible and enjoyable. First, I am indebted – once again – to my agent, Denise Marcil, and her delightful associate, Maura Kye, for all their efforts on my behalf. I was well represented!

The folks at Wiley were fantastic. I deeply appreciate their professionalism, expertise, encouragement, and, most of all, patience during both the acquisition and editorial phases of the project. The energy and passion associated with the *For Dummies* series is, indeed, infectious.

And, as always, I want to thank my loving family – Catherine, Rebecca and Chris – for yet another show of support for my life's work. They never disappoint.

Basically, we are all dummies when it comes to anger management – a field that remains a work in progress. I learn more every day about ways to harness this complicated and, at times, troublesome emotion, and being able to share this education with my readers is a pleasure. If this book changes the life of a single person for the better, then I am satisfied that the hard work that went into it was worthwhile.

Publisher's Acknowledgments

We're proud of this book; please send us your comments through our Dummies online registration form located at www.dummies.com/register/.

Some of the people who helped bring this book to market include the following:

*Acquisitions, Editorial and
Media Development*

Project Editor: Rachael Chilvers

Content Editor: Jo Theedom

Commissioning Editor: David Palmer

Development Editor: Charlie Wilson

Editorial Assitant: Ben Kemble

Production Manager: Daniel Mersey

Proofreader: Jamie Brind

Cover Photos: © Mark Sykes/Alamy

Cartoons: Ed McLachlan

Composition Services

Project Coordinator: Lynsey Stanford

Layout and Graphics: Ashley Chamberlain,
Tim Detrick, Christine Williams

Proofreader: Lauren Mandelbaum

Indexer: Ty Koontz

Contents at a Glance

Table of Contents

Introduction

A nger is a natural part of life – one of the rainbow of emotions all
humans feel and recognise. Anger is also a reaction that's built into
your nervous system – a survival mechanism intended to keep you safe. No
one chooses to be angry. In fact, anger is one of the first emotions mothers
recognise in their newborn infants. So, it's never too early to start anger
management.

On the other hand, the way you manage anger is down to you – your responsibility and your choice. You don't have to be a victim of your own anger –
you can choose how you respond when the world doesn't treat you the way
you want it to. You have just as much choice about how you express your
anger as you do about what colour shirt you wear, what you eat for breakfast, or who you choose to be friends with. You also have a choice about
how much of yesterday's anger you carry into the future and how you react
to anger you may feel tomorrow. If we didn't believe that, we wouldn't have
spent so many years of our professional lives working with people making
those choices!

No one is exempt from problematic anger. Anger is a very democratic emotion – it causes problems for men and women, kids and the elderly, rich
and poor, educated and uneducated, people of all cultures and ethnic backgrounds, believers and nonbelievers. Tens of millions of human beings need-
lessly suffer from what we call *unhealthy anger* – anger that literally destroys
happiness in life – each and every day of their lives.

Anger isn't something that can – or should be – cured. But you have to
manage it well – at home, at work, and in your most intimate relationships – if
you want to benefit from it. *Anger Management For Dummies* tells you how to
manage your anger by focusing on the positive – how to get a good night's
sleep, how to change your perspective on life, why owning up is better for
you than ranting, how to turn conflicts into challenges, and much more.
Anger management has moved far beyond the simplistic (if well-intentioned)
advice of years ago to 'count to ten' or take a couple of deep breaths every
time you get angry – and that's good news!

About This Book

How do you know when you have too much anger? Do you determine that for
yourself, or do you let other people make that call? If you're not physically
aggressive – physically hurting other people or punching holes in

walls – does that mean you're not angry? Does it really help to rant, to get things off your chest, or are you better off keeping your mouth shut in order to keep the peace? Can angry people really change, or do they have to go through life suffering because that's just the way they are? And what should you do if you're on the wrong end of someone else's anger? These are all important questions that *Anger Management For Dummies* answers for you.

When we wrote *Anger Management For Dummies,* we had four basic goals in mind:

- ✔ **We wanted to show you that anger is more than a four-letter word – it's an extremely complex emotion that has meaning well beyond the crude and hurtful words people use to express it.** Understanding all about anger is the foundation of anger management.

- ✔ **We wanted to illustrate all the various ways that anger can – and does – negatively affect your life when it occurs too frequently, is too intense and lasts too long.**

- ✔ **We wanted to explain that anger management occurs in three distinct time frames – yesterday, today and tomorrow.** The strategies we propose to manage anger will, of course, differ depending on whether you're trying to let go of some old anger, deal with the anger you face today, or prevent anger that you're otherwise likely to experience tomorrow.

- ✔ **We wanted to show you that managing anger is something that is entirely within your power – and not something you have to seek professional help for – if you're willing to make the necessary lifestyle changes outlined in this book.** It doesn't matter how old you are or how long anger has been a part of your life – it's never too late to manage your anger better.

Anger Management For Dummies isn't one of those 12-step books where you have to read (and follow the advice) of Step 1 before you can proceed to Step 2, and so on. It's a resource book containing all the information we have at our disposal after our combined experience of six decades of combined clinical practice with clients and scientific research on anger management. You don't have to start with Chapter 1 and read straight through to the end of the book. You can look at the Table of Contents, find something that interests you, and start there. You may want to focus on the area in which you're having the most trouble controlling your temper – with family, for example. Or you may want to head straight for a chapter on managing stress (one of the most common causes of anger). We're not even suggesting that you read the whole book – that's up to you.

Conventions Used in This Book

We didn't want *Anger Management For Dummies* to be yet another book written by psychologists for psychologists. This book is for everyone who wants to lead their life without anger interfering, so we've eliminated all the professional jargon, and used terms and ideas that we know work with the many different people we've met.

We've also tried to make reading *Anger Management For Dummies* an enjoyable experience. Just because anger is a serious topic doesn't mean that you need to approach it with a deadly serious attitude. If you can enjoy learning something new, you're more likely to remember it, and to follow it through!

Most important, *Anger Management For Dummies* is full of stories about people just like you, who have successfully overcome their difficulties with anger – even a lifetime of anger. The people you'll read about are combinations of many relatives, friends and clients we've known over the years, who've taught us what truly works for healthy anger management. The quotations and dialogues included in these stories are based on our memories of conversations we have had.

You don't have to know psychology to understand this book. But we do use a couple of conventions:

  ✔ When we introduce a new term, we put the word in *italics* and define it shortly thereafter (usually in parentheses).

  ✔ When we list an email or web address, we use a special font called `monofont` so you know exactly what to type.

And that's it!

Foolish Assumptions

We made a few assumptions about you when writing this book:

  ✔ **You may or may not have a problem with anger – but if you don't have a problem with anger yourself, you know or love someone who does.** If you didn't buy this book for yourself, you bought it for your husband, wife, brother, sister, son, daughter, father, mother, friend or work colleague. Or one of those people bought it for you.

  ✔ **You don't want to know everything there is to know about anger – you just want to know what you need to know to manage anger effectively.** Scientists have studied anger for years, but you won't find a list of scientific jargon in these pages. We focus on proven strategies to help you manage your anger, and that's it.

    ✔ **You're probably looking for useful information and hints about how to change.** We've laid this book out to make it simple to find what you're interested in, using the understanding we've developed through working with people facing exactly the same challenges. All of the information and examples you see have already worked for others – we hope you'll find in the following chapters those that work for you.

How This Book Is Organised

We've organised *Anger Management For Dummies* into six parts and 23 chapters. You can also find an online Cheat Sheet for quick prompts to deal with focused problems (see inside the front cover for the web address). Here's what you can find in each part.

Part I: The Basics of Anger

In the first three chapters, we acquaint you with some basic facts about anger as a natural human emotion, the role that emotions like anger play in your life, and help you decide whether anger is poisoning your health, work or relationships. Chapter 2 shows you how to measure your anger and distinguish between *healthy* and *unhealthy or destructive* anger. We want you to be free to decide how to respond to anger (and situations that trigger it) instead of just reacting in a knee-jerk way that almost always takes you somewhere you really don't want to go.

Part II: Dealing with Past and Present Anger

In this part, we help you tackle the challenge of managing anger *in the moment.* Most people get into trouble simply because they don't know what to else to do – apart from what they already know – when they begin to feel anger build up. In effect, it's what you don't know (for example, that all emotions are temporary) and don't do (for example, let the other person have the last word) that leads to anger mismanagement. Chapter 6 offers you a structured, multistep, *effective* method you can use to keep your cool.

If you're like either of us, you have found yourself getting much angrier than the situation you're in requires. You're left with the question: 'What on earth got into me?' Chances are you were influenced by some old anger you were unaware of at that moment that was just waiting for an opportunity to express itself. In Chapter 7 we offer some tips on how not to let today's anger become tomorrow's anger – strategies such as 'time's up!' and the ten-minute rant. In Chapter 8 we get into the details of achieving forgiveness as applied to anger management. We're not looking at forgiveness in a spiritual sense here, but rather as a tool for letting go of anger from the past that is no longer helpful and is long past its sell by date.

Part III: Preventing Future Anger

Chapters 9 to 12 show you ways to deal with anger *before it happens*. Stepping in early is a new approach – most anger-management strategies are designed to work after the situation has started to get out of hand. We believe it's more difficult (and sometimes feels impossible) to use the techniques and ideas for healthy anger management when you're in the middle of a rage! Preventing anger can be the most exciting aspect of anger management. In this part, we also talk about mental outlook (attitudes you learn and carry with you in your life), which influence what you expect and will tolerate from the world around you, why it's essential to stop disguising your anger and just say what you feel (but politely!), how to own up to yourself about your anger, how to become the type of person who doesn't trigger so much anger, and – perhaps most important – how you can use your anger positively. If you can make anger a positive influence, you no longer have to attempt to avoid it.

Part IV: Lifestyle Changes That Improve Your Anger and Health

We both believe that living a healthy lifestyle enormously improves your chances of not getting angry. Why? Because many hundreds of people that we've met and worked with, and tens of thousands of others, know through experience that treating your body well helps to steady body-based emotions like anger. In this part, we show you how unhealthy anger is a by-product of an unhealthy lifestyle. If you're on the verge of stress burnout, if your daily diet consists mainly of caffeine and alcohol (with some nicotine thrown in for good measure!), if your life is all out of balance (too much work, too little play), if you never get a good night's sleep, if you carry the whole world on your shoulders (unsupported by others or by spiritual faith), and if you're utterly depressed or feel hopeless, why on earth *wouldn't* you be angry? Change those things and you'll see some major changes in how angry you are.

Part V: Managing Anger in Relationships

Most of us sort our day-to-day lives into areas where we spend the most time – work, home and in intimate relationships. These two chapters are designed to address anger-management issues that are situation specific – what works at work doesn't necessarily work at home. The benefit of having an honest and personal discussion with family in an effort to reduce conflict may not be useful in a meeting with your bosses. Both chapters in this section offer a set of strategies aimed at turning hostility into harmony.

Part VI: The Part of Tens

If you're looking for quick ideas about how to raise a child with healthy anger balance, or you want some easy-to-remember anger-freeing thoughts or actions, you can find them here.

Icons Used in This Book

Icons are those little pictures in the margins throughout this book, and they're there to draw your attention to certain kinds of information:

We highlight case studies with this icon, as personal stories are often really useful for illustrating a point. (We don't use real names (apart from our own) to protect our patients' identities.)

This icon alerts you to important ideas and concepts that you might want to remember and that you can use even when you don't have *Anger Management For Dummies* to hand.

Every once in a while, we talk about scientific research, as a lot of very useful knowledge about anger and human behaviour comes from psychological and biological research scientists. When we do, we mark the paragraph with this icon. You can read these paragraphs if you want, but the information they contain isn't essential to your understanding of the topic.

The Tip icon suggests practical how-to strategies for managing anger. You can even transfer the ones you find useful to a card to keep with you.

This icon appears when we have words of caution for you, or when we suggest you may need to seek professional help.

Where to Go from Here

Each part and chapter in this book is meant to stand alone in its discussion of anger management. Just choose a topic that interests you, and dive in.

If you do read *Anger Management For Dummies* thoroughly and you still find that you're struggling with anger, we suggest you seriously consider getting the help of a professional. There's no shame in this – seeking help for habits that cause difficulties is the most common reason to talk to someone independent. Anger management is a specialist field and you need to find someone who has qualifications and expertise in this area. If you're interested in a medical remedy for abnormal anger – one that focuses on prescribed medication – you need to find a psychiatrist (a qualified doctor who specialises in mental health) who specialises in this area. If you're more open to *psychotherapeutic strategies* (where change results from an interpersonal relationship between you and a therapist), look for a chartered clinical psychologist, cognitive therapist or mental health professional. Either way, be sure to get the help you need. A book like this wouldn't exist if you were the only person who feels this way!

Part I
The Basics of Anger

In this part . . .

We talk about why anger is a universal emotion and help you distinguish between an emotional *reaction* and an emotional *response*. We show you how to quantify just how angry you are by answering two simple questions: 'How often are you angry?' and 'How intense is your anger?' With the information we provide in this part, you don't have to be a rocket scientist to figure out if you suffer from harmful anger.

Finally, in this part, you can discover the many ways in which anger can poison your life – robbing you of energy, affecting your health and career and harming those you love. You may be surprised about what anger says about your life now and in the future.

Chapter 1

Anger: A Natural Human Emotion

· ·

In This Chapter

▶ Examining the myths about anger

▶ Understanding how emotions affect your life

▶ Enlisting support

▶ Noticing your progress

· ·

*W*hat do people all have in common – whatever their age, health, wealth or occupation? They all recognise an angry face when they see it. Anger – along with joy, fear, sadness and surprise – is a universal emotion. All cultures around the world see and show anger as an integral and normal part of daily life.

So if anger is completely normal, why pick this book up? Anger is a normal feeling, but it can become too strong, happen too often and start to have a negative impact on your life or the lives of those around you. Anger management is a life skill, simply like building in a volume control, allowing you to feel your natural emotions without being tripped up by them.

Anger is part of a basic survival mechanism of human beings. When faced with a threat, like other animals, humans either run away or attack – fear triggers a reaction to get you ready for 'fight' or 'flight', and in 'fight' mode anger is often the fuel behind that attack. Both are built in for your survival, but excessive anger can also have the opposite effect and lead to serious health problems, even an early death. As Chapter 3 explains, too much anger can cause health problems, make you vulnerable to accidents and lead you to take serious risks. Anger truly is a double-edged sword.

Dispelling Common Anger Myths

Before you can manage your own anger well, you need to know what anger is and isn't. Unfortunately, myths about anger seem to abound. Here are some of the myths we want to dispel right from the start:

- **Anger is bad.** Anger serves a variety of positive purposes when it comes to coping with stress. It motivates you, improves your communication with other people, promotes your self-esteem and defends you against threats. People like Gandhi and Martin Luther King were angry about injustice, but they turned that anger into social reform that changed the way people live and made the world a better place.

- **Anger is good.** When it leads to violence to others, property damage, verbal abuse, drug addiction, self-mutilation or any other destructive behaviour, anger is definitely not good. Living with angry feelings, either constant fury or hidden grudges, can also have a damaging effect on your long-term physical health (see Chapter 3).

- **Anger is only a problem when you openly express it.** As few as 10 per cent of people act out their feelings when they get angry. The other 90 per cent either suppress their anger ('I don't want to talk about it!') or repress their anger ('I'm not angry at all – really!'). People who express their anger may get everyone's attention (aggression); people who repress or suppress their anger cause equal distress and need anger management just as much (passive aggression).

- **The older you get, the more irritable you are.** It's the other way around – as people age, they report fewer negative emotions and greater emotional control. Psychologists and researchers have established that people – like wine and cheese – do tend to mellow with age.

- **Males are angrier than females.** If by angrier you mean how often people feel anger, it's simply not true that men are angrier than women. Surveys show that women get angry just as frequently as men – about once or twice a week on average. On the other hand, men tend to report more intense anger and women tend to feel anger for longer.

- **Anger is all in the mind.** Nothing could be farther from the truth. All emotions have chemical and physical beginnings in the body. If anger were only a state of mind, why would someone say, 'I feel like I'm burning with anger?' or 'That makes my blood boil.' When you get angry that emotion instantly affects muscles throughout your body, the hairs on the back of your neck, your blood pressure, your blood sugar levels, your heart rate, your respiration rate, your gut, even your finger temperature – long before you're aware of what's happening. This is a biological response – you can't change it, but you can control it.

- **Anger is all about getting even.** In fact the most common motive behind anger has been shown to be the wish for authority or independence, or to improve your image – not necessarily to cause harm. Revenge is a less common motive. A third motive involves letting off steam over built-up frustrations – again, with no apparent intent to harm anyone else.

✔ **Only certain types of people have a problem with anger.** Actually, over the years we've spent helping people with anger management we've worked with all types of people – lorry drivers, university professors, doctors, housewives, grandmothers, lawyers, policemen, career criminals, poor people, millionaires, children, the elderly and people of different cultures, nationalities and religions. Anger is a universal emotion!

✔ **Anger results from human conflict.** Sometimes yes, sometimes no. Experts on anger have found that people can get angry as a result of being exposed to foul odours, pain or hot temperatures – none of which involve (or can be blamed on) the actions of others.

✔ **People who have problems with anger are bad people.** This is not true. The effects of poor anger management can be bad – for your feelings, your health, your relationships, your hopes. But why would you be reading this book if you enjoyed being angry and destructive? Only a tiny percentage of humans take pleasure from hurting or causing suffering to others.

Understanding the Role of Emotions in Your Life

Emotion is a compound word. The *e* stands for 'energy' and the *motion* means exactly what it says – 'movement'. Emotions *move* you to act in ways that defend you from threat, lead to social and intimate attachments, motivate you to take part in things you get pleasure from and lead you to explore your environment. Without emotion, life would be at a standstill.

Scientists understand the biological causes of anger to be similar to those of all strong emotions; for instance, intense love, triumph or terror. The sympathetic nervous system increases heart rate and blood pressure, and the adrenal gland produces the hormone adrenaline, which controls many of the body's responses to stress. The purpose is to prepare the body for 'fight or flight' and during this emergency response some body functions are temporarily unnecessary:

✔ Blood circulation to digestion is reduced (causing nausea or 'butterflies').

✔ Circulation to fingers and toes is reduced (which is why someone who's afraid might be said to 'have cold feet').

- ✔ Skin may become red in response to production of the hormone epinephrine (a similar response is seen in some animals).

- ✔ The heart pumps faster to deliver oxygen to muscles, raising blood pressure as the smaller blood vessels tighten, pushing blood to the parts of the body needed to fight or retreat.

- ✔ Sweating can increase as the body maintains temperature balance (which rises with increased breathing and heart rates).

Anger, then, has a big effect on your body. So, you want to have emotions but you want to be in control of those emotions. You want to let anger move you to write a letter to the editor in your local newspaper about some social injustice. You want your anger to move you to stand up for yourself when your boss is exploiting your talents at work. Anger that says to your partner, 'Hey, something's not working here' is good for a marriage. But if your anger causes you to hurt others – or yourself – then you definitely have a problem.

Think of anger as a tool that can help you throughout life if you know how to use it – and think of *Anger Management For Dummies* as a reference on how best to use that tool.

The real culprit when it comes to anger is *how much* of it a person experiences, *how often* and *how long* for. The logic here is simple: if you rarely get angry; if, when you do, it's not too intense; and if your anger is over in a minute, it really doesn't matter whether you keep it in or let it out. You don't have enough of it to cause you, or anyone else, a problem.

Similarly, if you're repeatedly angry throughout the day, your anger is extremely intense and you stay that way for the rest of the day or longer, it doesn't matter whether you're aggressive or passive-aggressive type – either way you have a problem. If you keep that much anger in, you'll pay a price – in the form of depression, heart attack, resentment, relationship problems and so on. If you let that much anger out, you'll pay a different price – in the form of legal fees, divorce, job loss and so on. The way you express excessive anger simply determines the type of consequences you pay.

Do you really want to change?

You're interested in making a change: you wouldn't be looking at this book if you weren't! Yes, hundreds of thousands of people have made changes to the way they handle their anger, and it starts with curiosity: 'Can I do it? How do I do it?' The worst thing about problems – including excessive anger – is that you can get used to them, and that makes it difficult for you to change. People aren't born thinking (language is learned later) and aren't born with patterns of automatic behaviour, or habits. These come as we go through life, and we rely on them to make life manageable. How difficult would life become if you had to concentrate as hard at 30 as you did at 3 on dressing yourself? How would you find your way home after a busy day? Of course, not all habits are healthy. Overweight people know they need to lose weight, but overeating and avoiding exercise become habits, just as smoking or heavy drinking do. Habits in our style of relating to others are also powerful in our life – unhealthy ones such as lying or blaming, or healthy ones such as openness and showing affection. The great news is that habits are learned. Anything you learned, you can unlearn, or relearn! It just takes the decision 'I really want to change this' and focus, so that you take every opportunity and keep on going until you succeed.

We believe in being honest with people, so we tell them from the outset that it's far easier to stay the same than it is to change. So, if you're looking for the easy way out, there isn't one. Not changing requires absolutely no energy, motivation or commitment on your part – but change does. If you want to try, this book is for you – and the rewards can be amazing. Our experiences, and those of friends and clients, include a more peaceful mind, more pleasure from life, seeing the funny side of frustrating daily hassles, better relationships (genuine ones!) with fewer hurt feelings, grudges and missed chances.

Getting the Help You Need

Everybody needs support – nobody can go through life completely alone. Humans are social animals. When you're embarking on a major change in your life, the help of other people is especially important. And managing your anger is a major life change.

Support comes in many forms. To manage your anger effectively, you need all the following kinds of support:

- **Emotional support.** You need people who are behind you 100 per cent, people who know about your problems with anger and are cheering you on as you work out how to manage it.

- **Feedback support.** You need people who are willing to give you honest feedback about your anger, as well as any improvement you've made – no matter how small.

- **Informational support.** You can have the best of intentions, but if you don't have the information you need about anger and how to manage it, it's hard to change. Here, you hold in your hands all the information you need to get control of your unhelpful anger.

- **Practical support.** Sometimes you need some hands-on support. An angry mother who's on the verge of losing her temper and abusing her child really needs her partner or friend to step in while she takes a break to calm down. Ten minutes of practical help can make all the difference.

To use all the support you need in order to succeed at anger management:

- ✔ **Keep in mind that most people want to be supportive – they're just waiting for you to give them a chance.** Take the initiative and ask your closest friends and family members for their support. Support that goes unrecognised or unused does you no good. Most people have far more support than they take advantage of. This is no time to think, 'I don't want to be a burden on anyone.' Trust us, you're more of a burden when you're angry than when you've gained control!

- ✔ **Be willing to give support to your friends and family in return.** Support must be a two-way street. In order to receive it, you must give it. A part of what you give back will come through taking control of your anger, and the benefit this brings everyone.

- ✔ **Remember that no one person can satisfy all your support needs.** One person may be able to offer emotional support, and another may help out in a more practical way.

Don't be too surprised if, at first, you have trouble getting support for your efforts at anger management. You may have hurt a lot of people with your anger over the years and they may have some remaining resentment, fear and uncertainty. That's natural. But if you're truly committed to managing your anger, the chances are much higher that people will eventually come around.

Knowing You're Getting There

Often people who've been successful at anger management have a hard time appreciating just how far they've come in their emotional life.

The author Gill had a moment of fury when faced with drunken abuse from someone she'd always supported, in front of friends and family, and at a funeral. Gill was so angry she couldn't speak, and was shaking when she walked away. Using many of the skills we outline in this book to calm down and regain her emotional balance, she delayed speaking to the woman again until she was sober and instead thought about those she was glad to be with (letting anger go). Gill had forgotten what that kind of shocking anger felt like. But after it subsided she realised that the reason it felt so awful was because this was the first time for a long time that she'd felt such a strong rush of anger.

So how will you know that you're getting there? Here are some ways you can tell you're succeeding in managing your anger:

- ✔ You begin to realise that you can see the things that used to set you off *before* you react to them. This gives you the time to make choices about how you handle them.

- ✔ People who know you well begin to give you unsolicited positive feedback about your improved temper.

- ✔ That angry 'fist' you feel in your chest, or the arguments in your head, day after day, are no longer there – replaced by a calm sense of control.

But in many respects the work of anger management is never done – you're always a 'work in progress'. Every day is an opportunity to exercise your anger-management muscles.

If you slip up and sulk, or have an outburst, don't fall into the trap of being irritated about being irritated or see it as a setback. Instead, we believe that each slip gives you another chance to practise what you're trying to learn until it becomes your new habit. Don't be angry with yourself – try using the energy to have another try. Turn the energy spent on anger into determination to succeed.

Chapter 2

When Is Anger a Problem? Assessing and Understanding Your Anger

*E*veryone gets angry. After all, anger is a universal emotion – along with sadness, joy and fear – that people throughout the world recognise when they see, feel or hear it. But people don't experience anger to the same degree. What you need to determine is exactly how angry *you* are and when.

How do you know when you have an anger problem? Some people say that any time you're angry, that's a problem. (This anger myth and others are dispelled in Chapter 1). Others disagree, arguing that anger is never a problem as long as it tells you that something's wrong in your life. In fact, your anger is a problem if it causes you a problem (in your view or that of others). Ask yourself a straightforward question – does your anger run you, or do you run your anger?

In this chapter, we introduce you to ways of measuring your anger. Many of our clients describe this step as one of the most helpful they make in developing better anger control. You'll be amazed when you look back in a few months and can see how far you've come. You can also seek the support of others by asking those close to you or regularly in contact with you to use the scales in this chapter to measure your anger as they see it – the results can be surprising, but try not to be discouraged – or angry!

Assessing How Angry You Are

Everyone recognises a difference between the *experience* of anger (how you feel; irritated, angry or enraged) and the *expression* of anger (how you show or don't show it). In this chapter, you only need to focus on assessing how often you *feel* anger and how *strong* it is, and to consider your triggers. In other chapters throughout this book we focus more on how you *express* it – what you do with your anger.

Defining anger

To focus on how you feel anger, you first have to agree on what anger is and what it isn't. People often define anger as the emotion that:

- Can be deadly to your health
- Does more harm than good
- Everyone else around you is most afraid of
- Expresses itself in revenge
- Gets your blood boiling
- Is negative in tone
- Is the opposite of fear
- Links to blame
- Most often happens with or before aggressive behaviour
- Signals that you feel personally threatened
- Triggers the *fight* component of your nervous system's fight-or-flight response
- You're most afraid of

These are just some of the ideas people hold about anger. They may not all be true (for example, fear is often linked to anger – refer to Chapter 1 for an explanation of the 'fight or flight' survival response), but your beliefs will influence the way you react to anger in yourself and in others.

A simple answer to anger?

Anger is a complex human emotion. By reading this book you can discover where your anger is coming from. What is it about you, your situation, your lifestyle, your thinking and your relationships that contributes to your anger going beyond the normal emotion that it is? It may be three things: being young, finding it difficult to communicate your point and the effects of recreational drug use, for example. Or it may be half a dozen – poor coping skills, a life that's badly out of balance, a cynical outlook, not having enough sources of support, the fact that you're a man and a high-stress job. The important thing at this point is to work out what contributes to your anger, recognise its harmful effects on your life and understand that you can change if you want to. Then you can use the information and resources in this book to find the right recipe for anger management and to bring your emotional life to a better place.

How often do you get angry?

Start by answering this question: How often during a typical week in the past month did you get irritated, angry or furious?

A. Not at all

B. Once or twice a week

C. Three to five times a week

D. One or two times a day

E. Three times a day

F. Four or five times a day

G. Six to ten times a day

H. More than ten times a day

Be honest. And don't just think of the times you flew into a rage – think of all the times you felt even the *least* bit angry.

Here's how to analyse your answer:

- ✔ If you answered B or C then your anger is within a healthy, normal range.
- ✔ If you answered D, you're more vulnerable to difficulties managing your anger.

> ✔ If you answered E, F, G or H then your anger is probably excessive (you're angrier than is healthy for you).
>
> ✔ If you answered A, ask yourself when the last time you felt anger or irritation was? Is it over three months? If so, what effect is banning one of the natural human emotions having on you or the people around you?

Most people who claim never to be angry aren't seen that way by others. Their efforts to hide or brush away their real feelings often have very negative effects on the people around them. Their behaviour is referred to as passive-aggressive (see Chapter 10). Of course, you may have a very calm temperament – but you may be disguising your real emotions and causing yourself problems as great as those who pour their anger out.

Kelly rarely shows any expression of anger. She thinks of herself as too nice a person. She has never sworn or hit out at anyone in a moment of rage. On the other hand, she's often disgusted with herself, distressed about her life in general and disillusioned by what's going on in her current job. The views and judgements about others that cause her to keep quiet are unlikely to be accurate, but she has no way to discuss and solve them. Kelly definitely has a problem with anger, but you'd have to be a detective to know it – her anger is disguised.

Most people tend to underestimate the extent to which they feel things. This is partially due to memory – only the more dramatic episodes of anger come to mind. Also, anger is one of those emotions everyone wants to forget as quickly as possible. Make sure that you're being honest with yourself about how often you feel angry.

How intense is your anger?

Now you need to measure the *strength* of your anger. Think about how you feel most of the time when you get angry and answer this question honestly: On average, how intense is your anger? (Circle one.)

1	2	3	4	5	6	7	8	9	10

Mild   Extreme

If your intensity rating is 6 or below, your anger is within a healthy, normal range. If your intensity rating is 7 or above, you probably have a problem with anger.

Of course, your anger may be more intense in some situations than others. But, by and large, feelings tend to be consistent from one episode of emotion to the next. Humans, after all, are creatures of habit!

Annoyances count

In one study 50 university students were asked to keep a weekly diary of how often they got annoyed or angry. They recorded 1,536 instances of emotion. The average student reported getting angry seven times a week, roughly once a day. However, the average student also reported feeling annoyed 24 times a week or approximately 3 times a day. In other words, their report of anger was four times greater when they included milder forms of emotion like annoyance or irritation.

What triggers your anger?

Psychologist Raymond W. Novaco, Professor of Psychology and Social Behavior at the University of California, has done extensive studies on the intensity and triggers for anger. He identifies five types of trigger:

- **Disrespectful treatment,** such as being ignored by someone you've spoken to, experiencing someone else's passive aggression (a sarcastic remark or dismissive expression), or being put down in public.

- **Unfairness,** such as being blamed for something you didn't do, or not feeling recognised for your efforts.

- **Frustration,** such as being prevented from doing something you need to do, or someone driving too slowly and holding you up.

- **Annoying traits of others,** such as foot tapping or nail biting, parents making no effort to control overexcited children, or dealing with people who promise but don't deliver.

- **Irritations,** such as unavoidable delays when travelling, being in pain, tired or hungry, seeing the last pint of milk bought by someone ahead of you in the queue, or other daily hassles.

Are any of these like a red rag to a bull for you? Do you recognise one or more of these as likely or guaranteed to set your anger off, before you take control?

For a detailed assessment of your triggers, you can use an online assessment such as the questionnaire at www.psychologistworld.com/stress/, based on the work of Professor Novaco.

Way beyond annoyed

Sandip, a client of Dr Gentry's, was reviewing an incident in which he lost his temper. As soon as Dr Gentry started to ask questions about what actually provoked his anger, Sandip literally sprang up from the couch, his face taking on a menacing look. He looked like a panther ready to strike. Dr Gentry asked him how he was feeling and Sandip said, 'I'm annoyed just talking about it.' When asked to rate the intensity of his emotion on a 10-point scale, Sandip said he was at a 5½ or 6.

'Well, I have news for you,' Dr Gentry said. 'You're way beyond being annoyed. A rating of 5 or 6 means you're angry, bordering on very angry.' Then Dr Gentry knew why Sandip had been referred to anger management. What he labelled as *annoyed*, most people call *anger*. And, what he called *anger*, they call *rage*.

Working Out Whether Your Anger Is Harmful

Certain subtypes of anger can be damaging, even lethal (see Chapter 3 for an in-depth discussion of harmful anger). Anger leading to aggression or violence is always going to have a harmful effect on others (physically and emotionally) and also on you. Hostility, ill will, cynicism, mistrust and paranoia are all harmful. To carry a grudge, or to be on permanent guard against everyone, is exhausting and takes your focus and energy away from making what you want of your life. This attitude also distances you from others, depriving you of friendship, trust and closeness, which are so essential for a healthy and contented life.

Other forms of anger are benign (not harmful) and really can't hurt you. The trick is to know which is which.

First, go to the 'How often do you get angry?' section, earlier in this chapter, where you indicate how frequently you find yourself getting angry during a typical week. If you selected B or C – 'once or twice' up to 'three to five' times a week – your anger is intermittent or *episodic* in nature. If you ticked D, you need to look more closely at whether you're feeling *irritated* or *angry* (see Chapter 14 for techniques if you recognise irritability as your problem). If you ticked any of the other answers – 'three times a day' through to 'more than ten times a day' – your anger is *chronic*. Generally speaking, episodic anger isn't a problem, but chronic anger is.

Now, go to the 'How intense is your anger?' section, where you rate the intensity of your anger. If your intensity rating was up to 3, we call that *irritability*. If your rating was between 4 and 7, we call that *anger*. And, if you rated yourself between 8 and 10, we call that *rage*. *Rage is always a problem.*

When two or more people admit to being angry, obviously they aren't talking about having exactly the same emotional experience. Anger is just a word until you break it down into something that you can measure.

Here's where things get interesting. The final step in assessing whether you have a problem with anger is to combine your anger scores in a way that generates six possible subcategories of anger, as illustrated in Table 2-1.

Table 2-1	Various Types of Anger Experience		
	Intensity		
Frequency	*1–3*	*4–7*	*8–10*
Less than once a day	Episodic irritation	Episodic anger	Episodic rage
At least once a day	Chronic irritation	Chronic anger	Chronic rage

Which category did you fall into? Does it make the problem more real when you put these types of labels on it? We find that most people are comfortable with terms like *irritated* and *angry*, but they don't like the label *rage* at all. There's something equally unsettling about the label *chronic*. And when you put the two together, people really get nervous! In the following sections we help you to see beyond the labels.

Episodic irritation

In a sample of the general population, roughly 25 per cent of 284 people surveyed fell into this category. That is, one out of every four people is like Cathy, a woman in her 60s who seldom finds herself experiencing even mild anger. Everyone regards her as upbeat, cheerful, easygoing and pleasant to be around. No problem here. If you fall into this category, your anger isn't harmful.

Episodic anger

Slightly more than a third (36 per cent) of people surveyed admitted that they got angry a couple of times a week. However, like Peter, their anger never amounted to anything. Sure, Peter gets angry on occasion – like when his secretary spoils his mood by starting the day with some negative remark – but he doesn't dwell on it and it passes fairly quickly. If you fall into this category, your anger isn't harmful.

Episodic rage

This is the first glimpse of what we call damaging anger. Around 15 per cent of those surveyed readily admitted to getting this angry occasionally, but not daily. If you fall into this category, you'll recognise some of the problems it brings. You may have outbursts only occasionally, but how do you feel afterwards? You may feel physical effects – a pounding headache or exhaustion; you may feel bad – you didn't get your point across; or others may feel bad – you're unpredictable and they're uneasy around you.

Chronic irritation

You may think that chronic irritation is a problem, but it's really not all that harmful. People may see you as moody or bitchy, but they still tolerate you most of the time. Interestingly, only about 2 per cent of people fall into this category.

Chronic anger

This is the second category of damaging anger. It included 11 per cent of those surveyed, people like Bill, a retired salesman who finds himself getting angry repeatedly every day about one thing or another. 'I get angry when my wife takes too long shopping, when things break around the house, when gas prices go up – just about anything that doesn't suit me,' he says. 'But don't get me wrong; I don't go off the deep end and rant and rave.' Like many people, Bill thinks he doesn't have a problem with anger because it never rises to the level of uncontrollable rage – but he's wrong. It's just not healthy to be angry as frequently as Bill is.

Chronic rage

This is the worst-case example of harmful anger. We're sorry to say that 12 per cent of those responding fell into this subgroup. If you find yourself in this group, your anger is *volatile* (as in volcanic!) and there's absolutely no question that anger is damaging just about every aspect of your life. This type of anger is dangerous and serves no useful purpose.

Recent research shows that people usually experience anger a few times a week. Between 43 and 58 per cent of anger episodes include shouting, swearing or screaming; less than 10 per cent involve physical aggression (this includes throwing small objects, pushing and so on). In adults who recognise a problem with anger, around 74 per cent of episodes include verbal aggression and 22 per cent involve physical aggression.

Calculating the Risks of Harmful Anger

You can calculate how at risk you are for harmful anger. Review the following sections and see how many of these factors fit you.

Are you male?

Men and women don't differ in how *often* they get angry, but men do tend to experience anger more *intensely* than women at all ages. Thus, men are more likely to experience rage as opposed to irritability or anger.

Are you under 40 years of age?

Growing older has some real benefits. The frequency and intensity of anger both tend to decrease with age – people actually do mellow over time (see Table 2-2). Anger is a much bigger problem during adolescence and young adult years (ages 13 to 39) and begins to decline steadily thereafter for most people. It's not that unusual for children and adolescents to throw temper tantrums, but if you're still doing that at age 30, you definitely have a problem.

Table 2-2	Age-related Changes in Anger	
Age	*Average Frequency*	*Average Intensity*
13–19	Daily	7 (very angry)
20–29	Daily	7 (very angry)
30–39	3–5 times/week	5 (moderately angry)
40–49	1–2 times/week	5 (moderately angry)
50–59	1–2 times/week	4 (mildly angry)
60+	1–2 times/week	3 (irritated, annoyed)

What's your temperament and personality style?

Temperament means your inherited, inborn traits that set the basic tone or quality of your emotional reactions. The two traits that set people up for damaging anger are *impulsivity* (an inability to wait for what you want or tolerate the frustration of a delay before your needs are satisfied) and *excitability* (how easily your emotions are triggered). More good news: both of these traits decrease with age.

Do you have too many triggers to anger?

Common sense tells you that the more provocation you have in life, the more chances you have to be angry. Take, for example, policemen and women who spend their days trying to get people to obey the law and who put up with a lot of abuse in the process. What about schoolteachers who have to put up with defiant, unmotivated children all day? Even nurses – we see more angry people waiting for appointments in the local hospital than almost anywhere else we go ('What do you mean the doctor can't see me yet?'). The same goes for family and intimate relationships – the style of some are more burdened with problems than others. The good news is that you can limit what the triggers do – how else could the people in these examples do their jobs?

Are you looking at life the wrong way?

Anger is in the eye of the viewer. It's not the things that happen to you that make you angry, it's the way you respond to those things. Here are four ways of looking at the world that tend to make it easy to be angry:

✔ **You're a cynic.** Do you wake up every morning expecting (and preparing yourself for) the worst? Do you anticipate that good things are *not* in store for you today? Do you mistrust others – even your loved ones? Are you constantly on guard in case other people somehow take advantage of you? If this sounds familiar, you're ready to react in anger at a moment's notice.

✔ **Everything is a catastrophe.** Would you agree that there are no little stresses in life? A friend was ten minutes late meeting you for lunch, you got stuck in a traffic jam on your way to work – everything is a big deal! What others might regard as a minor irritant you see as a big deal. If so, the strength of your feelings – panic not nerves, rage not irritation – reflects just how overwhelmed you feel most of the time.

✔ **You're compulsive.** Do you recognise the thinking style 'everything in life is either black or white' in yourself? Is it 'your way or no way'? Do you demand perfection in yourself and everyone around you? Are you all work and no play? Do you eat, sleep and breathe one thing: control? Are you always exhausted and never able to relax? No wonder you get angry so easily.

✔ **You're self-absorbed.** Is your life really 'all about me'? Are you the centre of your own little universe? Is everyone else just here to serve your needs? If someone does reach your targets, all's well, but if that person doesn't tell you what you want to hear, doesn't make you feel 'special', has her own needs or even (how dare she) talks about herself, there's hell to pay. If this sounds familiar, anger isn't far away (often passive-aggression if you fall into this trap).

Do you have an aggressive personality?

If you have an aggressive personality, you'll experience more anger than if you don't. You have an aggressive personality if the following are true:

✔ You like to dominate others.

✔ You're competitive.

✔ You're confrontational.

✔ You're demanding.

✔ You're forceful in pursuing goals.

✔ You're impatient.

✔ You're intense.

If you're not sure about this one, ask someone who knows you well what she thinks – but don't get angry if she tells you the truth!

CASE STUDY

Of course you're angry – you're the best

A colleague of ours was asked to consult with a company whose CEO was having difficulty getting his top executives to control their anger in day-to-day discussions. With considerable exasperation, the CEO acknowledged that he had, on more than one occasion, had to step in between two angry managers who were engaged in a physical confrontation. His question was: 'I pay these people very well and they have all the freedom in the world, so why are they acting like this?' It didn't take our colleague long to find the answer. Actually, it was quite simple. All of the executives were extremely aggressive personalities who'd clawed their way to the top of the organisation through a combination of ambitious and combative behaviour. Aggression was the fuel – the ammunition – that got them to where they were and kept them there.

Are you taking medicines or drugs?

Drugs – legal and illegal – alter brain chemistry and can lead to anger. Here's a list of some drugs to be aware of that can have a significant effect on your anger:

- ✔ Alcohol
- ✔ Amphetamines
- ✔ Caffeine
- ✔ Cocaine
- ✔ Hypnotics
- ✔ Nicotine
- ✔ Sedatives
- ✔ Tranquillizers

Do you stay irritable?

By irritable, we don't mean irritated. *Irritable* is synonymous with a general feeling of being:

- ✔ Aggravated
- ✔ Agitated
- ✔ Crabby
- ✔ Cross

✔ Grouchy

✔ Ill

✔ On edge

✔ Sensitive

✔ Tense

✔ Touchy

✔ Uneasy

✔ Unsettled

Irritability is a non-specific state of physical and mental discomfort that's often the by-product of life itself – hot weather, insufficient finances, hangover, illness, chronic pain due to arthritis or migraine headaches, boredom, second-hand smoke, memories of past hurts and grievances, being overweight and so on. The point we're making here is that a highly irritable person is a person who's ready to be angry.

Are you suffering from depression?

Mood and emotion go hand in hand. If you're in a positive, *euphoric* mood, you're apt to feel positive emotions like joy and excitement. If you're in a negative, *dysphoric* mood, the opposite, of course, is true – you're more likely to feel emotions such as sadness and anger. So, it doesn't take a rocket scientist to understand why depression and anger are so closely linked. If you're suffering from what psychiatrists call *agitated depression*, you experience anger often and express it in outrageous ways. If you have what's called *retarded depression*, you retreat into a world of angry silence. Either way, anger is a big part of your condition.

Why not tranquillizers?

Ironically, the drugs that doctors prescribe to calm you down may, inadvertently, make it easier for you to lose your temper. For example, the use of diazepam (Valium) tends to reduce anxiety, but at the same time can cause people to lose control and act aggressively. This begs the question: should tranquillizers be used in anger management? We would argue not. Some antidepressant drugs, on the other hand, appear to be both safe and effective in toning down a person's potential for anger. Head to Chapter 18 for more about antidepressants.

Do you communicate poorly?

Do you have a hard time saying what's on your mind but have no trouble whatsoever lashing out emotionally? Do you often find yourself saying things like 'Get off my back, you idiot!' or 'I've had it with you – you make me sick!' when what you really should be saying is 'I'm about to lose my job, I'm scared to death about our future and I don't know where to turn'? Anger communicates all right, but not the message you really need people to hear.

Do you lack problem-solving skills?

Are you the type of person who wastes a lot of time and energy being angry instead of fixing all the things that are wrong with your life? If so, you're a member of a very large club. Of course, you already know that an outburst of anger doesn't pay the bills, repair a flat tyre or get a person out of a bad relationship. Do you? Wouldn't it be better to save the anger or at least use it constructively to work out your money, change the tyre or tell your lazy partner to shape up or move out?

Are you too stressed?

Life is, by its very nature, stressful – but it's fair to say that some folks have more stress than others. Actually, it's the little irritants of life (psychologists refer to these as *hassles*) that upset you the most; most people handle the big stresses (*critical life events*) pretty well. Different types of stress exist, some more linked to anger than others. Stresses that persist over time (*chronic*), that build up over time (*cumulative*) or that are beyond your control and thus tend to overwhelm you (*catastrophic*) are the real killers. Sound familiar?

Are you too judgemental?

Anger, like other emotions, is a judgement. When you get angry, you're judging other people ('you treated me badly') and situations ('this just isn't what I want'). Anger is a statement – *your* statement – about right and wrong. The more you judge the world, the more likely you'll be angry about something.

Are you too much into blame?

Are you quick to assign blame to someone or something every time you suffer misfortune? Do you earnestly believe that no accidents exist in life – that everything is the result of someone else's intentional desire to frustrate, mislead or inflict harm on someone else? Are you forever reading some sinister motive into what others say and do that ends up hurting someone's feelings? Do you believe the idea that everyone's suffering at the hand of some kind of conspiracy? Then no wonder you're always angry and preoccupied with thoughts about how to even the score.

Are you constantly exhausted?

Are you like Pete, the worn out 32-year-old factory worker who couldn't stop rowing with his wife but had no idea why?

Pete referred himself for anger management because he thought anger was endangering his marriage. He didn't have a clue as to why he was so irritable all the time and quick to attack his wife over any little thing. Among other things, Dr Gentry asked him if he liked the kind of work he did and Pete said, 'It's okay, except for the fact that we're working seven days a week, ten hours a day.' And how long had that schedule been in effect? Five months. The poor guy wasn't just tired – he was exhausted! And that, of course, made every other thing in his life a strain. What was the message behind Pete's anger? Simple: 'I'm exhausted. I can't take any more. I need a break!'

Blame = anger = pain

For over 40 years now Dr Gentry has worked with patients who suffer chronic, often disabling, pain resulting mostly from work injuries. He confirms that they're an extremely angry group of people. Fifty-two per cent of those who completed his five-week outpatient rehab programme, for example, admitted to experiencing either episodic or chronic rage. Why is this relevant? Because studies have shown that work-injured patients who blame someone for their injury are less likely to remain employed, more likely to feel they received no benefit from medical treatment, more likely to suffer from psychological distress, more likely to anticipate greater pain and disability in the future and are less optimistic about further improvement. Those who had a no-fault view of their injury fared much better.

Who's around to help and support you?

No doubt you find life a struggle; so does everyone sometimes. In that struggle everyone needs help – a kind word now and then, some practical assistance (like a lift to the doctor or a loan until pay day), some sense of belonging to a world larger than yourself, or someone to reassure you at critical times in your life that you're simply okay and that this will pass.

But what if you don't have that support? What if you're struggling all alone, out there on a limb, by yourself? Wouldn't you be angry – angry that you don't have something (a resource) that other people have, angry that you have to reach out for help because no one is reaching out to you, angry at God for allowing your life to be like this? Of course you would – and you are.

Is your life seriously out of balance?

Is your life all give and no take? Are there too many downs and not enough ups? Are you all work and no play? Is there no room in your life for pleasure, messing around or those moments when you simply enjoy the ridiculous side of life? Do you spend far more time with those you work with than you do with friends and loved ones? Well then, your life is obviously way out of balance. Until you correct that imbalance, you're a sitting duck for anger.

Relax?

At the end of every first session we have with a new client – especially those who've come for help with anger management – we say, 'Tell me what you do to relax.' We often hear one of the following four answers:

- 'Relax?'
- 'What did you say?'
- 'What's that got to do with it?'
- 'Nothing!'

And then the problem is staring us in the face. Anger is one of a number of normal emotions everyone feels. However, to have no let-up from it isn't normal. Not making time to play or just let your guard down is harmful to the balance of life.

Chapter 3

Is Anger Damaging Your Life?

*I*n this chapter we show you the many ways in which anger can be harmful. We also discuss the second-hand effects of harmful anger – they're as dangerous to your health as second-hand smoke. If you find yourself feeling like a battery that's losing its charge, if you can't seem to lose weight or stop smoking, if you have headaches all the time, if you're taking blood-pressure medicine, if you're concerned about the health of your loved ones or if your working life seems like a disaster area, you'll find this chapter especially enlightening.

Draining Your Energy

Anger and tiredness go hand in hand. Emotions use your energy. The body requires energy to mobilise itself into an attack posture – heart pounding, blood pressure up, muscles tense from head to toe. By its very nature, anger excites you. Your adrenaline flows. And afterwards comes the recovery, where you feel physically drained – exhausted.

What about those of you who suffer from chronic anger? (Refer to Chapter 2 for ways to measure whether your anger is chronic or acute). You go through this vicious cycle of excitement and exhaustion several times every day. Consider how much of your day's reserves of energy this invasive emotion is soaking up. It makes us tired just thinking about it!

Vital exhaustion: Vital to avoid

Dutch medical researchers have coined the term *vital exhaustion* to describe a pattern of symptoms – excessive fatigue, increased irritability and feelings of demoralisation – that often precede a heart attack. They found that vital exhaustion and chronic anger separately increase a person's chances of sudden cardiac failure by 42 per cent. But *together* they increase it even more – by a whopping 69 per cent. This held true even when they considered other risk factors such as high blood pressure, smoking, diabetes and cholesterol.

Making You Ill

The link between emotion and physical health can be both direct and indirect. Anger, for example, has an instant effect on your blood pressure, but that effect is short lived and generally doesn't cause any immediate harm. Anger also elevates blood pressure through its link to smoking and obesity, and *that* effect is permanent.

In the following sections we fill you in on the damage anger may be doing to your health.

How anger indirectly affects your health

The best example of how anger can indirectly affect your health is shown by your risk of a heart attack. People who smoke cigarettes, are overweight, have high blood pressure and high cholesterol, or drink alcohol (or some combination of these) are at greater risk for some type of coronary episode – chest pain, heart attack or stroke associated with a history of heart disease. Anger contributes to all these risk factors.

Your risk, of course, is determined not by any one of these factors, but by how many you have operating in your life at any point. Jot down your answers to the following questions:

- Have you smoked cigarettes in the last 30 days?
- Do you have two or more alcoholic drinks in one go?
- Has a doctor ever told you that you have high blood pressure?

✔ Are you currently being treated for high blood pressure?

✔ Has a doctor ever told you that you have high cholesterol?

✔ Are you currently being treated for high cholesterol?

✔ Do you consider yourself overweight?

✔ Do you consider yourself obese?

It may surprise you to know that your answers to all of these questions may reflect how much anger exists in your life. In the following sections we explain.

Smoking

Your risk of ill health from being a cigarette smoker, believe it or not, is 65 per cent higher if you typically experience intense anger (rage) than if you typically experience mild anger (irritation).

Using nicotine reduces the likelihood that you'll react aggressively when you're provoked to anger. That's the good news. The bad news is that smoking is linked to heart disease (and cancer!). Angry smokers are far less likely to succeed in their attempts to quit smoking than non-angry smokers. In one published study, the risk of dropping out of treatment early or continuing to smoke after treatment was 12 times greater for angry smokers. Finally, anger is the second leading cause of relapse among ex-smokers – less than stress or anxiety but greater than depression.

Being hooked on cigarettes may also mean that anger is a habit. Without cigarettes, how would your anger control be? The use of habits like smoking for comfort can prevent you from ever trying to learn how to bring your anger down without them.

Drinking

Alcohol increases your risk of heart disease, and alcohol consumption is higher in people who experience intense anger. This may be a two-way street if you have a drink to calm down when you're irritated or angry. Unfortunately, the short-term effect you feel is outweighed by the disinhibiting effect of alcohol.

Alcohol is a numbing agent when it comes to emotions. People drink to forget not only their troubles but also what they're feeling at the moment – sadness, anxiety, shame, guilt and anger. The more you drink, the less connected you are to those feelings. Most people don't drink to make themselves feel good – they drink to feel less bad.

Alice was well into middle age before she finally admitted she had a drinking problem and got the help she needed to get sober. For years Alice blamed her excessive use of alcohol on her domineering mother and her equally angry, overbearing husband, both of whom provided her with a convenient excuse to continue drinking. What she failed to realise all along was that the real driving force behind her drinking was her own aggressive personality – and abiding anger – which she suppressed by staying drunk. Alcohol allowed Alice to be nice to the very people with whom she was the angriest. Ironically, all this came to light only after she began accompanying her husband to anger-management therapy – something he was now willing to do since she'd become sober. A further irony was the fact that as her husband began to control his temper she began to lose hers.

If you plan to continue drinking alcohol but you're concerned about anger, consider the following:

✔ **Alcohol initially acts as a stimulant, leading to increased arousal and excitation in the person who's drinking.** This increased state of arousal may set the stage for an angry reaction to some otherwise innocuous event or circumstance. Almost one million violent attacks in 2007–2008 involved heavy drinking. Alcohol was involved in around 58 per cent of attacks by strangers, and in 37 per cent of domestic violence incidents.

✔ **Even in small quantities, alcohol can cause you to misperceive the motives and actions of others.** What you might otherwise view as unintended or accidental you see as intended to inflict harm.

✔ **Alcohol lifts inhibitions in emotions and behaviour.** It lowers the nervous system's threshold for emotional experiences, allowing you to feel things you wouldn't if you were sober. It also transforms behaviour and makes you feel you have the 'right' to act opposite to your normal self – the quiet person becomes loud, the submissive person becomes dominant, the sweet person becomes angry.

✔ **Alcohol affects mood in the aftermath of drinking.** If you're a heavy drinker you can expect to feel more depressed after you sober up than if you use less alcohol.

✔ **If you're what's called an *angry drinker* (you get angry when you drink) you can expect to have a more intense hangover afterwards.** Angry drinkers are much more likely to experience headaches, stomach discomfort, diarrhoea, tremors and nervousness when they sober up. This is particularly true for men, but then again men are more likely to fit the angry-drinker profile.

If you want to know more about reducing your drinking, you can find information and advice at www.patient.co.uk/health/Alcoholism-and-Problem-Drinking.htm.

The recommended guidelines for the maximum amount of alcohol you should drink are two units per day (14 per week) for women and three units per day (21 per week) for men. And you may be surprised just how much alcohol your favourite tipple contains. Most home-poured measures of spirits are at least double those served in pubs, many wines are now 4 to 8 per cent stronger than those of 20 years ago and bottled beers can contain three units in a single bottle.

Obesity

Do you head for the refrigerator or the nearest fast-food restaurant when something annoys you? If you do, you're not alone! Food is, unfortunately, the solution that millions of people choose to quash their anger. And the resulting obesity is yet another risk factor for heart disease.

Amy is a self-acknowledged emotional eater. She currently weighs 100 pounds more than she did when she left school two years ago. She constantly finds herself holding back her feelings – even positive ones – because of her boyfriend's discomfort with any open expression of emotion. Hiding emotion under a facade of niceness is unnatural for Amy, who was raised in a family where everyone sat around to eat together in the evening and chatted about their thoughts and feelings with each other. She lives in emotional isolation day after day, self-medicating with food as a means of controlling her bottled-up anger. 'I hold in my anger as long as I can – usually for three to six months – but then I blow up and let it all out at once,' she says. But then the cycle begins all over again. She admits, 'I can't imagine how many hundreds of pounds I have put on and taken off because of all this anger, but it's a lot.'

People like Amy use food both to comfort themselves when they're upset with the world and also as a distraction – in her case, mostly from the anger she feels towards her boyfriend. In an attempt to hide her anger Amy may be a larger-than-life person but her health is now at risk. If you're like Amy, check out Chapters 10 and 11 in this book, which address the perils of suppressed anger.

Poor health habits

Researchers at the University of Texas Health Science Center at Houston have concluded that overweight children, especially girls, have poor health habits 'including anger expression' that contribute to a lifetime of obesity. Whereas non-obese adolescents show greater control over their anger as they grow up, overweight teens lag behind. They're able to acknowledge their angry feelings but they can't express those feelings in an appropriate way. For these children anger management is just as important as diet and exercise.

High blood pressure

People who have high blood pressure have a much higher risk of developing heart disease. And people who are habitually angry have a much higher risk of suffering from high blood pressure – in fact, three times the risk! (Only 15 per cent of not-very-angry people have high blood pressure, whereas 44 per cent of their highly angry counterparts have high blood pressure.)

The way you respond to anger also affects your blood pressure. If you keep anger in, your odds of having high blood pressure are 21 per cent. If you let it out, your odds are only 11 per cent. Of course, how you let anger out can make a difference too (Chapter 11 talks about how to do this constructively).

High cholesterol

High cholesterol, which places you at risk for heart disease, doesn't come from anger; it basically comes from your family history. But anger certainly aggravates the problem. When Dr Gentry asked people to tell him about how intense their anger was typically and whether or not they had high cholesterol, only 15 per cent of people with low anger had high cholesterol, compared with 22 per cent of the highly angry group.

Plus, medical studies have consistently shown that high levels of anger among those with dominant and competitive personalities are related to elevated levels of total cholesterol and LDL ('bad') cholesterol (the compound that has been linked to heart problems). People prone to verbal or physical anger and an antagonistic interpersonal style have unusually high levels of cholesterol. It's possible that when individuals experience anger and related emotions they release stress hormones, such as adrenalin and noradrenalin, which raise cholesterol in the body. Stress hormones release fatty acids which eventually become cholesterol, and also inhibit 'LDL receptors', which act to remove harmful cholesterol from the circulation (see Chapter 12 for more about identifying your temperament and Chapter 15 for more on your physical health).

When your doctor tells you that you need to lose weight and start exercising to lower your cholesterol levels, you need to follow medical advice. But also consider the potential benefit of anger management in achieving the same result.

How anger directly affects your health

Emotions aren't just distracting, they can also interfere with reason and cause you to make decisions or take actions that end up being hazardous to your health. In the following sections we cover three of the primary behaviours that can directly result from uncontrolled anger.

Unsafe sex

Anger, it turns out, often accompanies high-risk sex. When women, for example, are presented with an opportunity for unsafe sex, and they aren't angry at the time, they typically abstain or take reasonable precautions, such as using a condom. But if a woman is angry – for example, at a parent who's forbidden her to continue a relationship with her boyfriend – all that reason flies out the window. It's the old 'I'll show you I can do anything I want with whoever I want – *so there!*' mentality.

On-the-job injuries

You'll probably spend an awful lot of your adult life working. So if you're injured the accident is most likely to occur on the job – and that's true no matter what you do for a living. So, what does that have to do with anger? As it turns out, a whole lot.

Here's what we know about on-the-job injuries:

- ✔ In a survey of people who were injured on the job:
    - Up to a third of people admitted that they were experiencing some level of anger prior to the injury.
    - The angrier they were at the time, the more likely they were to be injured.
    - If they were extremely irritated, they were five times more likely to be injured than if they weren't irritated at all.
    - If they were extremely angry, they were seven times more likely to be injured than if they weren't angry.
    - If they were in a rage, they were 12 times more likely to be injured than if they weren't in a rage.
- ✔ Anger is more likely to lead to injury in men.
- ✔ Anger increases the odds of you injuring another employee and inflicting injury on yourself.
- ✔ Anger and alcohol use prior to injury are highly linked, and both independently increase a person's odds of being injured on the job.

Are you absent without leave?

The author Dr Gentry asked a large group of employees about their anger and about various health issues, including one question about absenteeism: 'In the past three months have you missed work because of illness?'

Interestingly, those who suffered from chronic anger – one or more episodes of anger every day – were five-and-a-half times more likely to have answered yes to that question than employees who got angry less often. Similarly, those who reported intense anger (rage) were three times more likely to miss work because of illness than those who were only irritated.

Findings like this lead us to believe that many employed people go AWOL when they get fed up with work, and illness provides them with a legitimate excuse.

Road rage

A recent Gallup poll shows that 80.4 per cent of UK drivers have been the victim of road rage. Twenty per cent said they'd experienced road rage more than ten times, and more than 70 per cent admitted to causing trouble themselves. Only 14 per cent showed any remorse, identifying bad mood as the most common cause of their actions.

The message? Anger is hazardous to driving! The effort you're making to learn healthy anger management can benefit every area of your life – and keep you safe! The bottom line is this: you may literally be putting your life in someone else's hands every time you get behind the wheel.

Road rage isn't about the road – it's about rage. According to researchers, high-anger drivers have the following characteristics:

- They're highly judgemental of other people's driving.
- They have contempt for how others drive.
- They have vengeful thoughts about other drivers.
- They take risks while driving – speeding, switching lanes, tailgating, running amber lights.
- They experience anger on a daily basis (what, in Chapter 2, we call chronic anger).
- They may get in the car already angry.
- They tend to express their anger outwardly – shouting, sounding the horn, gesturing, tailgating.
- They have less control of their emotions in general.
- They tend to react impulsively when frustrated.

Most of the things in life people call accidents really aren't accidents. And some people are really just accidents waiting to happen. Be honest about yourself, about your own road rage – you could not only be saving your life, but also the lives of everyone else on the road with you.

Reviewing the anger–health checklist

Take a look at the following checklist of medical disorders and diseases in which anger can play an active, direct role – either causing the illness or aggravating it. See how many of these apply to you or other angry people you know and love:

- ✔ Alcoholism
- ✔ Anorexia
- ✔ Asthma
- ✔ Bulimia
- ✔ Cancer
- ✔ Chronic fatigue syndrome
- ✔ Depression
- ✔ Eczema
- ✔ Fibromyalgia
- ✔ Headaches
- ✔ Heart disease
- ✔ High blood pressure
- ✔ Insomnia
- ✔ Irritable bowel syndrome (IBS)
- ✔ Impotence
- ✔ Lower back pain
- ✔ Neurodermatitis (inflammations of the skin)
- ✔ Obesity
- ✔ Phobias
- ✔ Psoriasis
- ✔ Stroke
- ✔ Substance addiction
- ✔ Teeth grinding
- ✔ Temporo-mandibular joint (TMJ) disorder

Do you really need a doctor?

Imagine that you're in a job that you hate, you're overdue for a pay rise, the boss keeps piling more work on you all the time, your co-workers are fools, you can't remember the last time someone told you that you were doing a good job, you feel absolutely stuck – and you're fed up about all of it!

Now, also imagine that it's 6.45 a.m. and you just got out of bed and are about to get ready for work. You didn't sleep well again last night, you're tired, your throat is scratchy and your head is beginning to throb.

All of a sudden a thought pops into your head: 'I can't go to work today. I'm ill. I'm going to call the doctor and see whether he can find out what's causing me to feel so bad. I think I just need some time to myself to rest and get well.' So, you call the office to let them know you're off sick and aren't sure when you'll be back in. You instantly feel better!

Here's what we think. We don't think you're sick at all – certainly not enough to see a doctor. Instead, we think you're sick and tired of going to work. You're full of anger and resentment and your body is telling you, 'I've had it. I've had enough. No more. I need a break.'

Maybe you don't need a doctor. Your doctor can examine you, run blood tests and even do x-rays, but the chances are he won't find out what's wrong with you. He may appease you by saying, 'I'm not sure what's causing your symptoms – you may just have a mild case of whatever's going around.' He'll probably tell you to just take painkillers, get some rest and maybe stay home from work for a day or two, and that should do it. But maybe what's wrong is your constant state of irritation while you're at work eight to ten hours a day. And painkillers and rest won't fix that! Anger is closely linked to fear and anxiety, and the worst you can do when you feel anxiety is to avoid the cause. Instead, try following up on the anger-management changes you're making, or make an appointment to talk things over with a cognitive therapist, counsellor or professional with a specialist interest in anger management.

Sabotaging Your Career

Not only can anger rob you of energy and end up making you ill but it can also drastically affect your career – and not in the way you want.

Here's an example. The author Dr Gentry was recently listening to a radio show that offered career advice. A 35-year-old unemployed man called the show to tell the presenter that he needed advice on how to get a good job. The presenter asked him about his educational background – he was a graduate – and enquired about his last job. The caller described what sounded like a pretty good job as a town administrator in a small community.

'How long did that job last?' the presenter asked.

'About 18 months and then I quit,' said the man.

'Why did you quit?' the presenter asked.

'They wouldn't give me the big pay rise I felt I deserved so I got angry and resigned,' was the answer.

'And what did you do before that?' the presenter asked.

'Same thing – city administrator for another small community.'

'How long were you at that job?' the presenter enquired.

'I think about two years, but again they wouldn't give me what I deserved, so I got angry and quit.'

The conversation continued until the caller had described six good jobs since he'd finished university, all of which he'd left in anger.

Finally, the host said, 'I get the picture but I think you're wrong about what your problem is. Your problem isn't how to get a good job. You've had six. Your problem is your inability to control your temper whenever your employer either can't or won't give you exactly what you want.'

The man was furious, shouting, 'You don't know what you're talking about! I'm not the problem; they are! You're not giving me any help here.' Then he hung up.

Obviously, what had started out as a highly promising career was now stalled and heading the wrong way – fast.

In the following sections we cover some other ways in which anger can sabotage your career.

Getting off-track early

In today's world, more than ever before, you hear the view that, if you hope to succeed at work then you need an education. Without an education your choices are extremely limited and you'll be lucky if you get what amounts to back-breaking, low-paying, here-today-gone-tomorrow jobs.

In fact, many thousands of kids struggle to attend school, particularly during their teens, and many more leave school after GCSEs and don't continue to A levels, a profession, a trade apprenticeship or university.

What does this have to do with anger? Well, those who drop out of school early or don't go on to use their skills and talents to reach a recognised level of expertise or qualification are very often the same kids who struggle most to control their frustration and anger. Poor anger control can sabotage the start that young adults make in trying to find and keep work. For some, they enter the job market already at a distinct disadvantage and never catch up.

Heading in the wrong direction

Most people want to have a better life than their parents and grandparents had. You want to make more money, have more creature comforts, drive a bigger car, live in a bigger house, wear more expensive clothes, eat in better restaurants, take more exotic holidays – and those are the incentives that may drive you to work longer and harder, year after year.

But not everyone follows that dream. Some people experience just the opposite – by the time they reach midlife they're actually worse off in terms of job security, job status and income than their parents. Why? The answer is anger. It turns out that easily angered people have more jobs over a lifetime, get fired or resign more often, are forced to take whatever jobs are available (instead of logically pursuing a career) and have a much more erratic employment history compared with those who are slow to anger.

To add insult to injury, many ill-tempered adults seek out jobs that tolerate their angry outbursts as long as the job gets done. In effect, they've found a niche for their anger. For example, how many of the major professions with a career structure – law, teaching, medicine, health service, police, army – could you work in if your anger outbursts are frequent, severe or long lasting? Instead, angry people may end up in a job where they're usually alone or where swearing and shouting are often tolerated, such as dispatch driving, security, labouring or factory work. Unfortunately, some of these jobs can be physically dangerous and low paying.

Asking the wrong question

Angry employees are typically more in tune with their *own* needs, expectations, wants, goals and so on than those of the company for which they work. If your boss comes to you late in the day and asks whether you can stay a little longer to finish up a rush order, you get angry and snap, 'Absolutely not! I have plans already. I've done all I'm going to do today,' before walking off in a huff. If you think you're entitled to a promotion but someone else gets it, you sulk and proceed to do as little as possible for your employer from that day forward.

You're always asking the same question over and over: 'Why aren't they treating me fairly?'

The question you *should* be asking is: 'Why do I get so angry whenever I don't get what I want when I want it?' Anger is like a mirror – your own personal mirror. Look into it and see what comes back at you. Maybe you're spoiled or you're a bit grandiose in what you expect of yourself and others at work. Maybe people at work aren't the problem – maybe you are.

Look around at the other people you work with. Are they as angry at work as you are? If not, and if they're doing the same work, ask yourself why. Why are you angry when they're not?

Improving your chances of getting re-employed

Every once in a while we run across a piece of research dealing with anger that really grabs our attention – like the one by Dr James Pennebaker at the University of Texas that linked emotional confession to an employee's likelihood of finding a new job. The strategy Pennebaker used to assist a small group of recently laid-off workers was amazingly simple. He had these 25 men spend 30 minutes a day for a week writing down their deepest thoughts and feelings about being laid off. The main emotion they experienced was outrage.

Although the men expressed instant relief after writing each day, the real benefit came from the fact that they were three to five times more likely to be re-employed several months later than a comparable group of employees who only received the usual types of employer assistance – help in updating their CVs. Dr Pennebaker surmised that helping these men come to terms with the anger they felt over losing their jobs enabled them to be less defensive and hostile when they went to interviews for other positions. In effect, they became more desirable candidates.

Engaging in unhelpful work behaviour

Have you engaged in any of the following behaviours at work lately?

- ✔ Come to work late without permission
- ✔ Made fun of someone at work
- ✔ Found yourself daydreaming rather than doing your job
- ✔ Behaved rudely to a client or colleague
- ✔ Refused to assist a colleague at work
- ✔ Blamed someone else for a mistake you made
- ✔ Tried to look busy while doing nothing
- ✔ Taken a longer break than you were entitled to
- ✔ Avoided returning a phone call to someone at work
- ✔ Intentionally wasted supplies
- ✔ Stolen something that belongs to a colleague
- ✔ Hit or pushed someone
- ✔ Made an obscene gesture or insulted a colleague

If you answered yes to any of these questions, you've engaged in what's called *unhelpful work behaviour*: an act at work that's clearly intended to hurt the organisation you work for or other employees. And which employees are most likely to engage in such behaviour? The angry ones, of course.

Now, ask yourself this question: if I act this way at work, am I likely to have a successful career – get a raise, get a promotion, get a pat on the back from the boss? Probably not.

Ruining Your Marriage

Angry people are difficult to live with, and anger is powerful enough to kill any positive feelings that a married couple has for each other. The idea that 'love conquers all' is a myth.

Take Alastair, for example, a young man who was married three times before he reached his 30th birthday. Alastair's explanation was that he was simply unlucky in his choice of partners – 'I seem to find one cow after another.' The truth of the matter, though, was that Alastair was a chronic rager, who easily became frustrated and violent when he and his wife faced any type of stress or conflict – problems sticking to a budget, how to discipline the children, how to satisfy both sets of parents. This problem was not a new one: Alastair's temper tantrums had begun when he was a small child and had gradually escalated over the years.

Is Alastair unusual? Unfortunately, no. Studies show that the divorce rate for men and women who were ill-tempered as children is twice that of even-tempered kids.

Making the healthy choice

Every day you're faced with choices. Some of those choices are simple, like which socks to wear, whether to have bacon with your eggs or whether to drink another cup of coffee. Other choices are tough choices. Do you let one of your employees go? Do you confront your teenager about the drugs you found in his dresser drawer? Do you keep your temper, even though you've good reason to lose it? Obviously, some of your options are healthy; others aren't.

Glenn was sent to the author Gill for court-ordered anger management after he assaulted his ex-wife. He wasn't all that motivated; he honestly felt that he hadn't done anything wrong, certainly nothing that should be regarded as a crime. His reasoning was: 'Basically, I hate conflict. I avoid it wherever possible, always have. I don't tell people – like my ex-wife – when I'm angry, because I don't want to hurt their feelings or make them uncomfortable. So, it builds up. I was trying to avoid a row, trying to leave rather than argue, but she stood in the door and blocked my exit. So I pushed her out of the way and she called the police.'

Gill asked him, 'If you had to choose between hurting your ex-wife's – or your current fiancée's – feelings or assaulting one of them physically, which would you do?'

He tried to avoid the answer, instead saying that he kept his emotions to himself in order not to hurt other people's feelings. Gill pressed him for an answer: 'I understand that, but I'm asking you to choose between possibly hurting her feelings versus hurting her physically.'

Once again, he attempted to avoid the choice. But after she pressed him a third time, he finally said, 'Well, of course, I'd rather hurt her feelings.'

Gill replied, 'Yes. You can recognise that what you did when angry went against your preferred choice. The last time you made the unhealthy choice, which has brought you here.'

If you choose to hold in your anger to the point where you finally explode in rage, the consequences of that rage are the result of the choice you made. If you want to have fewer negative consequences, then you've got to find how to make healthier choices. And that's what this book is all about – choosing solutions that 'defuse' your anger, rather than allow you to 'bottle it up' and then explode.

Affecting Those You Care About

If you're not all that concerned about the fact that your anger is poisoning *your* life, at least be concerned about what it's doing to those you live with and love. Living with a habitually angry – sometimes rageful – person is no different from living with someone who's a heavy smoker. Spouses of heavy smokers breathe in all that smoke and, as a result, have a 25 per cent greater risk of developing heart disease or lung cancer, even though they never smoke themselves. Well, the same is true of anger – all that anger that you're pouring out or holding on to over the years can rob your family of energy, make them ill and ruin their careers as well.

Sometimes the repercussions of being the spouse or child of an angry person are obvious – bruises, broken bones, scars, trips to the Accident and Emergency department. Most often, however, the effects are more subtle and less visible, but no less devastating or emotionally crippling.

Rhonda's father was, as she put it, 'difficult, always difficult', which turned out to mean he was a chronic rager. Growing up, Rhonda and her sister were used to him shouting, throwing things and being constantly disgusted by everything they did. Unlike her sister, who'd fight back even as a child, Rhonda's way of surviving her father's angry abuse was to escape by becoming invisible – that is, she behaved in ways that escaped notice, something she still did at age 56. The other legacies of Rhonda's early childhood – common to all victims of angry parenting – included

  ✔ Low self-esteem

  ✔ A lack of identity

  ✔ Suppressed emotions (most especially anger!)

✔ A feeling of estrangement and discomfort when in the company of others

✔ An insatiable need to please people

✔ Critical self-judgement

✔ An inability to experience intimacy in adult relationships

✔ A defensive orientation towards life ('I'm sorry – it must be my fault!')

✔ A lack of assertiveness

✔ A tendency to underachieve in her choice of occupation

✔ Frequent bouts of depression

Rhonda did one other thing common to children of angry parents: she married a man just like her father, a man she felt subordinate to, a man she was afraid of, a man who made her want to continue being invisible. So, all the symptoms and behaviours of her unhappy childhood continued throughout her adult years. Her father's anger affected Rhonda on every level – just as your anger affects those you love on every level.

A father's choices

Author Dr Gentry has first-hand experience of how an angry family member affects loved ones.

Growing up, our family wasn't poor, but we were just one step above it. Too many kids, too little money. My father was a good man, hard-working, intelligent and resourceful. But he had two black marks against him: he was an alcoholic and he had an awful temper.

My parents always argued about money. My mother was always on my father's back to earn more so that they could pay the bills and do some nice things for us five children once in a while. My father's answer most often was to simply get drunk and then turn violent.

Then one day he got a break. His employer offered him a white-collar sales job with higher pay. We were all excited, especially my mother. But things didn't go well from the outset. Dad just wasn't comfortable wearing a shirt and tie, working with his head rather than his hands

and keeping his cool with difficult customers. His boss eventually took the new position away from him and demoted him back to his old job in the warehouse.

And there we were, back to being nearly poor. My mother was furious with my dad. I don't think she ever forgave him for losing that promotion and I'm sure that had something to do with their eventual divorce a few years later.

Strangely enough, though, my father seemed relieved and happier with himself. He was back in his element, where he could get angry with his co-workers whenever he felt like it, stop off at the pub on the way home and end up fighting with his wife all night. Maybe that sabotaging this once-in-a-lifetime opportunity for advancement was a good choice for my father, but it sure wasn't for the family. Years later, my father died angry and broke – just as he'd lived his whole life.

Part II
Dealing with Past and Present Anger

'So, being asked lots of searching questions
sends you into an uncontrollable rage,
Mr. Houliston.....'

In this part . . .

We show you how emotions, like anger, are supposed to be transient – they come and go – and why you need to take immediate, decisive action as soon as you start to lose your temper in order to prevent anger from taking hold of your mind and body. In this part, you see why it's not always wise to have the last (angry) word and you find out how to ratchet down the volume of your own anger. Bottom line: Just because you have the right to be angry doesn't mean you have to exercise that right!

We also tackle the toughest challenge of all: managing anger from your past. We want you to be able to dig your way out from old anger that lies just below the surface and that can be triggered at any time for any reason.

To begin with, stop trying so hard to forget those old, unresolved grievances that create so much emotional harm. Your task is not to forget, but to forgive – and forgiveness is never easy. In this part, you explore what you have to do before you can get beyond your emotional past. Our goal in this part is to get you to stop playing the blame game and realise that the person who benefits the most from your forgiveness is *you*.

Chapter 4

Taking Immediate Action

- -

In This Chapter

▶ Creating emotional distance

▶ Striking while the iron is still warm

▶ Bringing yourself out of anger

▶ Breaking old habits

- -

*T*he first thing it may help to do when you feel anger coming on is to take immediate action. As the saying goes, 'He who hesitates is lost' – or for our purposes, a person who hesitates loses his temper.

Ninety per cent of people, unfortunately, don't act as soon as they start feeling angry, and all too often they quickly progress from a petty-annoyance stage to full-blown rage. This chapter shows you how to keep that from happening. The idea that emotions need to just run their course is a myth – and a dangerous one at that. The sooner you take control of your anger, the better off you are (and that goes for those around you too, who may end up on the receiving end of your wrath).

Drawing the Line – the Sooner the Better

Anger, by its nature, is meant to be short lived. It comes and it goes like a wave hitting the beach. For most people, anger is over within five to ten minutes. But for some people anger lingers and grows in intensity, accelerating under its own steam.

To change your angry response, try the following:

✔ **Giving yourself time.** Take a step back (you've probably heard the advice 'count to ten'.) Use the time it would take you to count to ten to ask yourself 'What physical reaction am I having?' and 'Do I have to react instantly?' You can put yourself at an advantage by making a plan. What do you really want to get out of this? Is it important enough to do something, or can you let it pass? What is most likely to happen if you react now?

✔ **Ask the right questions about your anger.** This may seem simple, but what exactly are you angry about? Is now the time to deal with it? If this is the seventh time your son has come in very late, but you've let the other six occasions go quietly, what do you want to say to him? If your friend's daughter has just broken your window, what will solve the situation? You're looking for a good outcome, not a chance to get rid of your physical tension with a rant.

✔ **Choosing how you react.** You know that you're feeling annoyed, irritated or angry. Others don't, unless you let them know. What's the expression on your face saying? And your body posture? What volume do you have to use to make your point clearly? Do you have to do anything, or can you just talk? If you choose to talk, focus on the problem and stay away from judgemental remarks.

✔ **Taking the consequences.** It's all very well feeling justified, in the right, but are you? If you lose your temper, others may be angry with you in return. Perhaps you've had an outburst at a birthday party or in the office. Other peoples' feelings are as important as yours – your behaviour affects their view of you. You can choose to behave in a way that brings you and others to a win–win ending, or leaves you having to resolve damage you've done.

✔ **Dealing with the bigger picture.** You're angry because your girlfriend didn't call yesterday when she promised to. Perhaps you just want to deal with what happened yesterday. However, it may not be that you're angry because you missed her yesterday, but because you can't rely on her keeping her word. Taking a moment to consider what one single situation means gives you the choice to focus on what really matters.

Settling for Just Being Irritated

Irritation, or annoyance, is the mildest form of anger. It lies at the opposite end of the spectrum from rage. Typically, you don't have to worry about managing irritation, unless it lasts and lasts, building up your tension levels.

Irritation is more commonplace than anger. Studies suggest that most people feel irritated several times a week. Because irritation is less intense than anger, people get over being irritated quicker than they do being angry. Also, irritation is more likely to go away on its own.

In short, being irritated is usually not a problem – if that's where it ends.

How do you settle for just being annoyed? The next time someone pushes your buttons, try the following:

✔ **Don't think of the incident or situation as more serious than it is.** Keep things in perspective. Does it really matter? If someone cuts you up in traffic, that's annoying, but it's not the end of the world.

✔ **Don't take it personally.** Was it aimed at you? That same woman who cut you up doesn't know you – she's probably oblivious to you, and even if she's acting out her own little road-rage drama, it's not about you in particular.

✔ **Don't blame the other person.** Is fault that important? When you start blaming someone else, it's easy to let your annoyance escalate. Sometimes people make mistakes. It's very rare that it matters enough to analyse whose fault it is. Calm people can just let it go.

✔ **Don't think about revenge.** Revenge is often the next step after you start assigning blame. It is a healthy way of 'getting your own back' to spend your energy on more useful things than revenge.

✔ **Keep striving for a calm way of coping with the situation.** So you're annoyed at that other driver. How can you deal with the situation without getting angry? Can you think about something else? Maybe you turn on your favourite music, look at the view around you or count the number of people you can see.

✔ **Refuse to see yourself as a helpless victim.** Take some type of action to adjust or correct what has annoyed you. It really doesn't matter what you do as long as you do something – other than just be angry. Take action to change the situation, around you or inside yourself.

✔ **Don't let a negative mood – like depression – magnify your emotion.** Anger only intensifies depression. Leave your mood aside, or make it a priority to get some help for your mood as well. Tell yourself: I'm not going to let this annoying situation add to what is already a down mood. Ask yourself: what would I do if I weren't depressed? And then do that.

Understanding Why Your Fuse Is So Short

Some people have a short fuse, meaning that their anger accelerates so quickly that they don't have much of an opportunity to take control of it before it gets out of hand. A number of factors determine the length of your fuse, such as:

✔ **How much sleep you're getting.** Without adequate sleep (six to eight hours per night), life becomes a real strain. Everything seems to take more effort. Your nerves are frayed. You're less effective at everything you do. And it doesn't take much to set off your temper. (See Chapter 16 for more on sleep and anger.)

✔ **Whether you have a defensive outlook.** If you have a cynical, hostile view of the world – expecting things not to go your way and thinking of everyone around you as potential enemies – you're always on the verge of lashing out in anger. Any little spark can (and will) set you off.

✔ **Your mood.** There's no question about it: if you suffer from certain types of mood disorders (such as agitated depression or bipolar disorder), it won't take as much to make you angry. Around 45 per cent of our angry clients also have a mood disorder (often undiagnosed).

✔ **Your personality.** Do you have a combative personality? Are you impatient, impulsive, confrontational, demanding and domineering in the way you deal with life? If the answer is yes, you're likely to have a short fuse – because you're always poised to move against the world at a moment's notice.

✔ **Your role models.** Often, the apple doesn't fall far from the tree. In other words, you pick up how to react to stress during childhood – from your parents and others who raised you. If they're quick tempered, it's likely you are too. The good news is that this is learned behaviour, and what you can learn you can relearn. It takes time to change habits learned in childhood, but then it took around 18 years to pick them up.

✔ **Your stress level.** There's normal stress and then there's abnormal, excessive, over-the-top stress. The farther away from normal stress you get, the shorter your fuse. Abrupt outbursts of anger are often your nervous system's way of saying, 'Stop! I can't take any more stress. It's killing me! Back off.'

✔ **Your temperament.** You came into the world wired differently from your brothers and sisters, your parents or your best friend. Anyone with children knows that they're different characters right from the start of life. These differences are evident even before birth and continue from cradle to grave. Some people are impulsive (acting quickly and without much thought) and others are more deliberate (taking their time to think things through before acting). You may be more excitable or reactive, which means that you're more physically aroused (your biological response is quicker) than someone who's slow, calm or careful by nature. Impulsive and excitable people have much shorter fuses.

✔ **Your use of chemicals such as caffeine, nicotine and alcohol.** Chemicals that affect your brain affect your emotions. That includes drugs such as caffeine, nicotine, alcohol, cocaine and tranquillizers, to name but a few. Both legal and illegal substances have a significant impact on emotional balance. If you regularly use any of these substances, you're more likely to have a shorter fuse. It's a myth that drugs and substances help to reduce anger – they help to suppress it. Turn to Chapter 15 for more.

The emotional toll of coffee and cola

Richard came to see the author Gill for help with his irritation and low moods. He insisted to Gill that he used to be content and had no major problems. A review of his lifestyle quickly revealed that he drank six cups of coffee at work each day, plus a caffeine boost drink in the morning if he felt down. He took recreational drugs every few weekends, but insisted that they gave him a good time and helped him to forget his problems.

Gill helped Richard to consider how chemicals that woke him up, gave him energy and made him feel happy and carefree might affect his body and mind when they wore off. Without anything in his system for the following month, he was amazed to find that he had his own reserves of energy and really was the steady person he believed he was. Caffeine, recreational drugs and alcohol were giving him brief lifts, but each had its own rebound on mood and anger control.

After two months of experiments with and without caffeine and other drugs, Richard said, 'Trying to keep myself steady was like trying to keep a car on the road when you're sharing the steering wheel.' Richard didn't really need to learn anger-management techniques; instead, he discovered that emotions such as anger all have a biological and physical element. Physical effects of his lifestyle just upset his normal, balanced approach to life.

Lengthening Your Fuse

You need to find ways to keep calmer and be slower to anger. So how can you lengthen your fuse? Well, you can't easily undo your childhood and you certainly can't change your temperament, but you can do a lot of other helpful things.

TIP

Try these anger-avoiding tips:

- ✔ **Ask for things instead of being demanding.** See Chapter 5 for tips on how to express your anger effectively.

- ✔ **Cut back on caffeine.** You find caffeine in tea and coffee, cold remedies, chocolate and some soft drinks. Consider each drink as one 'unit' and limit yourself to two to four per day.

- ✔ **Drink alcohol only in moderation.** Follow the guidelines and ask for help if your drinking has crept up to a level you know is too high.

✔ **Employ some stress-management techniques.** Chapter 14 shows you how to be a hardy personality.

✔ **Get counselling and treatment for depression.** Chapter 18 outlines the anger–depression link.

✔ **Get more sleep.** Chapter 16 can help here.

✔ **Try to have a more optimistic outlook.** Say something positive to yourself when you feel negative about what's happening – for example, 'I've managed more difficult things than this; I can do it.'

You can also try some other techniques that we cover in the following sections.

Walking away – but coming back

You have a built-in fight-or-flight mechanism that guides and directs your behaviour whenever you're faced with some type of threat – regardless of whether the threat is a physical one or a threat to your self-esteem. This explains why you probably respond to provocation either with some type of angry reaction (fight) or simply run the other way and try to avoid the problem altogether (flight).

The problem is that neither of these extreme options helps you manage anger. If you decide to stand and fight, you need to remain angry long enough to overcome the threat – and the intensity of your anger may become stronger. On the other hand, if you retreat from the threat, you end up taking your angry feelings with you. You can outrun the threat, but not your own emotions.

The good news is that a third, workable option exists – another way to take immediate action. You can disengage (walk away) initially, but return later, after you've calmed down sufficiently to discuss how to resolve the conflict. This is the most mature way to handle anger-provoking problems, but also the one most people are least likely to choose.

The choice of how you respond to provocation to a large extent depends on how angry you get initially. Table 4-1 shows how a group of 14 to 15-year-old school students responded when asked the question 'What would you do if another student got angry with you for no apparent reason?' As students got angrier, the chances that they would walk away and later return to discuss their anger decreased dramatically. Yet another good reason to settle for just being irritated (mildly angry) when things don't go your way.

Table 4-1	How School Students Respond		
If the Students Are . . .	Percentage Who Would Walk Away	Percentage Who Would Get Angry Back	Percentage Who Would Walk Away and Then Come Back to Discuss the Situation
Not angry	38	18	44
Mildly angry	21	51	28
Moderately angry	29	58	13
Extremely angry	0	87	13

Highly aggressive, combative personalities are poised to take on whatever is provoking them instead of disengaging and walking away. Even if calming down means winning, it just goes against their instinctive nature!

Giving the other person the last word

People get *irritated* with *things* – a leaky tap, a car that won't start – but they get *angry* with *people*. So, most anger occurs within the context of a social exchange. Somebody always has the first word – that's the provocation, the thing that gets the ball rolling. The question is, who stops the ball – who has the last word?

After you realise that you're angry, you can decide to let the person who had the first word also have the last. Do you always get what you wanted with the last word? It's unlikely. Why not let the other person take this risk?

Consider the following two conversations between a parent and a teenager and see which one you think is best. Here's the first conversation:

> **Parent:** I want you to clean up your room before dinner.
>
> **Adolescent:** I'm doing something now.
>
> **Parent:** (irritated) I said I want this room cleaned up.
>
> **Adolescent:** (angry) Leave me alone.

> **Parent:** (angry) Don't talk to me that way. Start cleaning up your room – *now!*
>
> **Adolescent:** (throwing book across the room in a rage) I told you to get out of my room!
>
> **Parent:** (very angry) Don't you *dare* throw that at me! Start cleaning this room right now. I mean it.

And here's the second conversation:

> **Parent:** I want you to clean your room before dinner.
>
> **Adolescent:** (irritated) I'm doing something now.
>
> **Parent:** (irritated) Yes, I can see that, but I want you to clean your room.
>
> **Adolescent:** (angry) Leave me alone.
>
> **Parent:** (irritated but not yet angry) Okay. That'll give you a chance to get started on your room.
>
> **Adolescent:** (angry) I'll do it when I feel like it.

Did it matter to the parent *when* the teenager cleaned her room when the parent first asked? Then why should it matter now? The point is, the teenager said she will clean her room, which was the parent's aim.

Often, people are so eager to have the last word in disagreements with other people that they totally lose sight of how out of hand things are getting. Anger management – having control of the volume of your anger – is more about what you do while a discussion is happening than it is about how it turned out. You can improve your anger control by letting the other person have the last word.

If you insist on having the last word – you just can't help yourself – then by all means make it a non-defensive and non-provocative one. Try to find a personal favourite and use that. You're much more likely to think of something when you aren't in the middle of angry feelings. When you've said your final word, walk away. You can clear up whatever's happened later.

Knowing That Sometimes It Pays to Feel Guilty

Guilt isn't necessarily good or bad. It depends on whether you feel guilty before you act out your anger or after you act out your anger. If guilt keeps you from harming another person with your anger – verbally or physically – that's a good thing. If you wait to feel guilty until after you've satisfied your thirst for revenge, that's bad.

Morality and religion

What we've discovered from exposure to different religions is that guilt is an inherent component of *all* religions – because religion and morality go hand in hand. Morality shows people right from wrong, what constitutes civil behaviour and where societal boundaries are.

Guilt is what society conditions you to feel when you cross those boundaries. Some of those boundaries have to do with anger and violence (for example, murder is wrong), and these boundaries are no less important today than they were thousands of years ago.

John gets angry with his wife whenever she shouts, 'Look out!' when he's driving the car. A couple of times, her nervousness has almost caused him to have an accident. He feels like shouting at her, 'Don't do that! You're going to get us killed.' But he doesn't. He loves his wife – a partner for over 40 years – and he knows that shouting at her will only hurt her feelings. So he lets it pass. John's brother, on the other hand, doesn't let *anything* pass. If he gets angry with his wife, she hears about it immediately and in the harshest terms. Sometimes, he just shouts; other times, he expresses his anger physically.

The next time you find yourself irritated (or just plain angry), before you act consider the consequences of what's in your mind. If you know the action is something you're going to want to apologise for later, don't do it. Think of a way of expressing your feelings that isn't hurtful. In this kind of situation, prevention really *is* better than cure!

Seeing How Distraction Works

You experience whatever captures your brain's attention. If you get aroused with anger, your brain turns its attention to that and away from other things. That's why anger can be such a disruptive emotion. The stronger the emotion, the more captivated your brain becomes. You can be irritated and continue to at least partially attend to other things. But rage, now that's a different story.

Intense emotional experiences – positive or negative – override your senses. That's how people end up 'blinded' by love or in a state of 'blind rage'. *Blind*, in this context, simply means your brain isn't paying attention to anything outside of your own emotion. (See Chapter 9 for more on blind rage.)

The good news, however, is that the brain can be distracted – meaning it can turn its attention elsewhere at any point in time. So the trick in anger management is to give your brain something else to attend to besides anger.

Changing your situation – getting some distance

In most people emotions are situational; in other words, something happening now irritates you or makes you angry. The emotion itself is tied to the situation in which it originates. As long as you remain in that provocative situation, you're likely to stay angry. If you *leave* the situation, the opposite is true – the emotion begins to fade as soon as you move away from the situation. Moving away from the situation prevents it from getting a grip on you.

Psychologists often advise clients to get some emotional distance from whatever is bothering them. One easy way to do that is to *geographically* separate yourself from the source of your anger – leave the area!

Andy employed this principle in dealing with his irritating boss. Andy had been referred for anger management with the author Gill after aggressively confronting his boss on two different occasions. The fact that he had good reason for doing so didn't matter. He was simply told that the next time he lost it, he'd be fired – immediately. With just a few years left before retirement, Andy wasn't eager for that to happen. Besides, his recurrent anger had also affected his blood pressure and his doctor had warned him of the possibility of a heart attack.

Andy and Gill talked about some practical ways to keep his cool even in difficult situations – which, unfortunately, occurred on a daily basis in his job. Gill asked Andy to pay more attention to his emotions, and as soon as he felt himself begin to get tense in an exchange with his boss, make a quick exit and calm down.

Guess what? It worked! Whenever Andy's boss began to confront him, and whenever Andy began to feel his blood start to boil, he'd politely say, 'Excuse me. Give me a minute. I'll be right back,' and then step away. Andy then used some of the techniques we talk about in Chapter 6 to defuse his emotions, returned to his boss (now more in control of his emotions) and said, 'Okay, what was it you wanted to say?' That was several years ago and Andy's still employed.

Why employees need breaks

A lot of companies have tightened up on allowing their employees to take work breaks. Apparently, every time you leave your workstation, employers feel like they're losing money. For the most part, we believe this is a mistake. Employees need work breaks, if for no other reason than to engage in some much-needed anger management. That's why so many people take smoke breaks and coffee breaks – these are legitimate, time-honoured ways of removing yourself from the stress (and irritation) that surrounds you at work. The fewer the breaks, the hotter the temperature in the office!

Stopping the rumination

What is rumination and what does it have to do with anger? Good question. *Rumination* is the human equivalent of a cow chewing on the cud – chewing food already swallowed to digest it. When you continue to rethink, reconsider, relive and rehash some incident that provoked your anger well beyond the point where it happened, you're ruminating. When you continue the conversation in your head, or angry thoughts pop in as you're doing something else, you're ruminating. This always intensifies the emotion. At first you may just be irritated, but the more you think and talk about it, the angrier you become. You can't let go of the thoughts, so you can't let go of the feelings – you're stuck!

 So, how do you get unstuck? Try using the thought-stopping technique. When you become aware that you're entering into the realm of repetitive angry thinking, say aloud to yourself, 'Stop!', and shift your attention to something else. Repeat the word as many times as necessary until you've let go of what's irritating you. If you use the technique quickly, before you get too far down that road of chewing too much on your anger, letting go isn't difficult. All you're trying to do here, really, is interrupt that pattern of unproductive thinking that can only make a bad situation worse.

 If the thought-stopping technique doesn't work, try ruminating about something *other* than your anger. You can engage in some *positive* rumination – otherwise known as daydreaming. Chose something you feel great about, or a place you'd love to be, and let your mind relive those feelings instead.

One of Gill's clients complained to her that she couldn't stop ruminating. She suggested that, rather than each slip being a failure, each is a chance to practise. Although you find it difficult, there will be lots of chances to practise.

Using imagery to transcend anger

Many parallels between anger management and pain management exist. Anger and pain can both be intense, chronic experiences – and you can easily find yourself ruminating about both (see the preceding section for more on rumination).

 So, what Dr Gentry found out from one of his pain clients has relevance here. Phillip was a man in his 50s who owned and operated an orchard. He enjoyed his life and found real meaning in everything he did – that is, until he was the victim in a car accident, which left him in incurable back and leg pain. Phillip needed to continue doing a lot of physical work in his orchard, but that tended to exacerbate his pain as the day went on. He needed a tool to help him alleviate the pain when it became intolerable so that he could get back to work. The tool Dr Gentry introduced him to was imagery.

Phillip found out how to relax and imagine his favourite thing – sitting by a pond fishing, all by himself. It was his version of heaven on earth. At whatever point in the work day when his pain was too much, he'd announce aloud to his wife and employees, 'I'm going fishing!' They all knew what that meant. Then he'd go to the back of the barn, sit down on the ground, close his eyes and 'go fishing' – in other words, imagine himself fishing. Phillip was good at imagery, so it was the next best thing to actually being there. After about ten minutes of this his pain would lessen to a point where he could once again bear it. He'd open his eyes, stand up and announce to everyone, 'I'm back. Let's get to work.' Simple, but effective.

You can do the same thing with anger. Here's how:

1. **Find a quiet setting.**

   You can't engage in imagery if you're distracted. Find a quiet place where you can be alone for at least ten minutes. If you're at work, that could be your office – if you close the door and put a 'do not disturb' sign on your door. Or you can take your break and find sanctuary elsewhere – an outside bench, sitting in your car in the car park, or – as one of our more creative clients did – sitting in a cubicle in the toilets.

2. **Rate your pre-imagery level of anger.**

   Rate how angry you are at this minute on a scale from 1 (mildly irritated) to 10 (extreme rage).

3. **Close your eyes.**

   Imagery is about visualising. If you're going to create internal images to use as an antidote to anger, you first have to stop visualising what's in front of you in the external environment. Closing your eyes is the first step in letting go – and you may find this difficult. It's all about trusting yourself and the world around you.

   If you aren't comfortable closing your eyes in the quiet place you've found, chances are you don't feel safe there. Try finding somewhere else.

4. **Release your hold on reality.**

   Letting go of the real world so that you can enter into the world of imagery takes more than simply closing your eyes. It also requires a receptive attitude. You have to grant yourself permission to let go of the situation that triggered your anger, and the feeling itself. This is no different from loosening your grip on the steering wheel in order to avoid road rage.

5. **Imagine something positive.**

   This is the fun part! You're free here to conjure up any positive image you want. What's your favourite holiday spot, where you're most relaxed? A lot of people say the beach, but it could be sitting on the decking in your own garden. The only requirement is that you choose a place where you're never angry.

6. **Be specific in your imagination.**

   This has to do with the *who*, *what* and *where* of the situation you choose. Are you alone or with someone else? Where are you and what are you doing? Lying in a hammock? Sitting on a dock, fishing? Working in your herb garden? Imagine what you're wearing. Can you see the colours of your clothes? What kind of day is it – cloudy, windy, warm, rainy, sunny? The more detailed you are about the image, the more you get into it.

7. **Stay with the image for at least five minutes.**

   This exercise is just for use in derailing anger that may otherwise get out of hand. It's not something that you need to do for a long period of time. You'll be surprised at how refreshing five minutes of positive imagery can be and how easy it is to release anger in that short interval. This has the effect of calming down your body's reaction to stress as well, reducing the chemicals produced for 'fight or flight'.

8. **Evaluate your post-imagery anger level.**

   While you're still relaxed and have your eyes closed, rate your anger on a ten-point intensity scale again. Is there a difference now? If so, you've obviously succeeded in your attempt to transcend anger for the moment. If there's no change or you actually find yourself *more* angry than you were earlier, let yourself have a few more minutes of positive imagery, trying to stay with the image. Or maybe you'll find the strategies we offer in other chapters more helpful. Don't be discouraged however – no single solution works for everybody.

9. **Linger in the moment.**

   If the exercise did what you wanted it to, why not linger a bit and enjoy the change in your mind and body – the lack of tension, the inner peace. Don't be in too big a hurry to get back to reality!

10. **Open your eyes and move on with your day.**

    When you do open your eyes, you'll realise that the world didn't go anywhere – *you* did. You took a short, refreshing trip to some imaginary, anger-free place that you call your own – and, in the process, you left behind the circumstances that provoked your anger in the first place.

You can use this imagery technique in two other ways:

✔ Instead of imagining yourself in another positive situation, imagine yourself in the same situation that caused your anger, but without any feelings of anger.

✔ Imagine yourself in the same (or a different) situation, but feeling a negative emotion other than anger (for example, sadness). Emotions compete with one another. Feeling angry and sad at the same time is difficult (if not impossible). In fact, that's why many people get angry in the first place – it's their way of not feeling sad. For example, imagine feeling sad (rather than angry) about the fact that the person who was just shouting at you doesn't appreciate what a wonderful person you are and how helpful you can be.

A simple, inexpensive, handy way to take immediate action when you find yourself getting angry is to suck a sweet until it's all gone. It only takes a few minutes but it short-circuits the natural progression of anger.

So why does it work?

- ✔ **This technique takes advantage of the link between the sucking reflex and achieving a state of calm that's evident in all newborn infants.** Any mother knows that giving an infant something to suck on alleviates the baby's distress. That's why dummies are so popular – and difficult for some children to give up as they get older.

- ✔ **The technique involves the ingestion of something sweet – sugar – and sweet sensations are associated at the level of the brain with pleasure, which is the antithesis of anger.** The sweet literally sweetens your disposition!

- ✔ **It buys you enough time to formulate a response to your initial anger, instead of just *reacting* to it (see Chapter 6).** An angry reaction is immediate, impulsive, thoughtless, predictable and typically leads to consequences that you later regret. An angry response, on the other hand, is more deliberate, engages the mind, takes advantage of past experience, isn't always predictable (what works in one situation may not work in another) and more often has positive consequences (see Chapter 11 for pointers on how to use anger constructively).

- ✔ **Patiently sucking on a sweet is out of keeping with the combative, dominating behaviour common in anger or rage.** Sucking is a passive response, not an aggressive one, and anger is essential only if you're moving against the world after you're provoked.

- ✔ **By putting something in your mouth to suck on, you can't say something angry that escalates the conflict between you and others or causes you regret later on.** Telling someone 'I'm sorry' after you've assaulted her with your angry words and tone of voice is useless and ineffective – it doesn't help you and it certainly doesn't help the other person.

Don't bite the sweet. It defeats the purpose of the exercise by shortening the length of time before you act on your anger and, more important, by indulging your aggressive personality. (Aggressive personalities seem to want to constantly 'bite' life rather than savour it.)

How some men handle grief

On more than one occasion we've worked with men – intelligent, successful men – who become extremely angry after the death of one of their children. Almost without exception, these men resist any effort on our part to tap into feelings of grief. (Who wouldn't be sad after losing a child?) The more we probe, the more defensive and angry they get. The look on their faces tells us, 'Believe me, you don't want to go there!' Translated, this means, '*I* don't want to go there!'

One man actually threatened the author Dr Gentry by saying, 'I'm warning you: if you ask me one more time how I feel about losing my son, I'm going to hit you. I mean it.' Some of these men become angry alcoholics. Some focus their anger on their spouses and end up divorced. Some alienate themselves from their other children (and thus compound their loss). Some take it out at work and end up unemployed. All in an effort not to feel sad.

Chapter 5

Avoiding Speaking Out in Anger

In This Chapter

▶ Avoiding the temptation to let it all out

▶ Finding the right language

▶ Staying focused

▶ Toning it down

▶ Paying attention to your voice

*W*hen it comes to emotion, communication is absolutely the key. It's not only *what* you say when you lose your temper; it's also *how* you say it.

Take Lisa, for example. Lisa is a newly married 26-year-old who finds herself constantly raging at her husband, Joe. In some situations Lisa has even physically assaulted Joe. There's no question that Lisa is frustrated by a number of things about her husband – Joe's friends spend all their time at their house, he doesn't help with even the simplest of household chores and he spends what little money he makes on drugs. When Lisa tries to talk to Joe about all this, he either ignores her or puts her off by saying, 'Okay, I'll get to it later.' Obviously, that's not the response Lisa is looking for.

When she first entered an anger-management programme Lisa expressed her anger towards her husband with expletives like, 'You @#$%head!' instead of articulating the *reasons* she was upset. But that's all changed now. She's found how to express her anger in non-inflammatory language (for example, 'I find that I'm a lot less angry when you're considerate and help me out'), while at the same time turning down the volume – from rage to just plain angry. Most important, she's discovered how to talk rather than hit, which gives her marriage a chance to succeed.

This chapter is all about finding out how to effectively communicate anger and how effectively communicating anger, in turn, benefits your health.

Stopping Ranting

Have you ever called a friend and said, 'I just have to rant'? Ranting is letting out stored-up emotion – that's the best-case scenario. At worst, it's like the dictionary definition of *ranting*, that says it's an 'angry outburst or tirade'.

But doesn't it help to release all those thoughts and feelings? To tell someone what's happened? Isn't ranting a good thing? Well, we're here to tell you that, contrary to what most people think, *ranting about your anger doesn't work*. Ranting doesn't provide the emotional relief you expect, nor does it resolve the real-life problems that trigger your anger in the first place. What it *does* do, unfortunately, is just the opposite: it makes angry people angrier and aggressive people more aggressive.

Screaming at someone that he's a '@#$%!' communicates nothing but raw anger. It doesn't tell the person why you're angry. On the other hand, if you tell him he's acting inconsiderately, then he may be forced to examine his own behaviour and see what needs correcting. If you use your anger constructively (see Chapter 11) it can be like holding up a mirror in which the other person sees a reflection of himself – his behaviour – and it's often a reflection that's unbecoming if not downright ugly. Many of the people you're angry at would *rather* you vent and call them derogatory names than articulate your anger, forcing them to take a closer look at themselves. In effect, by venting you may be doing the person you're upset with a big favour – but not the kind that lasts!

Dr Arthur Bohart at California State University conducted a series of experiments to determine the helpfulness of *catharsis* (the psychiatric term for ranting) in reducing anger. In one of those studies, he had three groups of distressed subjects do one of three things:

✔ Sit quietly in a room thinking about their feelings.

✔ Rant about their angry feelings into a tape recorder.

✔ Spend 20 minutes talking with a counsellor about how they felt.

Dr Bohart concluded that counselling was the most effective way of reducing anger because it involved both the sharing and understanding of your emotions. He also concluded that being silent (not speaking out) reduced anger more quickly than ranting – simply getting things off your chest and into a tape recorder.

If you're feeling chronically angry, then your best bet is to talk to a counsellor or therapist about your emotions so you can get to the bottom of them and work out how to move on. But if you're experiencing an isolated episode of anger, then you're better off thinking about your feelings quietly than you are ranting to a friend.

What was Freud thinking anyway?

The noted psychiatrist Sigmund Freud believed in a 'hydraulic' model of human emotion. As he saw it, emotions – including anger – are a natural by-product of everyday life, but they tend to build up over time, just like steam does in a kettle (or lava does in a volcano). As emotions build up, they create bodily tension that eventually seeks its own discharge. Freud thought that people remain healthy as long as they can freely and openly express their feelings. If you can't express emotion in some acceptable, adaptive way as you experience it, then the mounting tension within your body adversely affects your health.

Freud's term for helping clients discharge their residual anger is *catharsis,* which actually means a dramatic freeing up of deep-seated anger from the past – what we refer to in this book as *yesterday's anger.*

Many people (including lots of anger-management specialists!) misunderstand Freud's concept of catharsis, which was intended to be a therapist-guided, structured re-experiencing of anger that's at the core of the personality. Instead, people see catharsis as something akin to plain old ranting. But they're not the same thing! As far as we're aware, Freud never had his patients pound mattresses with a tennis racket, beat inflated lifelike dolls, rip up telephone books or scream to their hearts' content – all forms of conventional anger-management therapy at some time in the past.

Expressing Your Anger Effectively

If you want to express anger effectively you'd be wise to follow the advice of psychologist George Bach, a pioneer in the field of anger management, who suggests that constructive anger must not just be an exercise in hostility, but also have what he calls *informational impact.* You need to use your anger to educate, inform and share that part of yourself that's hurt, sad, frustrated, insecure and feels attacked with the person who tapped into these feelings. That's the message that needs to get out – anger is simply the vehicle. Following are some strategies that you can use instead of ranting.

Talking versus hitting

If you can't articulate your anger (clearly express how you're feeling through language) then you're likely to act it out through some form of physical aggression. When a man smashes his fist into a wall or, worse yet, into the face of another person, what exactly does that communicate, other than the obvious fact that he's mad as hell? How does that punching benefit him? It doesn't. Does that punch improve his relationship with the person he hits?

No. Is the angry person calm after he's slugged someone (or hit a wall)? Absolutely not. Expressing anger through physical violence has no upside.

So then, is it better to shout and scream out your anger rather than hit something or someone? Yes, if that's the only choice you give yourself at the time. But then again, verbal violence really doesn't get you anywhere either. No one feels better after he's given someone a good tongue-lashing, no matter what he says. And the person on the receiving end of all that yelling and screaming certainly isn't a happy soul either.

So what's left? Talking – using the gift of language to express your emotions (in this case, anger) in a constructive way.

The next time you get so angry you feel like hitting something (or someone), follow these steps:

1. **Come up with a label to identify the intensity of your anger.**

   For example, are you annoyed, irritated, angry, irate or in a rage? Start by saying, 'I feel . . .' Don't say, 'I think . . .' What you're going for here is your feeling, not your thoughts about how obnoxious the other person is.

2. **Identify the thing that triggered your anger.**

   For example, 'Every time I come home, his friends are here. We never have any time to ourselves.' Continue your conversation by saying, 'I feel _____ [insert the word you came up with in Step 1] because . . .'

3. **Ask yourself what it would take to help you return to a non-angry state.**

   For example, 'I'd appreciate it if he'd ask his friends to leave when I get home from work so we can have some time for us.'

When you're able to go through these three steps inside your head, see whether you can actually have that conversation with the person you're angry with.

Writing versus speaking

Some people find the written word a more powerful outlet than the voice.

A very nice woman – we'll call her Jane – came to Dr Gentry's office complaining of feeling emotionally 'burned out'. She dreaded getting up in the morning, was unusually tired, found herself crying for no apparent reason on more than one occasion and felt like there was 'a big fist in my chest' all the time. She had decided she was depressed and wanted to know what she could do to feel better.

After talking to her more, Dr Gentry found out that Jane was caught up in a very unhappy situation: she had spent most of her energy over the past several years caring for one of her grown-up sons who suffered from drug addiction, which continued despite all of Jane's well-intentioned efforts. Because she'd been so tied up in her son's problems, she'd long since stopped devoting any time to her *own* needs or wants – she wanted to travel, meet some new people, do things with her husband. She had, in effect, sacrificed her life for that of her son.

'Your problem isn't depression,' Dr Gentry told Jane. 'Your problem is that you have a ton of anger stuck inside you – anger at the way your life has turned out, anger at your son for not getting well and most of all anger at yourself for letting things get this bad. That's why you feel like you have a fist in your chest – you want to hit something, but you can't.' Jane agreed, adding that she had never been able to talk to anyone about how she felt and instead simply 'contained' her feelings behind a façade of niceness.

'Okay,' Dr Gentry said, 'let's start by having you write down your feelings about your son's drug problem and everything else that's not going right in your life.' He gave her 20 minutes to 'write from the heart, not the head' and then asked her to read what she'd written – just to herself, not aloud – and circle the emotional terms (for example, *angry*, *disappointed*, *upset*). Dr Gentry and Jane then discussed those words that she'd circled.

Two things were immediately apparent: it was easy for Jane to write a lot in a short time because the feelings were just beneath the surface, and she tended to circle issues (such as tiredness or lack of money) more than feelings. For example, Jane circled 'having no friends' – an issue, not an emotion. Jane was disconnected from the emotional side of her personality.

'This is good,' Dr Gentry concluded. 'Now go home and do this exercise for 20 minutes every day until you come back. That's how we're going to treat your depression.'

 Try this exercise for yourself. Find a quiet time, when you won't be disturbed, and a pen and paper, or your computer. As you'll be writing about anger, think ahead before starting and decide what you'll do to relax after you've finished. Set your alarm or a timer for five minutes, then try one of the following (you can try another next time):

- ✔ Start your first sentence with 'The thing that made me angriest this week was . . .' and keep writing for five minutes.

- ✔ Write a letter to the person you feel angry towards, but maybe haven't told, or perhaps just ended up shouting at. Don't think too hard, just begin with 'Dear . . . , I feel angry with you because . . .' Don't worry, you don't send the letter. You can destroy it or keep it somewhere safe.

- ✔ Write a letter to yourself about your true feelings, beginning with 'The thing I can't talk to anyone about is . . .'

When you stop, reread what you've written. Are you surprised by anything in there? Do you see any patterns in your anger? How do you feel to admit your anger to yourself? These are simple but powerful exercises – they show you where your anger crops up, help you to see where you're stuck and where you're dealing with emotions and events well, and allow you to put your point across with no interruptions, corrections or contradictions. Have a look at the language you use – all angry words or is your point coming across? Do you exaggerate or insult when you feel frustrated? And are you confusing other emotions or practical issues with anger (as Jane did)?

Now, take time out to relax – these are exercises to help you, not to tune you into chronic anger.

Leaving out the four-letter words

Lisa (see the introduction of this chapter) would be far better off and less likely to end up assaulting her husband if she referred to him as an 'empty head' – a head that apparently doesn't think about helping around the house or sharing some intimate moments with his wife – rather than a '@#$%head'.

Four-letter words are, by definition, incendiary. They add fuel to the fire and only heighten emotions and increase the probability of some type of physical aggression. They're meant to hurt, not educate. And they cause the person to whom they're directed to defend himself – either by withdrawing (tuning out what you're saying) or engaging in similar behaviour. So now you have two people swearing at each other.

Try to distance yourself from anger-laced profanity by starting with the word *I* rather than *you* – 'I'm furious' rather than 'You're a damn idiot!'. Better yet, enlarge your emotional vocabulary to include other words that are synonymous with anger, for example, *irritated, incensed, exasperated, annoyed, displeased, enraged, outraged, disgusted, riled, vexed* or *piqued.*

Put yourself in the other person's shoes and ask yourself how you would feel if someone called you a '@#$%head' or worse. If he were angry with you, what would you want him to say instead? Try to give some information, for example, 'You're late again. One more time and I'm cancelling my order.' Insults achieve nothing.

Staying focused

When you start speaking out in anger you may lose sight of the issue, problem or circumstance that initially provoked you. Your anger heads off on a tangent, jumping from one grievance to another, midstream. What starts out as 'I asked you to stop at the shop for me and you forgot' suddenly evolves into 'You never help out around here. You don't listen to me. You don't care about me at all. I don't know why I married you in the first place!'

You'd be surprised at how many of our anger-management clients describe some horrific incident involving anger but then when we ask them what started the angry exchange they say, 'I don't know. All I know is that one minute we were talking and the next minute I was shouting and pounding my fist into the wall.'

The more intense your anger, the more likely the emotion itself will distract you from the issue at hand. Blind rage (see Chapter 9) is so unfocused that after you calm down you probably don't remember anything that you said or did. One way to remain in control of your anger is to stay focused on what it is you're angry about. Keep your eye on the ball and things are less likely to get out of control.

Keeping it short – and breathing

Constructive anger expression should be a give-and-take exchange. You give out your feelings and let others take in their meaning. The best way to lose your audience, and ensure that the listener doesn't hear your message, is to go on and on and on . . . By all means, speak out in anger, but keep it short.

Neurological sciences explain that human beings can only digest (and remember) so much information at a time. After 20 minutes of general conversation, most people take a 'mental break', even if the conversation continues. When people rant, the increased speed of speech, volume, tone of voice and sheer hostility can be overwhelming, and are also major distractions for the listener, so they don't hear the message you're so desperate to get across. The longer the rant goes on for, the less attention the listener gives, and without attention, the human brain doesn't store information in the memory. So speaking out in anger for five minutes is like asking someone to remember a 50-digit number. It can't be done! It's no wonder children never remember what their parents tell them when the parents are angry – and you thought they just weren't listening.

Our advice is to speak out in anger one minute at a time. Then take a breath and let the other person respond. That also keeps the intensity of your anger from accelerating, which is what you want, right? If the person you're angry with reacts defensively, let him have his say – don't interrupt – and then resume expressing how you feel for another minute and take another breath.

You can use a traditional egg timer to get the hang of this. Take it in turns to hold the timer until the sand runs out. When it does, you *must* take a break and hand over the timer and give the other person time to speak. You may be surprised how much you hear when you know that you can only listen and wait your turn. You may also be surprised at how often you catch yourself preparing to speak, rather than listening!

It's Not What You Say, It's How You Say It

The louder you speak, the less people hear what you have to say. Your message gets lost in your overheated dialogue. Anger can be an effective means of communication, but if you want to be heard, then you have to pay attention to two aspects of your speech:

- ✔ **Volume:** The power and fullness of your words. The angrier you are, the louder you sound. You don't have to be a rocket scientist to tell the difference between a person who's irritated and someone who's in a full-blown rage.

- ✔ **Pace:** The speed or velocity with which you speak. As your anger accelerates, you find yourself speaking faster and faster. There's a pressured quality to what you're saying – as if the angry words can't get out fast enough.

Professor Aron Wolfe Siegman at the University of Maryland, Baltimore County, found that when people speak out in anger their speech tends to get louder and faster as they go. Anger arouses your nervous system and, among other things, your heart rate begins to increase. As your heart beats faster, it fuels the intensity of your vocal response. And the louder and more rapid your speech, the angrier you get. You're quickly caught up in a vicious circle that begins to feed on itself. (We'd be rich therapists indeed if we had a pound for every client who said, 'I don't know what happened – I was just telling my wife how irritated I was and the next thing I knew I was ranting and raving and scaring her half to death.')

The good news as far as anger management is concerned is that you can reduce the intensity of your emotion by slowing down your speech. You don't have to change what you're saying (unless it includes four-letter words!), just how you say it.

Professor Siegman also noted in his experiments that human beings tend to mimic or match the other person's vocal style. The louder you are when you get angry, the louder the other person is in response. And so it goes on. This type of reciprocal exchange also serves to accelerate anger to the point where it's often difficult to control.

This vicious circle of anger-arousal tone can have dire health consequences over time. And as Chapter 3 explains, people who engage in this type of escalating dialogue are far more at risk of developing coronary heart disease. So, not only are you taking the heart (and spirit) out of the person on the receiving end of your angry tirade, but you also may slowly but surely be killing yourself!

Whenever you find yourself on the verge of losing your cool, ask yourself this question: is this worth raising my blood pressure, straining my heart and even causing myself a heart attack? If not, it's time for some good old-fashioned anger management.

In his work with angry adolescents, Dr Gentry is often confronted verbally by a youngster who's obviously in an over-aroused state. He responds (not reacts!) in a firm, but even-toned fashion. The last thing the kid needs is for Dr Gentry to help exacerbate his rage. Initially, he may accelerate on his own, but Dr Gentry continues to respond to him without any change in the tone of voice. Often, the next thing that happens is that he begins to tone his angry rhetoric down – in other words, if Dr Gentry doesn't match the teenager's vocalisations (yelling back), then the teenager matches Dr Gentry's. This is a great way to defuse someone else's anger. So next time you're faced with someone who's getting upset, try to remain calm and defuse the situation.

Start paying more attention to *how* you speak when you get angry. If you hear yourself getting too loud, talking too rapidly and/or sounding shrill, adjust your speech accordingly. Think of this as an effort on your part to literally fine-tune how you speak out in anger.

Chapter 6

Keeping Your Cool

*M*ost people react angrily when they're provoked. You don't think about it – you just react. You react instinctively and your reactions are always the same. You scowl; you shout; you put down the person who provoked you; you lash out and hit something or someone; or you just stamp off in a fury. In other words, you lose your cool!

Losing your cool is easy. That's why millions of people do it more than they should. *Keeping* your cool is the challenge. Basically, it comes down to taking control of this thing called anger before it takes control of you. Responding to anger means just that – exerting some mindful control over your emotions rather than letting your anger play itself out in a mindless sort of way.

This chapter offers a simple, straightforward set of strategies for defusing anger at the very moment you begin to experience it. It's a set of strategies that only takes 90 seconds to accomplish. The key to this approach is to focus on your anger and your reactions to your anger, not the source of your anger (the thing that triggered it). This means turning your attention inward – on yourself – as a means of controlling how intense your anger is and how long it lasts. You can't manage anger if you're always trying to manage the circumstances (people, things) that unleashed it. For example, instead of focusing on your grievance – your daughter has borrowed the car and got another parking ticket in your name – focus on staying cool and calm. Let her know your view, and ask what she'll do to solve the problem. Asserting some self-control is how you manage anger in the moment.

CASE STUDY

Turning anger around: Ali saves his job

Ali, one of Gill's clients, started out with little belief in anger management but soon changed his mind. His warehouse manager had made it clear that she found Ali unpredictable; one day he'd offer a great idea for improvements to the dispatch system, but the next he'd be kicking a hole in the side of a box due to go out to a customer. Ali had been told very clearly that the next time he lost his temper, he would also lose his job. Ali came to therapy feeling desperate that he couldn't afford to have one more out-burst – everything was on the line. However, he made it clear to Gill that he didn't believe in talking as a 'cure' for anger. He didn't really want to spend time or energy understanding his anger, or doing exercises, he just needed it sorted out! Gill talked to him about his desperation and asked him what he had to lose. He agreed to give anger management a chance, and started

on the exercises in this chapter, after first taking time to measure his anger (refer to Chapter 2).

Only ten days later, he came for his third appointment and said 'You saved me from disaster! My manager changed my rota at the last minute, and told me I'd better not mess the job up as I had the largest load to do. I almost got straight in her face, but I remembered what you said about taking a step back and asking the right questions. She wasn't really threatening me, it's because she trusted me to get that load right. It's an important customer. I handled it totally differently. She even said sorry that she'd just talked to me like that!'

Gill reminded Ali that he was the only one who was there in each situation who could turn it around – it was his effort that had saved his job.

Choosing to Respond Rather Than React

Anger therapists who argue that anger is a choice always amuse us. We're sure they mean well, but they're wrong. The initial feeling of anger is no more the result of conscious choice than other emotions such as joy, sadness or fear. Anger just happens and it's based in the physical response the human body has to threat. Anger is your nervous system's intuitive reaction to some perceived threat or danger. The choice you have is to do with what comes after you feel angry – that is, how you act and whether you continue to feel angry. Ask yourself the following questions:

✔ For the rest of your life, do you want to simply react to your anger in the same old mindless, predictable way you always have?

✔ Do you want to always be a victim of your emotions?

✔ Do you want to continue to apologise for your angry reactions by telling those you hurt, 'I'm sorry, I don't know what came over me. I promise I won't act that way ever again.'?

✔ Do you want others to begin to judge you by your angry reactions (for example, 'Stay away from that guy; he's got a bad temper!')?

We're betting that your answer to each of these questions is a very clear 'No!' More than likely, you're ready for a change. So, before you do anything else, you need to make the decision to *respond* rather than *react* to your anger. Granted, this strategy is a mental one (as all choices are), but it nevertheless *is* a strategy, and a crucial one at that.

To begin to understand the basic differences between reacting and responding to anger, consider Table 6-1.

Table 6-1	Anger Reactions and Responses
When You <u>React</u> to Anger, You're . . .	*When You <u>Respond</u> to Anger, You're . . .*
Reflexive	Thoughtful
Impulsive	Deliberate
Predictable	Unpredictable
Out of control	In control

What happens, you ask, if I choose to continue reacting as I always have to my anger? Don't I have a right to react to my anger any way I want to? Of course you do, as long as you're willing to keep dealing with the same consequences you always have, or worse. You can keep apologising, trying to undo the harm your anger has done. You can continue down this path to a point where anger ends up poisoning your whole life (see Chapter 3). But then reacting is a conscious choice on your part. You can say loud and proud, 'I choose to lose my cool. That's just the way I am. So there!' That's fine. But at least that decision makes you responsible for the outcome of your reactive anger, no matter how negative, and you're no longer a victim of your emotion. And if you're not ready to take that different path now, maybe you'll be after you read this book, or sometime in the future.

But if you do want to start responding rather than reacting to anger, read on.

Breaking your lifelong habits of reacting to anger

Reacting to anger may be a habit you've formed over a lifetime, so don't be discouraged if you have trouble when you first try to avoid the reaction and focus on the response. The difficulty you're having may stem from things that have happened in your past that conditioned you to be a reactive person, or it may reflect an impulsive temperament that you inherited at birth. Either way, reacting is a habit that you need to break if you're going to get control of your anger.

Sam first began to have explosive anger when he was a teenager, defending himself from bullies in high school. His family moved into a new neighbourhood and he was an outsider. 'They picked on me and I had to take care of myself. I had to fight for everything I got,' he explained. Sam's problem was that he continued this fight for the rest of his life with his wife, children, neighbours and co-workers.

Linda grew up in an abusive, alcoholic family and found out early on that reacting in anger was a way of surviving. Unfortunately, at the same time, anger kept her from accomplishing all the things she wanted in life. 'My anger hurt me. It kept me from having things that people I grew up with had, like a university education and a good job,' she now laments.

Chris has always had a problem with outbursts of anger. His fuse is short. His anger doesn't build up slowly. It just comes on all of a sudden, as if someone flicks a switch. When he was a child, his mother would tell him, 'If people push you, you need to walk away.' Good advice. But he couldn't do it then, and he still can't do it at age 31.

Do you think childhood baggage might influence *your* tendency to be a 'hot reactor' when it comes to handling anger? It probably does if your parents were:

✔ Aloof

✔ Cold

✔ Demanding

✔ Difficult to deal with

✔ Distant

✔ Excitable

✔ Hard

✔ Highly strung

✔ Highly sensitive

✔ Nervous

✔ Not affectionate or tender

✔ On edge

✔ Reserved

✔ Rigid

✔ Stern

✔ Strict

✔ Tense

✔ Uncompromising

✔ Unenthusiastic

✔ Unfriendly

✔ Unloving

The nice thing about habits is that you can change them at any point in your life. Some of our most successful clients, in fact, have been in their 50s and 60s. Who says leopards can't change their spots?

Avoiding the company of other angerholics

Your attempts to stop reacting and make the choice to respond to anger may also be difficult because you're surrounded by people with excessive anger. You know what they say about birds of a feather – they tend to flock together, which means you've probably actively sought the companionship of others with the same temperament. Three reasons explain this:

✔ **Your style of reacting to anger leads you into life circumstances where your emotional behaviour finds a suitable fit.** For example, most of the corporate executives we work with tend to be very angry people. They pretty much all made it to the top of their organisation by using anger to compete with their peers and control their subordinates. To hear them tell it, anger works!

✔ **Angry, antisocial people tend to select peers who also engage in outrageous behaviour.** Tantrum-prone men and women, for example, are likely to date and marry other men and women who are also easily angered. In effect, you choose what's familiar.

✔ **By engaging in intense bouts of anger you're likely to be shut out by mainstream society; people who, for the most part, handle anger in appropriate and balanced ways.** Unfortunately, this means that you're denied an opportunity for corrective feedback that might otherwise come from friends and loved ones, who instead distance themselves from your anger. So, you seek out the company of those who both tolerate and condone your outbursts.

What you need are some anger allies, the kind of people who can help you form *new* habits of responding effectively to anger. Look for people who:

✔ Are compassionate; appreciating what a burden excessive anger is

✔ Are non-judgemental

✔ Are patient

✔ Are willing to be there for you at a time of emotional crisis

✔ Are willing to help, but are not willing to be responsible for your anger – that's your job!

✔ Don't assume that what worked for them in bringing their anger under control will necessarily work for you

✔ Don't pretend to have all the answers

✔ Have conquered their own anger demons

✔ Show by personal example how to express anger in a healthy way

✔ Will actively listen and support your efforts to bring your anger under control

You may have to distance yourself from the flock, whether that represents a group of angry peers or angry family members. Walking away from your angry friends takes a good deal of courage and a lot of willpower, but you can do it – and you'll see the positive benefits in your own life very soon! Alternatively, you can stay and show them how it's done – but do remember, not everyone is pleased to see big changes in someone close to them! You may not hear the positive feedback you hope for, because the person is still tied to their angry habits and may be angry with you for 'showing them up'.

Assessing Your Anger

The first, and most critical, step in managing anger at the moment you experience it is to assess the intensity of the feeling. We refer to this as the *rate-and-label step*.

To assess your own anger, follow these steps:

1. **Think of a number between 1 and 10 that best describes the intensity of your emotion, with 1 being mild and 10 being severe.**

   A rating of 2, for example, suggests a barely noticeable change in your emotional state, whereas a rating of 8 signifies strong negative feelings. Focus especially on the physical side of anger – how tense, wound up or agitated you feel.

2. **Convert the number rating into a label that aptly defines just how angry you are at this moment.**

   Basically, you experience anger at three distinct levels. A rating between 1 and 3 suggests that you're annoyed or irritated. A rating between 4 and 6 is typical of people who are angry. And, finally, if you rate yourself somewhere between 7 and 10, like it or not, you're in a state of rage.

Measuring anger with numbers gives you useful information:

- ✔ **Numbers tell you how close you are to losing control.** You're more likely to lose control when you find yourself extremely mad or at the point of rage than you are if you're just irritated.

- ✔ **Numbers tell you how much of a window of opportunity you have to retain control of your anger.** If you start out with a rating of 4, you obviously have more time to turn things around than if you begin with a 6, where you're only one tick away from rage.

- ✔ **Numbers provide a baseline from which you can measure progress.** If you start out with feelings of rage and, after employing the strategies we outline in this chapter, you find yourself just plain cross, that's progress.

Being Patient

Emotions, like anger, are by their very nature passing experiences. Each episode of anger has a beginning point (onset), a middle phase (where it peaks and begins to recede) and an end point (resolution). Emotions also work on the principle of gravity – what goes up must inevitably come down.

Anger always resolves itself and will actually do so without any effort on your part. The average adult is over her anger within five to ten minutes. You don't have to react in an attempt to make anger subside. The relief you're seeking from the tension and thoughts that accompany anger will come if you just give it enough time to pass. In fact, time is your ally. The real paradox here is that the more time you allow yourself to be angry, the sooner you'll be free of this emotion.

In order to give yourself enough time to feel your anger, follow these tips:

- ✔ **Remind yourself that time is on your side.** No one, not even the angriest person alive, stays angry very long.

- ✔ **Remember that patience is a virtue.** No one ever had a heart attack or died an early death as a result of being too patient.

- ✔ **Repeat to yourself as many times as necessary, 'This too shall pass.'** Sometimes a little wisdom goes a long way.

- ✔ **Say to yourself repeatedly, 'Less is more.'** In managing an episode of anger, it often pays to take a more passive posture.

Too angry? Walk away

Researchers asked a group of 115 Year 9 pupils how intense their anger was and how they reacted/responded when they got angry. Interestingly, the teenagers who reported the most intense anger and who also tended to react by taking their anger out on others took four times longer to calm down than did their counterparts who were just as angry, but who chose to respond to their emotion by walking away and letting their anger subside on its own. The teenagers who vented, on average, were still angry one to two hours later, whereas those who walked away got over their anger in less than 30 minutes.

Controlling Your Body

Anger arouses human beings. Your autonomic nervous system gets excited and floods your body with adrenaline. Blood pressure, heart rate, muscle tension, the hairs on the back of your neck – everything goes up! The angry person is instantly prepared for attack as a way of defending herself from impending harm. This is, in essence, the physical side of reacting in anger. Responding to anger requires that you begin to reverse this process and calm yourself down. In the following sections, we give you a few options for doing exactly that.

Using the relaxation response

Everyone has a natural protective mechanism to override the physical tension that accompanies anger. This protective mechanism is the *relaxation response*. To relax in the moment, all you need to do is pause long enough to take a few deep breaths. Breathing away the angry tension you're feeling and replacing it with a feeling of relaxation is as simple as one, two, three:

1. **Take a deep, exaggerated breath in through your nose, slowly.**

2. **Hold the breath for a count of one.**

3. **Now, breathe out slowly in an exaggerated way through your mouth.**

Repeat the exercise at least ten times (more if you want, depending on the intensity of your anger), staying fully conscious of your breathing throughout.

Think the word *release* with each exhale. This is your mind's command to the body to let go of this unwanted tension. Your body will follow the command – it's just the way the mind and body work!

Notice where in your body the tension is worst. Concentrate on this one area and let it relax. This has a knock-on effect in the rest of your body, triggering the full relaxation response as you keep concentrating.

Harnessing the power of quiet

Quiet is the natural state of the body at rest. Ranting about your anger verbally only adds more tension, further elevating your heart rate, blood pressure and so on. Just by being quiet for a few moments while you continue to formulate your response to anger, you'll begin to calm down. This simple principle underlies good anger management advice – the first thing the angry person should do is to shut up!

Lightening up

If you want to stay angry (or worse yet get even angrier), then by all means stay serious. Remind yourself that anger is no laughing matter. Don't even think about smiling. And, for goodness sake, do *not* try to find the humour in whatever situation provoked your temper.

However, if you're trying to calm yourself down, you need to lighten up. For example, if you feel compelled to say something to the person at whom you're angry, start by saying, 'You know, it's funny that . . .'

Or do what Fred, one of the author Gill's clients, did when another angry person shouted at him to 'Go to hell!' Fred thought for a minute and then said, 'Good idea. Except that I've already been there. Spent three years there, in fact, and I don't want to go back. It's called Milton Keynes.' Fred was laughing and the other man fell silent. (All kinds of people like Milton Keynes, of course – the point is to think of something that *you* find funny when you're angry, because it's hard to be angry while you're laughing.)

Talking to yourself

To inoculate yourself against the rising tide of angry tension, you can engage in positive self-talk by repeating (silently or out loud) phrases such as the following:

- 'Keep cool. Don't get so upset.'
- 'That person may not be in control, but I am.'
- 'That tension in my shoulders is normal, given how angry I am. If I just relax, it'll go away.'

✔ 'As the saying goes, this too shall pass.'

✔ 'I'm not going to give them the satisfaction of losing control.'

Asking Yourself Four Crucial Questions

You can't manage something that you don't understand. You have to analyse your feelings in order to respond to them in a healthy and appropriate way. You can do this quickly and easily by asking yourself the following four questions.

Who am I really angry at?

The answer to this question may, at first, seem simple: 'The person who just provoked me!' But if you look a little closer, the simple answer is often not the right one at all. The truth is that you may carry pent-up, unresolved anger from one situation or source to another, without realising it. Then you end up getting angry at the wrong person and experiencing angry feelings that are stronger than warranted at the time.

Consider the case of an angry youngster who comes to school each day, already angry at her parents and further irritated by having to deal with her peers on the bus. When the teacher tells her to take a seat, the child reacts by yelling, 'Don't tell me what to do!' Now, is this child really that angry first thing in the morning simply because the teacher invited her to sit down? The reality is, the child is angry with her parents and the other children on the bus.

So ask yourself: who am I really angry at?

Is this where I want to be angry?

Unfortunately, you don't usually get to pick the time and place of your anger. More often than not, anger finds you at an inopportune moment.

Nancy found herself angry at a co-worker just as she was about to leave work on Friday afternoon for a long-anticipated fun weekend with her friends. Clearly, she had a dilemma. Give in to her anger that afternoon and risk continuing to be angry and spoiling her weekend, or put her anger on hold and deal with it when she returned to the office on Monday?

Think about whether this is the right time and place for you to be angry.

Why am I angry?

It's possible that, because anger is often an instinctive, thoughtless reaction, you may actually not know *why* you're angry. You just know that you're angry, but you don't have a clue what the underlying issue is – the thing that sparked your emotion. The most common triggers for anger are:

- **Someone attacking your self-esteem through some type of verbal or physical abuse.**

- **Someone or something preventing you from reaching a desired goal.** This is even more anger provoking if you feel you're entitled to that goal or it's something you're strongly committed to.

- **Someone violating your basic moral principles – fairness, equity, honesty and responsibility.** Again, the more strongly committed you are to those particular values, the angrier you become.

- **A situation where you feel helpless, unable to correct or fix something that's gone wrong.**

Is the intensity of my anger at this moment consistent with why I'm angry?

Using the earlier example, even if the student is angry at the teacher for telling her to take a seat, does that justify a feeling of rage? Irritation maybe, but rage no. This is where most people get into trouble with their anger – the intensity of their anger is too much for whatever triggers it.

David kissed his wife goodbye and headed out for work one morning. He stopped to get a glass of orange juice from the refrigerator. Seeing that there was none there, he immediately flew up the stairs to the bedroom where his wife was and proceeded to yell at her for ten minutes. When asked whether he thought his rage was justified, he calmly said, 'Absolutely, she knows that I like my orange juice in the morning. She should make sure that we don't run out.'

You can often find justification for irritation and anger, but a justification for rage never exists.

Weighing Up Your Options

You can choose between an infinite number of responses to your anger. Some of those options are aggressive (yelling at or hitting someone). Others involve retreating from your anger (just walking away). Still others involve some type of assertive response on your part (standing your ground and saying that you're angry but in a non-aggressive manner). The real question is, what's the best way for you to respond in this particular situation? In the following sections, we fill you in.

Always giving yourself three ways to go

Give yourself a choice of at least three ways to respond to your anger. If you give yourself only one option (for example, swearing), you really have no choice about what to do next – choice requires at least two possibilities. Plus, no single option (even though it may be your favourite) fits every situation where you find yourself experiencing anger. For example, when you get cross over a disagreement with a friend, you could say:

- ✔ 'Fine, we'll just have to agree to disagree.'

- ✔ 'You're wrong, dead wrong, and I'm tired of listening to your moaning!'

- ✔ 'I think if we talk more I can convince you that you're mistaken in how you see things, but right now I'm too annoyed to do that. So, if it's all right, I'll get back to you later and we can talk again.'

Nothing's wrong with having an option that involves some type of aggressive response. The problem comes when that's your *only* option!

Considering the consequences of each response

When people *react* to their emotions, they never have time to consider the consequences. When they *respond* to these same feelings and circumstances, they do have time.

After you come up with your three options for responding (see the preceding section), and when you're next faced with a situation that makes you angry, take a minute and ask yourself 'What's likely to happen if I choose response option 1? What about if I try option 2? And what if I choose option 3?' Each of these options has different consequences, positive and negative, immediately and later on.

Emotions are temporary – they come and go. But you have to live with (and often pay for) the consequences of your responses long afterwards.

Consider what happens when you lose your cool:

- ✔ You feel a knot in your stomach.
- ✔ You feel ashamed, embarrassed and guilty.
- ✔ You feel depressed and unhappy.
- ✔ You feel like you're going to burst or explode.
- ✔ You feel nervous and agitated.
- ✔ You feel overwhelmed.
- ✔ You lose your concentration, focusing only on your anger.
- ✔ Your blood pressure goes up, in some cases dangerously high.
- ✔ Your heart pounds.
- ✔ Other people avoid you.
- ✔ Other people become defiant.
- ✔ Other people become indifferent to you.
- ✔ Other people have hurt feelings because of your anger.
- ✔ Other people lose their respect for you.

Now, consider what happens when you keep your cool:

- ✔ You and the other person leave the situation feeling good.
- ✔ You calm down quicker.
- ✔ You feel less agitated.
- ✔ You have lower blood pressure.
- ✔ You leave the situation not holding a grudge.
- ✔ You minimise future conflict.
- ✔ You're a much more agreeable person.
- ✔ You're more empathetic.
- ✔ You're more likely to come up with constructive solutions to problems.
- ✔ You're more likely to understand the other person's point of view.
- ✔ Other people maintain their respect for you.
- ✔ Other people are more likely to approach you.

Motives matter

Given a choice of how to respond to anger, females most often act in a way that lets the person who made them angry know what they're feeling and what they're thinking, whereas males are much more likely to choose a response that allows them to blow off steam. Unfortunately, the pleasure males feel from the immediate release of angry tension is far outweighed by the long-term negative consequences associated with such outbursts. Anger management is, to a large extent, about delaying the instant gratification of answering anger with anger so that you can experience the eventual satisfaction of being in control of your emotional life.

Choosing not to always exercise your right to be angry

If we had a pound for every time some angry person has said to us, 'I have a *right* to be angry!' we'd be very rich indeed. Our answer is always the same, 'Of course, you do – but that doesn't mean that you also have the right to express anger any way you feel like it.'

We believe in freedom of experience, including the freedom to experience emotions. But wisdom sometimes dictates that you hold back on the expression of that experience. To feel without acting is a choice, a difficult choice sometimes and a mature, courageous choice, but a choice nonetheless.

Taking action: responding

Eventually, you have to decide how you want to respond to your anger. So think about your options, consider the consequences of each and think about whether you want to exercise your fundamental right to express anger in this situation. Then go ahead and respond.

Most likely, you'll respond in a way that benefits you more than it hurts you. But if you choose to respond in an aggressive manner (for example, by shouting), so be it. If you've really taken the time to consider the consequences, though, you probably won't waste your energy yelling. (And if you do, you'll see the consequences of your yelling and, next time, you may think even harder before you respond in that way.)

Advantage females

When 518 adolescents were asked how they would react/respond to anger from a peer, the most prevalent response was to answer anger with anger. Forty-two per cent of boys chose this reactive means of protecting themselves from the other person's angry behaviour, compared with 32 per cent of girls. Contrast this with the finding that only 28 per cent of the boys chose to respond in a more mature fashion – by walking away in order to cool down and then returning to discuss the problem they had with the other youngster – whereas more girls (39 per cent) chose this response. Females have a clear advantage, even at this early age, in managing their anger, a trend that appears to continue throughout life.

Rewarding Yourself

If you decide to respond (not react) to today's anger in a different way than you have in the past, feel good about yourself. Nothing's like the feeling of being in charge of your emotions. You need to celebrate the moment by rewarding yourself for making a healthy choice. That's how one-time experiences become lifelong habits.

A long-held tradition of the science of psychology is that human beings learn to behave as a function of consequences. It's really quite simple: if you do something and you get a reward, you repeat the same behaviour, looking for the same reward. If you do something and you get no reward or, worse, you're punished for what you did, you won't repeat the behaviour. Rewarding positive behaviour is how habits – patterns of behaviour that persist over time and that you do automatically, without any conscious effort on your part – are formed. Repetition by itself is not enough to build a new habit; you must follow it with a reward.

So whenever you use the anger-management strategies that we outline in this book, be sure to do something to reward yourself. Here are some possibilities:

- ✔ Privately pat yourself on the back and say 'Good job!'
- ✔ Say to yourself or aloud, 'Good for me. Couldn't have happened to a nicer gal.'
- ✔ Sit quietly and reflect on the feeling of success you feel at this moment.
- ✔ Share your triumph over today's anger with someone you care about.

✔ Treat yourself to something special. Buy a book or a CD that you've been wanting, stop for a coffee mocha or buy a lottery ticket (keeping your cool may really pay off!).

✔ Put a pound coin in a special anger-management jar. When you accumulate enough money, use it to indulge yourself. Seeing that jar filling up will be a pretty strong reward in itself.

✔ Share your triumph over today's anger with a higher power in a moment of thankful prayer.

✔ Think for a minute about all the negative consequences you *didn't* have to face this time because you kept your cool. Experience the joy of what didn't happen!

✔ Repeat with conviction, 'I have control of anger; anger does not have control over me.'

CASE STUDY

It's never too late to figure out how to keep your cool

Frank, a client of Dr Gentry's, had a terrible temper his whole life. It ruined his health, caused him to lose most of his friends, but most of all it led to an estranged relationship with his only child. Frank had been so angry during those child-rearing years that he found himself increasingly distant from his son – both geographically and emotionally. Frank said that whenever his son called home and Frank answered, his son would immediately say, 'Let me speak to Mother.' The only things Frank knew about his son (or his grandchildren) he found out second-hand from his wife.

But then Frank did a curious (and courageous) thing at the age of 58: he entered an anger-management programme and figured out how to control his temper for the first time ever. Now when his son calls and Frank says, 'Wait, let me get your mother,' his son replies, 'No, I wanted to talk with you. How are you feeling? What are you doing?' Frank and his son enjoy a relationship that neither one of them thought would ever be possible. By learning to keep his cool, Frank, now 67, gained a son. And he's a very happy man!

Chapter 7

Letting Go of Past Anger

. . . .

In This Chapter

▶ Understanding why anger lasts

▶ Examining your fears

▶ Living without the ending you want

▶ Deciding when it's time to let go

. . . .

*A*nger is an emotion, and emotions are meant to be short lived. The biology of your anger means that the chemicals you produce wear off quickly. Excitement, fear, sadness, surprise, irritation – all these emotions pass through you throughout the day. But for some people anger persists, and through its persistence anger is harmful.

In this chapter we discuss some of the reasons why people hang on to anger. We also offer some solutions for letting go of angry emotion.

Digging Yourself Out of Anger

When you get angry, do you have trouble letting go of your anger? When something or someone triggers your anger, does it tend to consume you, transforming you into an entirely different human being? When you're cross, are you deaf, dumb and blind to the world around you – listening only to your own hostile thoughts? Do you have trouble seeing beyond the anger so that you can focus instead on the issues behind it? Do you stand by help-lessly as your mood progresses from irritation to anger, and finally to a state of full-blown rage? If your answer to any of these questions is yes, then you need some tools to dig your way out of your anger.

CASE STUDY

Releasing anger, lifting depression

Joanna was referred to Gill by her GP with feelings of low mood and depression, which had lasted for many years. After very little time spent discussing her life and her feelings, it became clear that Joanna was depressed because she had no help from her family of three boys and a girl, all in their twenties. Two of her children had families of their own, but Joanna looked after them also. Soon Joanna began getting in touch with some very angry feelings. She was furious at having no time to herself, and that she couldn't see an end to her hard work, but couldn't say this directly. She believed strongly that a good mother 'should be there for her children' and 'should never turn them away

when they need their mum'. Gill spent time with Joanna, examining these beliefs in detail. Only after recognising that allowing her children to solve some of their problems independently of her also allowed them to become healthy adults, and also accepting that she'd done a good job for many years, could Joanna say, 'But they're not children any more.' Recognising that her children were independent adults allowed Joanna to make more balanced choices, and to recognise the role of anger in her previous despair and exhaustion. Within six months her depression had lifted.

Knowing that resistance equals persistence

Ever try not to think about something? Try not thinking about the word *elephant* for five minutes and see what happens. The more you resist that thought, the more it persists – elephant, elephant, elephant!

It's the same with emotions like anger. The more you tell yourself, 'I'm not angry; I'm not hurt; it doesn't bother me,' the longer you stay angry. All that you can focus on is the anger.

CASE STUDY

Sarah had recurrent headaches for most of her adult life – that is, until her husband's untimely death at the age of 60. Shortly after her husband died, Sarah's headaches stopped completely. The reason: Sarah no longer had to resist expressing the anger she felt towards her husband, a man who she said, 'was angry all the time about almost everything and took it out on me.' Her husband would explode with verbal rage and five minutes later would be fine. But not Sarah. She held on to her anger for days – sometimes weeks – expressing it through silence and pain. 'When he lashed out at me, I couldn't let it go. Staying silently angry was my way of telling him, "You're not going to get away with this!"' But who was Sarah really hurting by hanging on to her anger? Herself.

Isn't it time you stopped resisting both feeling and expressing anger in your life? If the answer is yes, start letting go by following these seven steps:

1. **Identify the source of your anger.**

   What person, event or situation provoked your anger? How long ago was this?

2. **Acknowledge your angry feelings.**

   Say aloud, 'I'm angry because . . .' Then decide how angry you are (what we refer to in Chapter 6 as *rate and label*). Rate the intensity of your emotion on a scale of 1 (mild) to 10 (extreme). Ratings of 1 to 3 translate into irritation, ratings of 4 to 6 suggest that you're annoyed or angry and ratings of 7 to 10 show that you're heading for a state of rage.

3. **Accept your anger.**

   Remind yourself that you have a right to feel anger, just as you have a right to feel happiness or excitement. You don't really need to justify your anger – anger is, as one workshop participant noted, 'one way I know I'm alive!'

4. **Give yourself permission to express anger.**

   Anger has a bad reputation because people all too often associate it with violence, rudeness and disrespectful behaviour. But you can express anger in lots of healthy, constructive ways (see Chapter 11 if you want some examples). So your goal is to constructively express your anger.

5. **List three ways in which your life is better off by letting go of anger.**

   For Sarah, letting go of anger – after her husband's death – ended a life-time of headaches, gave her peace of mind 'every time I walk through the front door and don't have to worry about seeing that angry face staring back at me', and the freedom to live a life without anger. Months later Sarah was off on yet another adventure and enjoying life to the fullest.

6. **Decide how best to express anger without hurting yourself or others.**

   Don't misunderstand us – we're not suggesting that you let go of anger by ranting and raving for everyone to hear. That's neither healthy nor constructive. If anything, ranting tends to *maintain* anger not *relieve* it. But you can talk about your anger more openly (see Chapter 8), use exercise to drain away your angry feelings or put pen to paper and 'confess' your anger in writing (see Chapter 11).

7. **Get started.**

   Now you can move forward and carry out the plan(s) you made in Step 6. You can change if you make the choice to.

Identifying the fears that hold you back

Most people hold on to anger because of fear. Some common fears that may keep you from letting go of anger include:

- Fear of making another person angry
- Fear of hurting someone else's feelings or losing their love
- Fear that letting go of anger (forgetting) will mean you forgive the person who made you angry
- Fear that you'll lose your reputation as a 'nice' person if you express anger
- Fear that when you start to express anger you'll lose control of your emotions
- Fear of other emotions (for example, sadness) that underlie your anger
- Fear that others will see you as weak or vulnerable
- Fear that if you let go of your anger, you're letting the other person off the hook
- Fear that anger will cause you to lose something you value (for example, a job or a friendship)
- Fear of admitting, once and for all, that you're only human

What are you afraid of?

Being nice doesn't mean being powerless

Who says 'Nice guys finish last'? Pretty much everyone – because people learn to associate niceness with powerlessness. But, as it turns out, one doesn't necessarily mean the other.

The dictionary defines a nice person as someone who's pleasant, agreeable, courteous, considerate and delightful. It doesn't say anything about you being a victim of other people's bad behaviour. It doesn't say that you can't stand up for yourself. It doesn't say you don't deserve to be respected, to be safe and to be treated fairly by others.

If you see yourself as truly powerless then you tend to store up feelings of anger instead of letting them go. In an effort to be seen as ultra-nice, you say you're 'fine' when actually you're irritated. And those irritations linger and – slowly but surely – accumulate into feelings of anger and rage. How many times over the years have you read in the newspaper about someone who went into a public place and started shooting innocent people for no apparent reason?

And how many times have neighbours and friends described the killer as a 'really quiet, nice person'? Too many.

If you hang on to anger today, it becomes both yesterday's *and* tomorrow's anger.

Hiding your anger but making others suffer

You've probably heard the term 'passive aggressive'. What's nice about anger dressed up as polite behaviour? If you fall into the trap of saying 'I just don't get angry' you may be shocked to know that this is often not how other people see you. Some of the most severe bullying we have come across has been inflicted by those who see themselves as 'nice', who never express or admit to anger but achieve their rigid and narrow view of what they want by sulking, being deceitful, exaggerating or by cold revenge. Many of our clients give examples of others around them who are demanding, rigid and selfish without ever showing or owning up to their own anger. Although passive aggression may suit the 'nice' image you have of yourself, others know you by the negative atmosphere you create.

If you're silently angry, ask yourself: who knows what the problem is or what you need? Whose responsibility is this? You may be angry with someone, and think you're nicer because you're silent, but is it a calm silence or full of resentment and spite?

Seeing who hangs on and who lets go

Letting go of anger in a timely manner doesn't come easy to everyone. It can be especially difficult if you're:

- ✔ **A believer.** If you're religious or spiritual and believe in a higher power – regardless of doctrine or denomination – you've probably been taught to 'turn the other cheek' when faced with hostility. However, it's distorting this perspective to believe that expressing anger – even irritation – is an unspiritual or unholy act. You were made with the full range of feelings and not to hide half of them!

- ✔ **An introverted, avoidant or dependent personality.** These types tend to avoid conflict and emotional discomfort. Their reluctance to experience or express anger is motivated by fear – fear of confrontation or the loss of a relationship on which they believe they depend for their very survival. This unhelpful way of seeing the world guarantees a passive aggression which, at worst, leads to constant suppression of negative emotions. The effects on your health, as well as your relationships, are destructive.

Highly aggressive personalities can also hang on to anger, but for different reasons. They need to stay angry in order to satisfy their competitive, win-at-all-costs style of dealing with the world around them.

✔ **An ethnic minority.** Being part of a minority group is associated with a tendency to suppress anger. In a hierarchical society, where power tends to be concentrated at the top, anger rarely flows upwards. Those at the bottom tend to complain but otherwise 'grin and bear it'. Alongside this, many cultures don't support the expression of anger in healthy ways.

✔ **An intellectual.** Some people intellectualise anger – think it to death – while others just get upset. Intelligence is a wonderful thing, unless it gets in the way of constructive anger expression.

✔ **Emotionally illiterate.** You may be surprised by how many adults can't find words to describe what they're feeling. If you ask them how they feel about something, they respond by telling you what they think ('he isn't being fair') or what they did ('I just walked off'). Early on in anger management we find it helpful to run through an emotion list. Try it: can you list ten feeling words from the wide range of human emotions? See Chapter 18 for a list of positive and negative emotions. Check your words against these lists – are all the words you've used feelings, or have you included reactions (such as 'storming off') or behaviours (such as 'sulking') as well?

✔ **Female.** Across all age groups women tend to hang on to anger longer than men. Men's anger tends to be more intense, but they get over it quicker. Women more often do a 'slow burn' when they get angry. This may have a lot to do with social expectations that women should be kind, gentle and nicer than men.

✔ **Guilt ridden.** You should reserve guilt for those occasions where you've done something intentionally wrong, spiteful or harmful. Feeling responsible is a more healthy and balanced state. Frequent guilt can lead either to hiding or denial of other emotions, or using passive anger to avoid making hard choices or ignore the feelings of others.

✔ **Suffering from depression.** The influential psychoanalyst Sigmund Freud thought of depression as 'anger turned inward'. If you feel uncomfortable expressing your anger directly, you're more likely to either sit on it or turn it on yourself. Expressing anger also takes energy, something that people who suffer from depression often lack.

✔ **The child of nice parents.** People who hold their anger in, rather than let it go, have parents they describe as loving, warm, easygoing and relaxed; in other words, nice. Those who express their anger openly and without reservation tend to have the opposite kind of parents – cold, distant, strict and excitable.

✔ **Too angry.** Obviously, the more intense your anger, the harder it is to let it go. Letting go of irritations – or even normal anger – is relatively easy. But rage, passive or active, needs active management.

✔ **Young.** The younger you are, the harder it is for you to let go of anger. As people age, they tend to get angry less often and let it go more quickly. Perhaps they find that staying angry too long takes too much energy!

Trying the ten-minute rant

One of the reasons people have difficulty letting go of anger is that they express it a little bit here and a little bit there over a period of time, rather than all at once.

At the end of each day, if you're angry, try allowing yourself a ten-minute rant. If you always use the time (and want more), it's likely ranting just fuels your anger. If you never use the time, it's likely you're caught in passive aggression – no less deadly!

Living without Resolution

Maybe you're the kind of person who holds on to anger until you can resolve the problem that caused it in the first place. That's a great approach if you're dealing with a solvable problem. But what if you can't resolve the problem at all – or at least not completely? What purpose does hanging on to anger serve then?

You encounter lots of problems, conflicts and situations in life that, despite your best efforts, never have a happy or satisfying outcome. These situations you have to live with – without resolution. Examples include:

✔ Being raised in an alcoholic home

✔ Birth defects

✔ Childhood abuse

✔ Chronic illness

✔ Disability

✔ Disfigurement

✔ Irreversible loss of income

✔ Loss of loved ones (through death, divorce or abandonment)

✔ Natural catastrophes (like floods or hurricanes)

✔ Sexual assault

✔ War

Running out of steam

In a meeting with Alan, an angry client, and his family, everyone was putting each other down for a holiday that had gone badly thanks to a dodgy tour operator. There was an obvious undercurrent of anger and resentment. So Gill suggested, 'I'll tell you what we need to do here: each one of you takes a turn saying every angry, hateful thing you can think of about holiday companies. Each of you will have ten minutes to get it all off your chest. No one will interrupt you, so go for it!'

Alan got the ball rolling and ranted for about seven minutes before he began to run out of steam. 'Keep going,' I told him. 'You've still got three more minutes. We want to hear it all.'

Then, one after the other, the other members of the family had their say, pretty much all complaining of the same things. Like Alan, each person had trouble filling up the ten minutes.

At the end, the family were emotionally exhausted. The exercise demonstrated both that there were things worth saying, but also that they weren't news to the others and so not worth going on and on about. Ranting fixed nothing and certainly didn't affect the holiday company that had triggered all the anger.

 The next time you get angry, ask yourself these questions: can my anger correct the situation? Can it undo what's been done? Or, is this one of those times when 'after the toothpaste is out of the tube, you can't put it back!'? If so, then let it go.

Time's Up: Knowing When to Let Go

Here's the big question: how long should you hang on to anger? How long before it begins to hurt you? How long is too long?

Our answer is simple: 25 minutes at the most. Why 25 minutes, you ask? As Table 7-1 illustrates, most people let go of today's anger in less than half an hour.

Table 7-1	How Long People Stay Angry
Length of Time	*Percentage*
Less than 5 minutes	29.4
5 to 10 minutes	27.3
Less than half an hour	14.0
Less than 1 hour	12.9
1 to 2 hours	4.9
Half a day	5.2

Length of Time	Percentage
1 day	2.8
More than a day	3.5

Think of this as the 25-minute rule: the next time you find yourself angry, look at your watch to see what time it is. If you don't wear a watch, ask the person you're angry with for the time. Keep checking the time so that you know when 25 minutes have passed. If your anger has already subsided, good for you. But if it's still there, say aloud, 'Time's up!' Then let go of the anger and focus your mind on a new topic. (This book is full of simple, easy, practical exercises for letting go of anger that you can use during that critical 25-minute window of opportunity.)

The angry smoker

A statistical link exists between cigarette smoking and how long people stay angry. Smokers take longer to let go of anger than nonsmokers. Or, put another way, people who have trouble letting go of anger are more likely to smoke cigarettes.

One explanation is that some people self-medicate anger with nicotine (for more details see Chapter 14). Another possibility is that smoking, along with the intensity and duration of a person's anger, is linked to an impulsive temperament and may reflect how your body's 'wired'.

Chapter 8

Moving Forward: The Power of Forgiveness

....

....

*J*ack's in his 50s. His health is poor, he's not working, he's lonely and he has little to show for his life. Why? Because he's let anger poison him. All his life Jack has held onto his anger at his mother, who had to put him in an orphanage for a brief time when he was very young. 'She abandoned me – left me with strangers – and I'll never forgive her for that!' he shouts, with tears in his eyes, 45 years later. His mother – who's now in her late 80s and suffering from dementia – came back to get him after a year, when she'd found her feet again, and from then on she gave Jack a stable home. But none of that matters to Jack. As he sees it, his mother had committed an unforgivable crime and he'll punish her – and himself – for the remainder of his life. And so Jack carries that anger, anger that on more than one occasion has resulted in physical violence, cost him two marriages, the relationship with his only son, his steady job and in the end his health. And yet, even today, and with plenty of regrets, Jack hasn't forgiven his mother.

This chapter offers strategies for letting go of old feelings of anger and hurt that are tied to past grievances and grudges. It provides you with both a rationale and a road map for handling what we call *anger hangovers*. This can be one of the most difficult types of anger to manage. To move forward and achieve your goal of better anger control you have to find antidotes. Working with many different people has shown us that forgiveness and acceptance of other points of view are crucial to progress. You can do it!

Knowing that Forgiveness Is Never Easy

Forgiveness rarely comes easily to human beings. Anger, now *that* comes easily – but forgiveness, no. You were born with instinctive biological capacity for anger, but forgiveness is something you have to learn. It's a 'life skill' really – no different from learning how to ride a bicycle, give compliments or speak a foreign language.

You may be one of those lucky people who was raised in a tradition of forgiveness. You learned to forgive by seeing the forgiveness that your parents showed one another. Or you learned it through your participation in organised religion – in church, synagogue, mosque or temple. If so, forgiveness probably comes easier for you than it does for many because you were raised with a set of beliefs that value the idea that it's not your place to judge.

Of course, not all situations are the same. Some examples of life experiences that are most difficult to forgive are:

- Assault
- Being abandoned (by death or divorce)
- Betrayal or infidelity
- Death of a child
- Death or injury of a loved one due to crime
- Emotional abuse (being regularly neglected, unfed, put last)
- Physical abuse (severe or regular physical punishment, violence)
- Rape or sexual assault
- Sexual abuse (however brief or limited)
- Traumatic workplace injury
- Unexpected job loss
- Violations of trust or innocence

You need time

Forgiveness is a process. No magic wand exists when it comes to forgiving those who have wronged you; forgiveness is a journey you go through. The longer you hold your anger, the more your way of dealing with what happened becomes a habit. It takes time before you reach that point of resolution called forgiveness. Jack (in the introduction) has been angry at his mother for over 40 years. Even if he sets off to forgive her today, it'll be some time before he reaches his goal. The good news for him is that time is on his side. His mother's still alive and if he can forgive her before she dies, he'll undoubtedly have less painful grief, guilt and regret after she's gone.

Ask yourself, is today the day you're ready to start this journey – to free yourself from your anger hangover?

You need support

Humans are naturally social, instinctively preferring to be in groups, organisations, communities and relationships. Forgiving someone takes personal strength, courage, wisdom – and some of that you can draw from those around you. Who do you know who can serve as your forgiveness supporter? Who's already been encouraging you to let go of anger from the past? Who can serve as a positive role model – someone who's forgiven what happened to her and moved on with her life by looking ahead?

It's true that forgiveness is a voluntary act. No one can (or should) force you to forgive another person. As therapists, we've never advised a client to forgive someone. What we do, though, is offer forgiveness as an option that each person should consider in her efforts to find peace of mind. But the choice is entirely hers. And, of course, we offer to support the person if she makes this healthy choice.

Ask yourself, do you have the support you need to begin this journey?

 Spend five minutes thinking quietly. Picture people you know – those who are close, those you know a little, those you may admire from a distance. When you think of other people, what do you admire about the way they are towards others who hurt them? How do they deal with it? What are they saying inside? What do they do, say or believe that you respect? Now imagine yourself dealing with your anger and grudges their way. Try it – you don't have to let on! This kind of mental exercise gives you practice at changing your habits. You can choose to run different approaches through your mind and find the ones that suit you best.

Support is only support if . . .

Support is only support if you use it. Your support network is the people you can count on to help you deal with tough times in life. But you have to be willing to accept that help. Some people have a small network but feel a tremendous sense of support as they live their lives. Others have a huge network and yet feel isolated and alone. The irony is that people who are full of anger and resentment, who need support the most, are the least likely to accept it. You aren't weak when you accept help, but are weaker without it.

You need to sacrifice

Now comes the hard part. In order to forgive someone, you have to give something up. Something has to give; the question is, what? Consider the following possibilities:

- ✔ You have to let go of what made you a victim.

- ✔ You have to give up the myth that 'life must always be fair'.

- ✔ You have to give up your use of anger to protect yourself from emotional pain.

- ✔ You have to give up reliving what happened day after day.

- ✔ You have to give up this hold you're letting the other person have on you by keeping her alive in your thoughts.

- ✔ You have to let go of your 'right' to revenge and blame.

- ✔ You have to give up the idea that holding on to anger somehow undoes the injustice done to you.

- ✔ You have to give up the idea that you're entitled to the good life – the life you imagined that's free from stress, misfortune, pain and sadness.

- ✔ You have to give up the belief that everyone – especially those closest to you – must always approve of you and treat you with consideration.

- ✔ You have to give up the idea that forgiveness is a sign of personal weakness.

Ask yourself, are you ready to sacrifice keeping the past in the present and look ahead instead?

Choosing to Forgive

You choose to forgive. No one can make you. By choosing to forgive, you remain the one in control. Timing is everything. Conditions need to be right before you can honestly expect to begin a journey of forgiveness.

You have to be safe

Anger does play a protective role when life is threatening – situations in which mistreatment is ongoing, you're on guard against it happening or you believe your physical or emotional survival is under threat. To ask yourself to forgive someone who's actively harming you here and now is, we think, too much to ask. You have to be safe first.

Liz couldn't forgive her alcoholic father for his regular drunken outbursts of spite and violence, always followed by tears, apologies and promises never to do it again. She tried hard to protect her younger brother and her mother, but as a child she couldn't keep them safe or happy. Eight years after her father left his family he died alone. Liz and her family were safe. Only when she and her brother were collecting the few belongings he still had from his landlord did she discover from papers and a neighbour that he'd been married before, losing both his wife and baby when a drunk driver ran them over. As she saw her father's life with new eyes, she felt the first ever feelings of forgiveness.

Ask yourself, are you safe enough to start a process of forgiveness? Has the threat you originally protected yourself from gone now?

You have to acknowledge the frailty of human nature

The thing you mostly need to forgive others for is being human. Humans are actually very weak creatures, despite all our marvellous advancements in technology and lifestyle. People make mistakes. People hurt others' feelings – deliberately or accidentally. At times, people are far too selfish. People say 'no' when they should say 'yes'. We could go on and on.

Most people mean well. Most people do the best they can under the circumstances. But often, that's not good enough. So people end up blaming each other for what? For being human.

You probably get angry with people because they don't do what you expect of them. But do you expect too much? Nobody's an absolutely perfect parent, child, boss, spouse or friend. And if you can't forgive yourself ('I hate myself. It's my fault. I never do anything right.'), is that because you hold yourself to an unrealistic, all-or-nothing standard of performance? Then, the chances are, you have this standard for others too!

Doing a Cost–Benefit Analysis

You can make this calculation yourself by weighing up the pros and cons. If you're going to forgive someone, there definitely has to be something in it for you. You have to believe that it's in your best interests to let go of yesterday's anger. And that basically comes down to two questions you need to ask yourself:

- ✔ Who are you letting off the hook?
- ✔ Do you deserve to live happily?

Who are you letting off the hook?

The person who benefits the most from your forgiveness is you. Forget about the other person – do it for yourself! Forgiveness should be about *your* anger, not *her* bad behaviour. In fact, thinking that you're doing something good for a hurtful person can only stand in the way of you starting this journey.

First, consider what it's costing you to hang on to old anger. How does it compare with what you win if you let go? Here are some of the costs of hanging on:

- You constantly relive the painful past.
- Old anger finds its way into your present and future relationships.
- You feel drained, untrusting or sour as a result of all that anger.
- You see your life as permanently damaged by what happened.
- You tune out of the good things and choices in your life.
- You remain in a constant state of mourning.
- Your health is affected.
- You see yourself as guilty too.
- You remain constantly ready to deal with threats, always tense and guarded.
- Your anger turns into bitterness, mistrust and hostility.

And here are some of the benefits of letting go:

- You have energy free to use on happiness.
- Your life is now focused on the present rather than the past.
- You no longer feel so vulnerable.
- Your outlook becomes much more optimistic.
- When you forgive, others tend to forgive you.
- It becomes easier to forgive yourself – for being human.
- Your health improves and your risk of illness falls.
- You experience an inner peace that you haven't felt before.
- You have a newfound sense of wisdom.
- You move beyond the pain of past transgressions.

Ask yourself, is it time yet to let yourself off the hook?

Dave saves his marriage

Dave started out with no belief in forgiveness. His first marriage ended when he discovered his wife's affair. Since then, he'd tell anyone who'd listen, 'The only person you can trust is yourself.' This view of the world spoiled every day for Dave, who was always on guard against betrayal, certain that truths people told him covered up for lies, however small. Only three years into his second marriage – to a woman he truly loved – Dave started to check up on his wife. With his mind constantly repeating thoughts of betrayal, he started looking for proof. Their relationship was heading for disaster. His constant suggestions that she didn't love him meant that Dave's wife didn't trust him either. Only when he made a cost–benefit analysis (by weighing up the pros and cons) did he stop and question why one person, 12 years ago, still had so much power over his thoughts, feelings and priorities in life. Dave was able to say, 'That was then. I'm with someone completely new now.'

Do you deserve to be happy?

You aren't entitled to happiness, but you do deserve it. But the answer to the question is really something you have to decide for yourself. If you agree, then you have to let go of memories of past wrongs, the blame you attach to the other person's behaviour, your desire for revenge – all the 'shoulds', 'oughts' and 'musts'. Of course, bitterness and happiness are incompatible. If you keep one, you sacrifice the other.

Ask yourself, is there some reason you feel you don't deserve a chance at happiness? Perhaps you can start your journey of forgiveness with yourself.

Accepting the Finality of Being Wronged

One obstacle on the journey of forgiveness has to do with accepting the finality of being wronged in some way. It really has happened. Do you say to yourself in an angry moment, 'Why shouldn't I be angry? That's natural until I get justice. Things need to be put right again, or I need somehow to even the score'? Well, good luck, because that day will never come. What in the world can a parent do to truly even the score when her child dies at the hands of a drunk driver? How does the wife of an unfaithful man get true justice? How do you set right the fact that your employer went out of business, causing you to lose the best job you ever had? How do you make up for parents who neglected or abused you?

When we say that in order to forgive someone you have to accept that she did you wrong, we're not suggesting that you ignore what she did – absolutely not! Nor are we suggesting that you approve of the person's hurtful behaviour or make excuses for her. Instead, you can accept that you were hurt, but choose not to replay it. You're choosing not to let the damage done in the past continue to damage your life now, or in the future.

Angelo came to Gill's clinic after becoming a victim of serious violence. Gill talked with him about how often he made angry remarks about justice. His attacker had been prosecuted and given a sentence of less than two years, while he had lost the sight in one eye. Angelo's most common preoccupation was 'When am I ever going to get justice?' His hopes that he'd feel better after the court case were dashed, and now he was angry at his attacker *and* at 'the system' (the Courts and the law). Instead of feeling better, he felt much worse, constantly distracted by thoughts that no one cared about the terrible injuries he'd suffered and the changes to his appearance. Working steadily over several months, Angelo started to recognise that he wasn't expected to forget, but equally, he wasn't expected to spoil his life with resentment he could never use in any positive way. When he left therapy, he reflected 'Now, all I've lost is my eye. I almost wasted years and could have lost a lot more.'

You don't have to forget the past

When clients who've suffered some trauma come to us, often the first question they ask is, 'When will I get over this?' Our honest answer, one that no client likes or at first understands, is, 'Never.' We then explain that human beings don't get over bad things; if they're lucky (or accept the right kind of help), they just get *beyond* those things. The bottom line is, you'll never forget whatever it is that you have trouble forgiving. But you don't have to. The memory will probably linger, although not nearly so strongly or so often. What you're trying to do is get to the point where you can remember without anger. That's forgiveness.

The harder you try to forget something – the more you try not to think about it – the more you remember it. Try this instead: close your eyes and focus on something else. When the memories return, allow them to take a back seat. You're busy focusing on now! If those things hadn't happened, what would your energy be focused on instead?

The age of forgiveness

Forgiveness requires a certain amount of maturity. And maturity means using wisdom – your learning from life – to make a positive difference. Young children can be quite unforgiving because their minds are self-centred, unrealistic and dominated by emotion. The same can be true of adolescents, who for the first time begin to see that the adult world is complex, imperfect and at times unfair – but still a world in which we have to live. This, in large part, accounts for the heightened levels of anger in these early years (more about this in Chapter 2).

As you grow older, forgiveness is one of your choices. Child logic no longer rules. You have a more balanced, realistic view of yourself and others. You come more and more to see and accept that no one's perfect. The world isn't as simple as black and white, as easy as right and wrong. People hurt each other, deliberately or not, as they go through life. Forget that it shouldn't be that way – it *is* that way!

Choosing pain over anger

Most people hang on to old anger as a way of avoiding other painful emotions. That makes perfectly good sense – because anger (particularly rage) is such a strong emotion that it can mask even the most severe physical and emotional pain. But sooner or later, you're going to have to deal with the pain anyway. It's like the old saying, 'You can run but you can't hide!'

CASE STUDY

Holding on to the past

Mandy's family brought her to see Dr Gentry because they were facing yet another difficult Christmas after the untimely death of Mandy's youngest daughter. Clearly, Mandy didn't want to be seeing a therapist, and she did everything she could to appear pleasant, assuring Dr Gentry that she didn't have any psychological problems. That is, until Dr Gentry asked about her daughter, whereupon Mandy suddenly became visibly angry and snapped, 'I don't want to talk about my daughter. That's none of your business. She died and there's nothing else to say.'

Dr Gentry asked a few more questions about the daughter's death – how long ago it happened, what time of year it was, the cause of her death – and Mandy became increasingly agitated. Then Dr Gentry asked Mandy to verify what her family had said about how, every Christmas, she brought out all the wrapped presents for her daughter that were under the tree four years earlier at the time of her death. Mandy acknowledged that she did that, so Dr Gentry asked her why. She burst out in rage, 'So she'll have her presents when she comes back!' 'What do you mean "comes back"?', Dr Gentry replied gently. 'She's dead.' The pain on

(continued)

(continued)

that poor woman's face was obvious as she shouted, 'Don't you say that! Don't you ever say that! My daughter is coming back to me. If not this Christmas, then next. And her presents are going to be there – right where they were when she went away.' The woman stormed out of Dr Gentry's office with her distressed family in tow, and he never saw them again.

Mandy wasn't full of forgiveness. She couldn't forgive the fact that her daughter was gone for ever. Anyone who spoke the truth, who said otherwise, received her anger. She couldn't forgive life for letting this terrible thing happen to her and her family. She couldn't forgive her family for trying to get her to move on with her life. She couldn't forgive her husband and remaining children for not wanting their Christmas ruined. She couldn't forgive herself for being a mother who couldn't protect her child from a life-ending illness. And she couldn't forgive Dr Gentry for confronting her with the reality of her tragic loss. All these things that she couldn't forgive left Mandy consumed with anger.

The only way Mandy can get beyond the anger is to let go of her demands that life is fair, that her daughter should be here. Without these demands, she has a chance to share her energy and focus with the family she does have, people who've lost someone too.

Part III
Preventing Future Anger

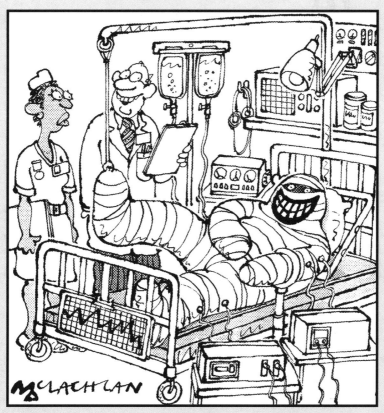

'This patient runs an anger management group and they came to visit him today.'

In this part . . .

We explain how to manage anger before it happens. You can avoid getting angry tomorrow by the things you do today. In this part, we show you how to create your own recipe for defusing your capacity for anger. If you don't want to be a victim of blind rage, you have to open your eyes to the way life *is* instead of dwelling on how you *want* it to be.

Here you also discover why you need to stop saying you're 'fine' when you're not. Hiding anger may be civilised, but it certainly isn't healthy. In this part, you find out why you're so dissatisfied with your life and what you can do to remedy that. First, you need to make your own private confession about just how angry you are and why. Then you can make anger your ally rather than your enemy – this approach is called *using anger constructively,* and it's a whole new way of dealing with your emotion.

Chapter 9

Adopting a New Outlook

*Y*ou aren't born with words for thinking or speaking. You learn to put words to what happens and why, and as you do you develop your own style of explanation in life, your own perspective. The great news is that you can relearn the way you see things and what you do about them. Certain styles of explanation are much more likely to trigger your angry feelings. In this chapter we cover aspects of thinking style and perception that our clients recognise are often at the root of uncontrolled anger or constant irritation.

Paul is in his early 50s, likeable, intelligent, good at his trade, but always quick to see some bad intent in the actions of others. If he emails a friend and they don't email back within a day, Paul's first thought is, 'Is he ignoring me? That's not right; he's supposed to be my friend. Some friend he really is if I don't matter.' It doesn't even occur to Paul that the person he's now irritated with has other important things to do as well, or that he's at home poorly with a cold, or that he's a good friend who doesn't imagine for a moment that an answer when he's got time to relax and chat is an insult! As far as Paul is concerned, only one possible explanation exists for not hearing back immediately – a lack of respect – and that's why Paul's angry.

If this were a one-off situation it wouldn't be a problem. But if you're like Paul, this is the way you view everything that comes your way throughout the day. Every time someone cuts in front of you in traffic, every time you have to wait more than two minutes before a waiter appears at your table in a restaurant, every time your partner forgets to pick up your dry cleaning, it's just one more example of bad intent – and one more time when you feel that your anger is justified.

This chapter is all about the 'mental' or 'thinking' side of anger. You really can choose how you view the actions of other people, and you really can influence your choices and behaviours and the way they affect your emotional life. We explain some alternative ways of perceiving events that clients we've worked with have found helpful; for example, we look at why provocation is terribly overrated. We also distinguish between hostility and anger and explain why the two are inextricably linked.

Seeing that Anger Is In the Interpretation

Humans are the only living things we know of that have a choice about how they view the world. Cats, dogs, squirrels, hamsters, goldfish – they're all creatures of instinct, which means they respond in predictable ways that are pre-wired into their nervous systems. Instincts are universal – scratch a dog's tummy and he'll instantly begin shaking his hind leg. All dogs have this instinct and nothing can change this.

The great thing about being human is that you aren't ruled by instinct. You have choices about how you respond to the world around you (for example, when someone mistreats you). Before that even happens, you also have a choice about how you perceive or interpret people's actions in general, and that person's actions in particular.

Do you think he did that on purpose? Was it an accident, or did he do it deliberately? Did he direct the mistreatment at you personally? Do you view what is happening as a catastrophe – a life-altering event? What reason, other than you, might he have had for saying this? Is this something that you think shouldn't have happened? These questions are all ones your mind considers, although you aren't always aware of it, before you have a chance to react or, better yet, *respond* to provocation (see Chapter 6 to better understand the difference between reacting and responding).

Looking to childhood for answers

You might say Mike is a born pessimist, but actually that's not true. Human beings aren't *born* with attitudes – those attitudes come from life experience. What *is* true is that Mike is the product of an alcoholic home, where things could be going well one minute and in complete chaos the next. He found out as a child not to expect the good times to last and that he and the rest of his family were always just one beer away from a family crisis. So, for all of his adult life, Mike has expected that most things will eventually turn out badly, given enough time. No matter how loving his wife is or how co-operative his children are, in the back of his mind he expects that any minute things will change for the worse – and he's ready to react in anger when that moment comes. Why does he get angry? It's Mike's way of defending himself against chaos, a way of feeling in control – unlike when he was a child hiding under the bed while his drunken father ranted and raved well into the night.

Mike is unaware of how his early childhood influences his view of the world. Like most children of alcoholics, he thinks that because he survived those unpleasant years (physically at least), he's okay. He also has no clue why he loses his temper so easily.

Understanding why it's called 'blind' rage

The more intense your anger is, the more it overpowers your central nervous system – in other words, your brain. When you're in a state of rage, you are, to all intents and purposes, deaf, dumb and blind to everything that's going on around you – something that's *not* true when you're merely irritated or just angry (see Chapter 2 for details on how to distinguish between these three levels of emotion).

While in a rage, people only hear and feel their own anger and only see the target of their wrath. After they calm down they often experience emotional amnesia – they can't even tell you exactly what triggered their outrageous behaviour in the first place, nor do they remember any of what they said or did during their tirade. Ironically, they're often shocked by the harm they cause, and they can be genuinely remorseful. The problem is, because the brain can't take in and store information under extreme emotional pressure, these people are blind to how extreme a level their own emotions reach, and they have difficulty learning from these experiences.

The only way to effectively manage rage is to prevent it from happening in the first place – to act *before* you enter into that state of uncontrollable emotion. That's why it's important to take immediate action when you first realise you're getting angry (see Chapter 4) and to follow our advice about how to keep your cool (see Chapter 6).

Arguing in a state of rage

We've treated quite a few people who reach rage – or screaming point – very early on when facing a problem or disagreement. Claire came to see the author Gill complaining that she'd had an argument with her husband and that they hadn't solved their disagreement because he was still upset about something she'd said while they were arguing. He said she'd called him 'useless', but she couldn't remember saying that, and to make matters worse she denied that she'd have said anything hurtful because she loved her husband.

Throughout this first meeting Claire seemed to want to understand what was happening, but her focus was on her husband. How could he believe she thought that he was useless? She suggested to me that he was confused, trying to distract her with a new argument, or was saying that she was a nasty person. She found it impossible to describe to Gill how her anger had started or turned so quickly into rage, and decided that she probably wanted marriage counselling rather than help for herself.

She returned two weeks later. This time, following her rage, her husband had asked her to leave because (so he said) she'd told him she wished she'd never married him. It became apparent that Claire regularly had arguments that she couldn't recall. Gill encouraged her to consider why she should be so definite that her husband was in the wrong for reminding her of insults she'd thrown 'in the heat of the moment'. Recognising that her rage robbed her of the ability to make her point, or to remember her husband's answer, shocked her. This time she was motivated to learn some new choices for behaviour when she felt angry and over the next few months she made changes that ended the hurtful insults and provoking remarks – and her loss of memory. She didn't reach the rage state any more: she took the blinkers off and started paying attention to all the things that were stressing her out before the dam broke and she released all that pent-up emotion.

Choosing the lesser of two evils

The first few years after one of the authors, Gill, moved to London she found herself experiencing a lot of road rage. She had lived in several other cities and it seemed to her that London drivers were a bunch of idiots who were all out to kill her. Talk about being angry! She'd be driving down a road and a driver would cut her up, forcing her to swerve, and she'd think, 'That so and so did that on purpose!'

One day Gill finally got tired of being angry all the time while she was driving, so she decided to adopt a different perspective on the driving behaviour of Londoners. Now she tells herself, 'They're not out to get me. They're not purposely trying to force me to hit my brakes and swerve. They just aren't all good drivers – it's not deliberate.' Based on her new perspective, she now always prepares to move out as soon as she sees a car that could potentially pull out in front of her, no matter how close or far away. That way, the other person's problem doesn't become her problem.

Gill's new point of view is what you call choosing the lesser of two evils: she chooses to perceive drivers in London as unaware rather than malevolent. Her altered perspective doesn't mean that she's happy about the way some people drive, only that she doesn't get angry any more. She chooses to make it relevant that she's safe from bad drivers and irrelevant why they drive badly.

Think of a situation that has left you feeling irritated, angry or in a rage lately. Ask yourself: what did that person do that set this emotion off? And, more importantly, why did he act that way? Now, see whether you can come up with two other alternative explanations for that person's behaviour. Take a piece of paper and write down all three points of view – your initial one and the alternatives. Consider how you'd feel if each one was the true explanation. Then pick the one that produces the *least* adverse emotional consequences – in other words, the lesser of three evils.

For example, say you're irritated at your dentist for running late for your scheduled appointment. Your first assumption is, 'This guy's so greedy for money that he's packed his day with too many patients, and now we all have to wait!' Okay, maybe that's the case. But try to come up with two other reasons why your dentist could be late. Maybe he had to spend extra time helping a patient who was really afraid of dentists. Or perhaps his mother is ill and he had to take a phone call from her doctor about her condition. Now, which of these scenarios upsets you the least? Maybe it's the poorly mother. So now, just for the sake of your own stress level, assume that his mother is ill. Take it another step and try to empathise with him. Wow, it must be hard to have to see patients and keep up such a cheerful façade when he's upset about his mother. Maybe if you're understanding of him, you'll help make his day a little easier. (And if nothing else, you'll have kept your irritation from turning into anger and ruining your day.)

Accepting Life for What It Is, Not What It Should Be

Wouldn't it be nice if everything in your world was the way you thought it should be? You wouldn't get angry if:

- ✔ The red light turned green when you thought it should
- ✔ Your wife paid as much attention to you as you thought she should
- ✔ Your kids respected you the way you thought they should
- ✔ Your work compensated you the way you thought it should

- Your retirement fund increased the way you thought it should
- Government officials did what you thought they should to control the deficit
- Tyres lasted as long as you thought they should
- Your clothes fitted the way you thought they should
- Your children got the kind of grades you thought they should
- God answered your prayers the way you thought He should
- You had all the rain or sunshine you thought you should
- People laughed at your jokes the way you thought they should

The problem everyone faces, unfortunately, is that things don't always work this way. You're forced to deal with life the way it actually *is,* rather than the way you think it 'should' be.

Begin paying attention to how many times you think or say the word *should* in the course of a day. Each time you hear yourself saying 'He should . . .', stop and ask yourself the following three questions:

- **Who says he shouldn't act that way?** Where is that written down? Is that a fact or simply your opinion? At what point in life did you start deciding how other people should act?

- **Why shouldn't he act that way?** Isn't he entitled to the same rights of free speech and expression as you are? Shouldn't he act according to how he sees things? Why does your point of view count more than his?

- **Is the fact that he's not acting as you feel he should worth getting angry about and perhaps ruining your day over?** Why do you believe that your lives are so linked that you can't get on with your own day? Are there other choices that you haven't considered?

Considering the parent–child dilemma

If you don't want to be angry off and on for about 20 years running, don't have children. Most of the anger we see between family members, especially parents and children, has to do with differences in their perceptions of how things *should* be. For instance, parents think their kids should obey their every command, keep a respectful tone and in one form or another show their gratitude for all their parents do for them. Children – certainly adolescents – on the other hand, believe they should be free to do what they want, should be able to talk to their parents any way they feel like and think parents are only doing what they should be doing for them, so they shouldn't need any thanks. Negotiating around all these *should*s is what makes or breaks a parent–child relationship.

Becoming More Tolerant

Anger is the emotion of intolerance. Intolerance means that you don't accept another person's point or view or behaviour. Anger says that you think you're right and the other person is wrong. It's as simple as that.

Intolerance defends the listener against any change in his way of thinking. Instead of accepting the challenge of an honest difference of opinion (including differences in style of behaviour), the intolerant person resorts to intimidation, insult or withdrawal – all fuelled by anger – as a way of rigidly holding on to his beliefs.

Re-thinking your approach

The more intolerant your thinking is, the more intense your anger. So it's important to find new ways to deal with people and their actions so that you can feel calmer inside.

The next time you find yourself getting angry about something another person says or does, try the following:

- ✔ **Remind yourself that if you're secure about your view, you have absolutely nothing to defend.** Just because someone else thinks differently from the way you think doesn't mean you're wrong or that you necessarily have to justify your own beliefs and actions.

- ✔ **Instead of being defensive (that's what intolerance is all about!), try being curious.** Say to the other person, 'Tell me more about that. How did you arrive at that opinion? This is your chance to educate me.'

- ✔ **Don't personalise the conversation.** Concentrate on issues not personalities. Focus on the point of the conversation (for example, 'I disagree that parents should give contraceptive pills to their teenage daughters') rather than the *person* on the other end of the debate ('You're stupid for thinking that way!').

- ✔ **Look for points of agreement.** For example, parents who are discussing whether to give contraceptive pills to their daughters can begin by agreeing (out loud) that they are, of course, both concerned about the ultimate safety and well-being of their kids.

- ✔ **Avoid the use of expletives.** Swearing and cursing only insults the other person and reduces your chances of putting your view across. Why do that if you believe in what you think? Instead, you could try saying, 'I really don't know what to say when you act like that,' rather than saying, 'You're an idiot, and you know it!'

✔ **At all costs, avoid contempt.** Contempt is any expression of superiority over an inferior (for example, sighing or rolling your eyes). It not only shows your intolerance, it tells the other person you think he (and his thinking) is utterly worthless. It's just a way of saying, 'I'm better than you!'

As we describe in Chapter 1, when angry many more people are motivated to assert their authority or to regain a feeling of control over something they feel threatened by, rather than to harm other people. Contempt is an example of a behavioural habit you can exhibit when you're angry. Changing this habit means recognising that it doesn't help you achieve what you're trying to do – that is, to put your view across.

Seeking diversity in all things

The good news is that, as far as we know, intolerance isn't inherited. It's an attitude that people pick up through life experience. If you grow up in a family that tolerates differing points of view, you tend to be like that yourself. The same is true if you're raised in an intolerant family.

One antidote to intolerance – an *all-or-nothing* or *black-and-white* view of life – is to look for diversity. Intolerant thinking is a way of trying to simplify an always changing, complicated world. Diversity (variety) helps you expand your horizons and see that the range of ideas, beliefs and behaviour is huge and endless. Uncertainty is everywhere: truth, or what is correct, lies somewhere between what one person thinks and what another believes.

Variety of experience is easier to achieve than you might think. Here are some ways you can become a more tolerant person:

✔ **Read about ideas or subjects you wouldn't normally spend time on.** Make a start with a *For Dummies* book; they cover a wide range of subjects. Consider finding out more information on something you've already decided you're against – this is an interesting experiment in which you can't lose. Either you'll find more confirmation that you have good reasons to hold your view, or you'll find out something interesting and adjust your view. Being able to change and be flexible is a sign of being confident and relaxed in yourself.

✔ **Look out for news about places and countries you don't know much about.** Newspapers from a friend or relative away or abroad; the world affairs or international sections of Internet news websites; meeting people who don't come from your community or area and having curiosity about their life or views – all of these are ways of helping yourself to become more tolerant.

✔ **Every other time you go into a restaurant, try something new.** This forces you out of your comfort zone. Being flexible with your food can be an easy and fun way to become more able to change.

✔ **Be adventurous throughout life.** It's fine to know your own limits and preferences, but try to take some opportunities that keep you trying new things. For some people this may be to change their routine while on holiday, for others it may be taking up an extreme sport.

✔ **When you go to a party, look for people you don't already know and start up a conversation.** If you only talk to the people you know, you're less likely to discover something new.

✔ **Travel as extensively as your budget allows.** Try to go to different regions of the country (or the world). When you're there, spend some time talking to the locals.

✔ **Make a point of socialising with people from racial and ethnic backgrounds other than your own.** Most cultures and communities welcome interest in their customs, behaviours, ideas and lifestyles. As well as introducing you to variety, you're likely to be with people who feel goodwill towards you because of the interest you show them.

✔ **Visit museums, art galleries, and music and theatre venues.** You can understand a lot about the beliefs and lifestyles of people through the creative arts. Far from being 'for the few', most writers, artists, composers, sculptors and poets create their work for everyone to enjoy.

✔ **Talk to people of different ages.** You'll be amazed at how differently people, much younger and much older than you, think.

✔ **Attend free lectures by local and out-of-town authorities on various subjects.** Most communities offer lecture series or similar cultural experiences. If you live in a very small town, look to a bigger town nearby and make a point of travelling there to take advantage of these things.

✔ **Keep your eyes open and your mouth shut.** Learn now, debate later.

Tired of listening to yourself?

One of Gill's client's, Hugh, was a senior executive, and in many ways very successful. However, in therapy after a bereavement and reoccurrence of his low mood, Hugh said, 'For most of my adult life I was an outspoken, opinionated person, who – even though I didn't realise it at the time – tried to force my viewpoint about how the world works on anyone who would listen. Well, that all changed when I went through a five-year period of depression during which I was forced to finally listen to what others had to say for once.'

'After I recovered from the depression, I found that I was tired of always listening to my own voice and I rather liked being an active listener. For the first time in my life, I found that I was, and always had been, surrounded by many intelligent, interesting people, including my wife and children, who were eager to share their own personal views on life, if allowed. What a delightful surprise!'

Considering the media's effect on you

A free press comes with a price. Any media can choose to present information in their own style and with their views or editorial attached. Some channels, broadcasters, Web content and publications express extreme points of view on virtually any topic you can imagine. Exchanges between 'experts' are often deliberately intense, loud, argumentative and at times angry. Instead of imparting new information, some media rely on unpleasant exchanges and a climate of intolerance. If you weren't angry *before* you started watching a discussion programme, you will be shortly.

What people accept as normal changes all the time. In the early days of television, programmes were more factual. Now an element of viewer participation can exist, and to encourage this producers choose stories or issues for their controversy. What are you taking in about how people behave and what's acceptable? Is everything up for debate or can you just peacefully accept new ideas and consider them before having a view? Why is bullying at school or work unacceptable, but unpleasant practical jokes, humiliation or repeated demanding questioning from interviewers acceptable?

Although televised and visual media are without doubt more stimulating and entertaining than a newspaper, they also arouse more passion. If you're just interested in knowing what's happening in the world around you – without all the angry commentary – you might find it helpful to use media that don't involve any delivery using vision or sound, until you feel you can manage any emotional responses.

Rarely do the media offer you 'good news' – it's slanted towards the negative. If you already have a pessimistic, cynical outlook, or you're in a bad mood, the last thing you need is more negativity – which is just one more thing that predisposes you to anger.

Figuring Out Where Hostility and Resentment Come From

Hostility is an attitude – a feeling of ill will – that you attach to people and circumstances around you. Like resentment, hostility is a perspective that has a circular relationship with emotions like anger and aggressive behaviour. In other words, hostile people more often find themselves angry, and anger tends to incite hostile thoughts. And unlike anger, which comes and goes, hostility can really last.

So where do these negative attitudes come from? Two sources really:

- ✔ **From your family.** Like many other things, you can learn hostility early in life.

- ✔ **From your unexpressed, unresolved anger.** Think about a cup that you use to drink tea out of every day. Now suppose you never wash out that cup. What happens? Each time you drink tea a slight residue stays in the cup, eventually discolouring the insides of the cup and giving the tea poured into it each day a bitter taste. That's exactly what happens when you hide your emotions (see Chapter 8) or when you have an unforgiving nature (see Chapter 13). Hostility becomes that bitter taste you have that discolours how you view and interpret life around you. People generally don't become hostile and resentful overnight; it's a slow and gradual process.

Hostility and resentment usually come from past experiences that carry over into the present and future. They illustrate, in fact, exactly how yesterday's anger can become today's anger, and how today's anger becomes tomorrow's anger.

To avoid being a hostile and resentful person, use the anger-management strategies we offer throughout this book, including:

- ✔ Recognise your anger as soon as you feel it.

- ✔ Use your anger to understand and manage yourself better.

- ✔ Express your anger without ranting.

- ✔ Stop saying you're 'fine' when you're not.

- ✔ Think of anger as part of you rather than your enemy.

- ✔ Find healthy ways – like exercise – to let off steam.

- ✔ Think of anger as a normal emotion, just like love and happiness.

- ✔ Let yourself off the hook by forgiving others first. Be more tolerant.

- ✔ Live in the present, not the past.

- ✔ Turn your resentments over to a higher power.

- ✔ Stop playing tit for tat – there's no such thing as getting even.

- ✔ Establish healthy boundaries between yourself and those you love the most. Make clear your views and respect the view of others.

- ✔ Come back and discuss the reasons for your anger after you walk away.

- ✔ Look for the enjoyment in life to balance out the difficult times.

Who's more hostile – men or women?

Research by psychologist Wolfgang Linden and his colleagues at the University of British Columbia challenges the long-held notion that women tend to suppress anger more than men, which can lead to an increase in resentment. On the contrary, Linden found that women tended to use different anger coping techniques – for example, seeking social support from other women with whom they discussed their feelings – than their male counterparts, who relied more on overt aggression (attacking the source) as a means of expressing their anger. This suggests that women are more likely to resolve their anger in a reasonable time and not experience the side-effects of chronic hostility.

Being Assertive

If you lack assertiveness and never stand up for yourself, you're probably full of resentment – and understandably so. Why? Because you're a virtual storehouse of accumulated frustration and anger. You never let your emotions – especially negative ones – see the light of day, so you never let go of them.

Try to go into a situation prepared to be assertive. Feeling relaxed and confident is helpful; a bad mood or being physically uncomfortable (for example, cold or hungry) are not. Find the word or words that describe what you're feeling. Work out why you're irritated or angry – what are you thinking about? Put this into clear language without including swearing or insults. Finally, say what you'd prefer to happen, or explain your point of view. Being assertive means remembering that others don't have to agree when you've finished!

Consider asserting yourself in the following ways:

- ✔ If you're not satisfied with the service you get in a restaurant, say something to the waiter or, better yet, the manager.

- ✔ Practise politely saying 'no thank you' when people (for example, aggressive sales staff) invade your personal space.

- ✔ If someone asks you to do something (or, worse yet, demands that you do it) ask why (with curiosity, not confrontation) before you act.

- ✔ Get used to returning faulty goods to shops without feeling embarrassed or being apologetic. Don't be afraid to discuss the problem with salespeople – it's your money after all.

- ✔ If someone pushes into a queue ahead of you, say 'Excuse me!' and then nicely let him know where the end of the queue is.

Chapter 10

Saying What You Mean

. . . .

In This Chapter

▶ Identifying important reasons to speak up

▶ Recognising the drawbacks of being 'polite'

▶ Asking yourself, 'What am I not thinking (and talking) about?'

▶ Showing healthy anger

. . . .

*T*he author Gill was recently at the park with her godson, Jacob, when Sarah and Amanda, two friends, arrived with their sons. Sarah is very interested in health and fitness and always carries fruit and cut vegetables for her son. Amanda is less careful with her child's diet. Before Sarah could react, Amanda reached into her bag and gave each of the three kids a chocolate muffin. Amanda said to Sarah, 'You don't mind, do you? They need the energy.' Sarah smiled quickly and said, 'No, of course not,' but her face was tense and she said to her son, 'No more treats today.' When Amanda moved away for a moment, she turned and smiled at Gill, saying, 'I do try to balance out how much sugar he gets.'

How often do you find yourself, like Sarah, saying things are fine when they're not really? If you often hide your real feelings or tell 'white lies', what effect do you think that has on you? What effect does it have on people who know you or deal with you, even strangers? For example, what message does Sarah give her child about anger? What do you believe would happen if you were more open and honest about the things that make you angry? What effect are you really achieving when you tell yourself you're 'being nice'?

In this chapter we guide you through answering those questions and show you how to allow yourself to express healthy anger. This chapter helps you say what you feel rather than what you tell yourself other people want to hear – and the more you can do that, the better you're able to manage your anger.

Seeing Why Hiding Your Emotions Isn't Healthy

Emotions are naturally brief, passing experiences. Typically, they come and go throughout the day, moving you in various directions, shown by changes in your behaviour. Anger, for example, triggers a fight-or-flight response that's pre-wired into your nervous system and body. Not acting on an emotion like anger is unnatural and, in some instances, can be unhealthy. Emotions reflect changes in physiology – increases in blood pressure, heart rate, blood sugar and muscle tension – that are usually harmless because they're short lived (that is, if you express the feelings). But if you don't express emotions they can continue to affect your body, causing continued physical and biological tension, – and that can be harmful and even, in the worst cases, deadly.

Realising there's no such thing as hidden anger

Suggesting that anger is either expressed or unexpressed is actually untrue. All anger is expressed – the question is how. You probably think that you're expressing your anger when you do so in a way that other people can see, hear or feel. Otherwise, you tell yourself that you're not expressing it.

The reality is that you express *all* anger – some of it in ways that you can't see straight away. For example, you may not *look* or *sound* angry, but your anger may be expressing itself in your cardiovascular system (through high blood pressure, a racing heart or headaches), your digestive system (through irritable bowel syndrome [IBS] or frequent indigestion) or your musculoskeletal system (through neck, jaw or tension pains, or headaches).

Your anger may express itself in negative attitudes – pessimism (expecting the worst), cynicism (doubting the motives, goodness or trustworthiness of humans), hopelessness (no belief that things can improve), bitterness and stubbornness. Or you may express anger with some form of avoidance behaviour (giving people the silent treatment), oppositional behaviour ('I don't *think* so!') or passive-aggressive behaviour ('I'm sorry – did you want something?'). Anger may also sour your mood and leave you feeling down or depressed. You suddenly lose the enthusiasm you had previously. (For additional examples, take a look at the anger–health checklist in Chapter 3.)

The non-body injury

Over the years, doctors have recognised that many people suffering from back pain actually never had an injury to their back. A colleague's client – a really nice guy – who came in complaining of unremitting pain in his lower back said that it began when he put his foot on a shovel to dig a hole in sand, something he did countless times in his work. That was the injury that caused him unbearable pain, resulted in extensive medical treatment and meant he was unable to work.

Upon further investigation, it turned out that this man had quit working for his current employer some years before because he was dissatisfied (angry) about low pay, lack of benefits and a disagreement with his foreman. He had taken a much better job in another town and was quite happy at work until his new employer unexpectedly declared bankruptcy. He was then forced to return to his old job – same low pay, lack of benefits and foreman – all the while feeling both defeated and dejected. His way of coping was to 'grin and bear it', absorb whatever mistreatment came his way and never – I mean *never* – let himself get angry.

Then, one day – like any other day – his back suddenly went out. The result: he could get paid without returning to work (sick pay) and also avoid dealing with his boss. We agree that the man had been injured, but it was his *spirit* that was injured, not his back. After he went through a pain rehabilitation programme, where he got insight into the inner dynamics of his back pain, he found new employment and his back pain was no longer a problem for him.

Noting that dissatisfaction can be lethal

Being chronically – morning, noon and night – dissatisfied can be dangerous to your health. Dr Ernest Harburg and his colleagues at the University of Michigan did a study asking people how satisfied they were with their jobs. They specifically asked the people how satisfied they were;

- ✔ That their job offered an opportunity to earn a higher salary
- ✔ That they had an opportunity to work with people who were friendly and helpful
- ✔ With their ability to acquire new skills in their line of work
- ✔ With job security (were they unlikely to get made redundant or fired)
- ✔ That they were allowed to do those things they were best at in their jobs
- ✔ That they had an opportunity to get ahead at work (be promoted)

Dr Harburg also asked questions to understand whether they tended to habitually express or suppress their anger. Interestingly, the data showed that those employees who were highly dissatisfied at work but who suppressed their anger had, by far, the highest blood-pressure levels on average, compared with those who were highly satisfied with their work or dissatisfied workers who expressed their anger in some way. The increase in blood pressure resulting from this combination of chronic dissatisfaction and suppressed anger was enough to place the employees at risk for potentially lethal heart attacks and strokes.

The same, it turned out, was true when Dr Harburg asked similar questions to determine how satisfied these people were with their home/family situation. Again, those who were the most dissatisfied but least expressive about their anger had the highest blood pressure.

CASE STUDY

Focusing on your own part – and letting other people focus on theirs

His company's human resources manager referred Carl for anger management. A man in his late 50s, who'd worked in the same job for almost 20 years, Carl was now being disciplined for several recent rather uncharacteristic outbursts of anger, directed at his immediate supervisor. Carl had been given an ultimatum: learn to keep your cool or you're fired! To make matters worse, recent stresses at work had suddenly caused Carl to have problems with his blood pressure and cholesterol levels, even though he'd successfully managed both with medication for years. The problem, as Carl saw it, was that his boss was young, inexperienced and incompetent – in his words, 'an idiot who doesn't have a clue about how we do things around here'.

Clearly, Carl was dissatisfied – not with his own work, but rather with how his new boss did his. He had tried for the longest time to let things ride and keep his dissatisfaction to himself, but lately he had boiled over with anger. Given his age, Carl couldn't afford to lose his job and benefits and he most assuredly didn't want to 'stroke out' because of his job, but he was at a loss as to what he could do to resolve his anger.

Carl came to see Dr Gentry for anger-management counselling. Dr Gentry suggested that Carl make a compromise – that he be content to be satisfied with how he did *his* job and let his boss answer to those above him for his own mistakes. 'Do your part as well as ever, sign off on it, and if your boss screws things up after that, that's his problem,' Dr Gentry said. 'Just be responsible for yourself, not for the whole world.'

It worked. We're not sure how his boss is doing, but Carl's blood pressure and cholesterol levels are once again stable, he hasn't had any more outbursts and his human resources manager is delighted with how things turned out. And he's still working!

Being Civil Doesn't Always Mean Being Nice

Being civil simply means being polite – operating within the social rules of a society. It means acting towards others in ways that show mutual respect.

It means not being rude, insensitive, thoughtless and deliberately aggravating. On the other hand, it doesn't mean that you're always nice, tolerant or accepting of whatever mistreatment comes your way. It doesn't require that you be passive, someone's doormat or the proverbial pushover. And it certainly doesn't mean that you never feel or show reasonable anger.

Civil people get irritated and angry, but they express their feelings in constructive ways (see Chapter 11 for examples). They respond to their angry feelings instead of reacting in some mindless, shoot-from-the-hip kind of way. In the right situation, they speak out in ways that inform and educate those within hearing distance about the issues that underlie their anger.

Stop saying 'I'm fine' when you're not

You may have found how to avoid taking responsibility for your anger by always saying 'I'm fine!', even in circumstances where that's far from the truth. This response is an example of what politicians call a *non-response response*. It's a passive way of saying, 'I'm not going to tell you how I feel. Maybe I don't trust whether you'll accept my feelings. Maybe you'll get angry because I'm angry. Or maybe I don't trust my own feelings – should I really feel that irritated?' You'd be surprised how many of our therapy clients, when we ask them how they are, say, 'Fine.' Our immediate thought is, 'Well, if you're fine, why are you here?'

The next time someone asks you how you feel about something, choose an emotional label that fits the situation – for example, happy, sad, angry or glad. Being honest about how you feel helps you to practise naming your feelings correctly, reduces your physical tension, communicates something clearly to others and can help keep you from getting any angrier.

Stop saying 'I never get angry'

It may be true that you almost never feel irritated. Perhaps you have a very calm or easy-going temperament. However, such people are very rare! Instead, most people who say this to us do so with obvious self-satisfaction, as if they've achieved a goal of being above anger.

Passive-aggression is an inactive refusal, or obstructive or sabotaging resistance to the views, feelings or expectations of others. It's a common problem for people who declare they never get angry. You may say you're not angry, but in a variety of ways you show that you are. Your facial expression (for example, sour or distant), body language (very inactive, disinterested), behaviour (failure to get things done, or doing them badly) and general attitude ('why should I do what you want?') certainly give away an anger more severe than irritation.

The headache that is passive-aggression

Laura was suffering from severe headaches when she came to see the author Gill. She didn't really believe her doctor's suggestion that a psychological approach to her problems might work. Her resentment about coming to therapy was obvious to Gill, in her tense and sometimes sulky expression, her sighs when Gill asked questions she couldn't see the importance of and her 'polite' little smiles with no warmth in them. She complained about the small details of how people around her did things, until Gill wondered why anyone would want to be around this constant smiling criticism.

Laura displayed a range of passive-aggressive behaviours: her expression, her sighing, the contradiction between her expression and what she said, and her difficulty in admitting to any emotion she thought was 'bad' or admitting that she had a serious problem with anger management. Her only way of admitting her difficulty came through her headaches. Her chronic pain came from emotional pain.

Laura was able to learn some relaxation techniques and use these when she could admit to feeling tense. By linking her tension to situations in which she felt resentful or irritated, we found some ways in which Laura could admit to and allow her normal feelings of anger.

The bottom line is, everyone gets angry sometimes, and telling yourself that you aren't cross doesn't do you, or anyone else, any favours.

Stop apologising for what others do

Are you such a 'nice person' that you try to take responsibility for others' mistakes?

When someone bumps into you out in public, don't say, 'Sorry' or 'Excuse me.' *You* haven't done anything wrong – *the other person* has. *You're* not the one who made the mistake here – *the other person* is. So why should you apologise? Apologising is what people do when they take ownership for some misdeed. Unless you're the one who bumped into someone, you shouldn't apologise. If you want to say something, you could say, 'Excuse you!' It's a civil way of giving the person feedback about her behaviour. (We're not suggesting that everyone who bumps into you does it intentionally – you still want to give people the benefit of the doubt.)

If 'Excuse you!' feels a bit rude (and it depends on your tone too), you might prefer to say 'Pardon you' – it still puts the responsibility where it belongs.

Expressing your anger without worrying that you're being stroppy

Despite the advances women have made worldwide – political, economic and social – differences in standards of acceptable emotional behaviour among men and women remain. These also vary between cultural groups. Even today, women who show signs of anger and who express themselves in some assertive way may be labelled stroppy for doing so. No such reference is made to men who do exactly the same thing. Many women are sensitive to this double standard and hesitate to be completely honest about their feelings, unless those feelings are positive ones. The reverse is true when it comes to feelings such as grief, fear and depression. Men who openly acknowledge such feelings tend to be viewed – by themselves and others – as weak or feminine.

If being stroppy means you admit it when you're irritated or even angry, if it means setting limits on the bad behaviour of others, if it means saying 'Well, pardon you!' when it's deserved, then our advice is to be stroppy.

Having Feelings Rather Than Issues

One of the catchphrases used these days to describe people who are in some type of conflict is, 'She's got issues.' *Issues* are those problematic situations that trigger emotions like fear, sadness and anger. The problem we see, though, is that many people are so focused on their issues that they lose sight of what it is they're actually *feeling*.

The following conversation between the author Dr Gentry and one of his anger-management clients illustrates how difficult it can be to get a person to stop having issues and start having feelings:

Dr Gentry: How have things been at work this week?

Client: The same. My supervisor is still not including me in things that go on in the office, like going out for lunch with one of our staff members who's leaving. Everybody else, it seems, knew about it but me.

Dr Gentry: And how did that make you feel?

Client: I didn't think it was fair.

Dr Gentry: That's what you thought. I want to know how you *felt* about it.

Client: (Pause) I'm not sure what you want. It's just another example of how I'm excluded around the office.

Dr Gentry: I get the part about being excluded. What I want you to tell me is how you *felt* when you realised, once again, that you'd been left out.

Client: (Exasperated) I told you – I thought it was unfair! I don't know what else you want me to say.

Dr Gentry: Try this: when you found that you'd been excluded from going out to lunch, did you feel happy, sad, angry or glad? Choose one.

Client: You keep asking me how I feel about things. I don't know. None of those fit. I just thought it was unfair. (Looking perplexed.)

His employer had referred this client to Dr Gentry because he was seen as being uncooperative with co-workers and insolent towards his boss, both of which he denied. 'I don't know why they want me to come to anger management, because I'm not angry,' he said. The problem, as Dr Gentry saw it, was that he *was* angry (a natural response to being excluded). But instead of being able to say how he felt, he acted out his anger through what his superior saw as oppositional behaviour. When he said he wasn't angry it was because he didn't realise he was.

Practise what we call *feeling-cause language.* Start with how you feel ('I am irritated . . .') and then identify what happens to cause the feeling ('. . . because I always seem to be excluded from whatever is going on in the office'). Feeling-cause statements reduce hostile behaviour and increase empathy – a concern for your welfare – in the person with whom you have an issue. Would the client we mention earlier have continued to be excluded by his supervisor if he'd simply told him how he felt and why he felt that way, instead of communicating his feelings the way he did? Possibly, but you never know.

Having a good cry isn't always the answer

A study of 177 female university undergraduates found that crying was a symptom of suppressed anger, which in turn was associated with a higher risk for depression and anxiety. Younger women tended to cry more often than older women. This suggests that crying frequently should make you think about the possible reasons for your tears. If you think that anger may be part of the cause, have a look at Chapter 11, using some of the ideas to help you identify underlying anger. If this is true for you, then having a 'good cry' may, in fact, not be as good for your health as mental health professionals once thought (although refer to Chapter 5 for more information on the health benefits of catharsis, or emotional expression).

Walking Away and Still Having Your Say

If you give people a choice of how to respond to someone else's anger (or their own anger at someone else's behaviour), they'll typically either stand and fight back or run away. The old fight-or-flight response is built into your nervous system. Unfortunately, neither of these choices results in an effective resolution of whatever it is that underlies the emotional response.

You can classify both fight and flight under the heading of *resentful anger coping* (taking your anger away with you to brood over, or taking it out on others). It's much better to aim for *reflective coping* (for example, talking to someone about your anger after you've cooled down). Or you can choose a middle-of-the-road response – walk off until you cool down and then return later to the source of your anger and say exactly why you feel the way you do.

Try the following exercise:

1. **Think of some recent situation in which you felt someone treated you unfairly or unjustly but you didn't say how you felt at the time.**

2. **Write down the situation in as much detail as possible.**

3. **Read what you've written.**

4. **Write down how you felt about the situation – not what you thought or what you did, but how you *felt* (your emotions).**

   It's okay to list more than one emotion – for example, 'I was angry and hurt.'

5. **Write down the cause of your feelings ('She made an unkind remark about my weight').**

6. **Write down what you want to say to the person with whom you were angry.**

   Be sure to use feeling-cause language, starting with feeling and then the cause (see 'Having Feelings Rather Than Issues', earlier in this chapter). Avoid using inflammatory language (swear words, or opinion that goes beyond your message).

7. **Now, ask yourself how you feel – better, relieved?**

8. **Reinforce what you've done here with a positive self-statement – 'Good for me! I can speak up for myself now I know how I feel.'**

Make this a weekly exercise until you get better at expressing your feelings on a day-to-day basis.

Emotional maturity: You're not born with it

You don't start out life knowing how to manage your emotions well. You have to discover how to manage your emotions as you journey through life – a journey towards emotional maturity. Some of our angry clients are irritated by the term 'mature'. They react as if it's an order not to have fun, or to do what other people want. But emotional maturity isn't a restriction, it's the ability to

✔ Balance your emotions.

✔ Deal with as much as you can while the feelings are strong.

✔ Be clear and respectful when you communicate your feelings.

✔ Understand that you have a volume control on any of your emotions.

✔ Use your life experiences to guide you to make choices that work out well for you.

You can choose to pay attention to your feeling now, or later. Emotionally mature people understand that emotions use a percentage of their total energy for that day. They choose how much of their energy they use, and when, and balance this with what they gain from spending that energy.

If you want others to see you as a mature person, you have to handle your emotions – including anger – in something other than a childlike manner. Tantrums may be a normal occurrence for two-year-olds, but not for those who've supposedly reached adulthood.

Chapter 11

Owning Up to Your Anger

. . . .

In This Chapter

▶ Knowing whether you need to confess your anger

▶ Understanding how a journal differs from a diary

▶ Finding a safe way to express anger

. . . .

A colleague was teaching an anger seminar at a local college. One evening, he asked the students to begin by quietly writing down how they were feeling. He told the students to focus specifically on negative feelings, but the feelings could be about anything or anyone in their day-to-day lives – work, grades, relationships, family, finances . . . Some students began writing immediately, but others protested, 'I don't have any negative feelings. I'm fine! I don't have anything to write about.' He encouraged them to try anyway.

After a few minutes the students were writing furiously, filling up page after page with emotion. At the end of 20 minutes he told them to stop and asked them how they felt. One young woman, who had been reluctant to do the exercise in the first place, said, 'I feel terrible – like I'm going to explode! I don't know where all these feelings came from – about my anger at my mother and my friend. I was fine and now I feel awful.' Other students reported similar experiences. Some were tearful. Many felt relieved, as though they had unburdened themselves. Most of them were amazed at how powerful this simple exercise was in tapping into their underlying emotional life.

In this chapter we walk you through an exercise called *emotional journaling*. It's a technique that allows you to own up – to yourself – what it is that you're feeling but is not necessarily on your mind. Writing a journal makes you aware of feelings – like anger – that you've deliberately tucked away because they make you feel uncomfortable and you don't want to deal with them. The problem is that these emotions build up over time and eventually come back to haunt you. By not dealing with today's irritations, you carry them forward into tomorrow. You end up doing the very thing you've been trying so hard not to do: you get angry.

Give your health a boost!

Professor James W. Pennebaker, Chair of Psychology at the University of Texas and author of *Writing to Heal: A Guided Journal for Recovering from Trauma and Emotional Upheaval* (New Harbinger Press) has conducted many studies of the effects of *disclosure* (talking about events and feelings) on physical health. Studies with children and with adults over the years have repeatedly shown that simply writing down events or feelings is good for you. No one else has to know or discuss with you what you write about, and you can destroy or throw away your writing afterwards. No negative emotional effects of focusing on distressing feelings have been shown (as some

people fear) – in fact, just the opposite is true. The benefit comes from putting your feelings and experiences into words.

Pennebaker's research on disclosure has shown that writing about an event that caused you serious distress or trauma can result in a measurable boost to your immune system (your physical resistance to illness), your body functioning (such as blood pressure) and your emotional health, and that the effects last for the remainder of your life. Because one in four people need help with their mental wellbeing in their lifetime, this is a big reward for a very small effort!

Owning Up: It's Good for You

Behavioural medicine (the science that connects mind and body) advises that excessive inhibition (holding in) of emotions, especially strong emotions like anger, is unhealthy. That's right – holding back on emotions can actually make you ill. It makes sense if you think about it. Holding back on emotions is unnatural for humans. As a baby, you begin life by crying whenever you're uncomfortable – hungry, thirsty, lonely or in pain – but then life teaches you to do just the opposite: to keep your feelings to yourself and, in effect, cry inside. Your body wants to let go, but your mind tells you to hold back.

So, you end up in a state of emotional paralysis, which shows itself in a variety of emotional and physical illnesses. Chapter 3 has the low-down on how anger damages you. Common ailments include high blood pressure (hypertension), insomnia, headaches and depression.

Will confessing your negative feelings on a regular basis result in a decrease in your need for the doctor, or in how often you end up being off work because of illness? Current science suggests that the answer is yes.

10,000 Israelis can't be wrong

A fascinating study of 10,000 Israeli male civil-service employees looked at a total of 90 medical, social and psychological factors that might explain the development of high blood pressure. Four of the factors that made a real difference in a person's odds of having high blood pressure were:

✔ Brooding over feeling hurt by a co-worker

✔ Brooding over feeling hurt by a supervisor

✔ Restraining from retaliating when feeling hurt by a supervisor

✔ Keeping conflicts with your spouse to yourself

The study found that restraining and repressing emotions have the same effect on blood pressure as cigarette smoking and obesity do.

Seeing Who Can Benefit from Owning Up

If you're still somewhat unsure whether you really need this exercise in order to control your anger in the days, months and years ahead, the following sections describe the types of people who need to (and will benefit from) keeping an anger journal. If you see yourself in any of these categories, what do you have to lose by trying it?

Men in general

Two distinct types of men tend to exist:

✔ Those who express their emotions as they experience them

✔ Those who deny their feelings and act cool

The latter group far outnumbers the former, interestingly even when it involves getting angry. For every man who loses his cool in public, nine more keep their feelings under control – to the point where some don't even realise that they're angry.

Women who cry a lot

Women who cry often are more likely to suppress angry feelings than those who don't cry. Crying because you're slicing onions or have an allergy doesn't count!

People who are prone to guilt

Guilt is a real barrier to emotional expression. For example, one study Dr Gentry was involved in found that women who felt guilty about expressing anger towards their parents had higher blood pressure than women who weren't sorry about their angry behaviour. Many women, we suspect, discover early in life that it's easier to bottle up anger than it is to get rid of guilt.

People who are too empathic

Normally *empathy* (being in tune with another person's emotions) is a good thing. But when you have too much empathy, it can cause you to hide your true emotions so that you don't hurt someone else's feelings. Your feelings have the same value as theirs. How honest is it of you to keep yours hidden, in the belief (and you may not be right) that showing them hurts someone else?

People who are hostile

Hostility is an attitude that all too often leads to anger. The combination of hostility and anger-suppression tendencies can be lethal when it comes to your health. Your hostility is also a protection against the way you believe the world is – somehow you need to be on the alert, always defending yourself from attack. If you're sure you're right, what do you have to lose by trying a journal for two days?

Introverts

An *introvert* is a private person, someone who tends to be shy and timid. His emotions aren't available for public scrutiny. He tends to be serious and cautious about life, and he plays by the rules imposed by society – usually without complaint. Introverts are the proverbial nice guys and gals who tend to say things are fine when they're really not. Introverts are self-contained personalities, so emotional journaling should come easy to them. Of course, they're also more likely to fall into passive-aggression: saying, 'No, really, everything's fine,' but thinking, why can't he see I'm unhappy? (Turn to Chapter 10 for more on passive-aggression.)

People who've suffered a lot of trauma

The more that people suffer unusual, intense, traumatic experiences – such as child abuse, rape, death of a child or the breakdown of a marriage – the more likely they are to spend a lot of energy defending themselves from future hurts. One way to do this is to ignore your feelings about what goes on in your day-to-day life: going about your business, smiling and reassuring everyone that you're 'okay' no matter what. Journaling is a process by which you can heal, by both admitting to and letting yourself grieve over the damage the trauma caused in your life.

People who are chronically ill

Some people who live with severe chronic, progressive and disabling illness – such as multiple sclerosis, arthritis, fibromyalgia, diabetes or asthma – can experience a whole host of negative emotions. Anger is also well recognised to be associated with chronic pain. Bottling up emotions like anger and sadness only serves to heighten their struggle to maintain some quality of life.

Young people

As people grow older, they tend to be more open with their feelings. Maybe it's because at their age they believe they have less to lose by being honest about how they feel about life. Or maybe somewhere along life's way they achieved a measure of wisdom about how to deal with emotions in a healthy way.

CASE STUDY

Finding a new way of life by releasing feelings

Gill worked with a client who had a nervous breakdown aged 38. Working extreme hours in the City, drinking huge amounts, with little sleep or time for balance in his life, Geraint became deeply depressed and unable to go out. Over the following three years he met with Gill and talked through the start in life that had led to his breakdown. Raised in an alcohol-abusing family, he'd learned early on not to depend on his parents to be consistent, kind or honest. At school, Geraint had found it hard to trust others enough to make good friends, and feeling like an outsider just reinforced that he must be right to keep his distance. Although married and with a child of his own, he kept his distance through work, finding himself in a career that took time away from belonging to a close and loving family.

Out of Geraint poured his fury at the childhood he couldn't control, his sadness at having no friends to rely on, his hopelessness at being on a treadmill at work that he couldn't stop or climb down from, and his fear that he'd lose his own family. Being listened to without judgement allowed him to build his own view of how he'd come to be unwell.

A year after therapy, Geraint has stayed focused on his new goals. One breakdown is enough! He now drinks at celebrations but not to relax, finding his happiness playing with his children and joining his wife every other weekend in a quiz team. He works hard but always takes the holiday he's due and at work can discuss the occasional problem with his boss and colleagues, using feeling words and a calm approach to make his point or look for support. His last words at his review session with Gill were, 'I haven't just recovered; I've started a whole new life.'

Understanding the Difference Between a Diary and a Journal

Keeping an anger journal isn't the same as keeping a diary. *Anger diaries* can be useful in monitoring anger throughout the day. They allow you to keep track of how many times you experience anger, how intense the feelings are each time and how long your anger lasts – information that helps you measure just how angry you are (see Chapter 2 for more). That's all an anger diary does.

An *anger journal* does much more. In an anger journal you need to put your feelings into words, not numbers, and describe the situation in which your feelings arose. An anger diary might typically read: 'Got angry at 11.30 a.m.; rated as a five on ten-point scale; lasted about 20 minutes.' An anger journal, on the other hand, might read: 'I really got angry at lunchtime when my friend, Amy, once again failed to show up. I can't believe she's that irresponsible! I'd never treat her that way. She obviously has no respect for me whatsoever. I don't understand why I let people treat me like this.'

As you can see, anger journals are more revealing. They tell you something about yourself, more than just the fact that you got angry. In this example, the writer can begin to appreciate the fact that his anger isn't the result of his irresponsible friend (the world is full of those!), but rather his willingness to let other people treat him badly without standing up for himself. His real confession here is: 'I don't respect myself enough to ask respect from others.'

Some people keep anger diaries to see whether their anger experience is changing over time – the diaries provide an opportunity to look back and answer the question, 'Am I becoming a less angry person?' Journals, on the other hand, are only useful at the time you write them – you write, you read, you learn and then you discard them. With journaling, each day is a new day!

Telling Your Story Your Way

Owning up, in this case about anger and other unpleasant emotions, is about telling a story – *your* story. How you construct that story, however, makes the difference between whether or not this exercise is a therapeutic one. Just like Catholics who make their confession to their priest follow rules, there are rules about owning up like this. In the following sections we cover some of the more important rules to follow when working on your anger journal.

Making yourself the audience

In confessing the emotions that made up your day, you're taking both sides of a private conversation that's for your eyes only. You won't share your writing with anyone and owning up will end when you complete the exercise. So there's no need to construct a story to impress, teach or make someone else feel better.

We can't emphasise this enough: your anger journal is meant to be a conversation between you and yourself, not between you and someone else. When we ask clients to keep a journal, we make it clear from the start that we won't read what they write, nor do we want them to read their journals to us after they finish. The exercise is for the clients' benefit, not ours! All we ask when they finish is that they tell us how they feel and to summarise what, if anything, they discovered about themselves in that few minutes.

Using the first person

Writing in the first person (using *I*) may be the most difficult aspect of owning up. Most people are so used to describing and understanding their feelings in terms of *other* people's actions that they feel out of control. To illustrate this, think about how you and others you know talk about anger:

'My **mother** made me so angry.'

'My **boss** ruined my day.'

'If **they** didn't push my buttons, I wouldn't get so mad.'

If you think about your emotions like this and you write this way in your journal, everything you discover will be about your beliefs about other people and not about yourself. Writing in the first person makes you responsible for your emotions:

'**I** got so angry at my mother.'

'**I** let myself be annoyed by my boss.'

'**I** get angry when they make so much noise and keep me awake.'

If you write in the third person about your emotions, you'll feel more like a victim – a victim of the other person's behaviour. Victims end up feeling *more* angry when they finish writing, not less. Feeling more upset is exactly the opposite of what you want to accomplish with this exercise.

Relaxing about grammar

You don't have to be a writer to keep an anger journal. What's important here is putting your true feelings into words for your eyes only. This gives you a chance to let go of some of the physical tension you use to hold on to unexpressed emotion, and also teaches you about your own emotional self.

Grammar, spelling, handwriting and punctuation are completely irrelevant. Who cares! Our advice instead is to

✔ Write spontaneously (be natural).

✔ Write carelessly.

✔ Write with abandonment (say whatever you want).

✔ Write continuously.

✔ Write without a clear sense of purpose (not with a plan).

✔ Write with your heart, not your head.

✔ Write with passion, not perspective (perspective comes later).

✔ Write for no one but yourself.

✔ Write as if this is the last conversation you'll ever have on earth.

✔ Write just for the hell of it!

✔ Write first, read later.

Focusing on the negative

There's no medicinal effect to owning up to positive emotions. Storing up feelings of joy and satisfaction doesn't make you sick, whereas storing up emotions such as anger and sadness does. So the focus of an anger journal must be on anger and other negative feelings. What you're trying to do here is to purge those feelings that can poison your life as time goes by (more about this in Chapter 3). Think of it this way: holding on to positive feelings leads to contentment; holding on to negative emotions ends up in resentment. The aim of the anger journal is to avoid the latter.

You may confuse feelings with thoughts and actions such that, if asked about how you feel, you answer, 'Well, I thought he was stupid!' (thought not feeling), or, 'I just got up and left after I realised that she forgot we were meeting' (behaviour not feeling). Emotions are simply statements about how happy, cross, sad or glad you are, not why you feel that way or what you're going to do about those feelings.

You may not be fluent when it comes to emotional terminology. Even the most intelligent or educated people can have difficulties with feeling words. Your *emotional vocabulary*, the words you use to describe how you feel, may be limited to a few general terms like *upset*, *angry* and *scared*. Here's a list of words people often use to describe the emotion of anger. If you're at a loss for words to describe your feelings, you may want to choose some from this list.

✔ Annoyed

✔ Disappointed

✔ Disgusted

✔ Displeased

✔ Dissatisfied

✔ Enraged

✔ Fuming

✔ Furious

✔ Incensed

✔ Indignant

✔ Irate

✔ Irritated

✔ Livid

✔ Outraged

✔ Vexed

Finding the cause of your feelings

After you've worked out what you're feeling, try to identify the causes of your negative feelings. In other words, as you write in your journal you need to ask yourself exactly *why* you felt angry, sad or hurt. Although simply owning up to uncomfortable emotions through journal writing can get rid of those feelings (and the tension that accompanies them) from your mind and body, that alone doesn't provide the insight and understanding of why anger plays such a big role in your emotional life. The understanding – which is how you eventually gain greater control over your anger – comes from giving meaning to these feelings.

Here are some excerpts from an anger journal kept by Carol, a 22-year-old single mum, who was trying to understand why she was irritated so much of the time:

> 'I got really annoyed **because** the kids wouldn't stop running through the house when I told them not to.'

> '**Why** do I always have to get mad before anyone understands that I need some help getting everything done around here?'

> 'I think I'll go crazy if one more person tells me that there's no **reason** for me to get so upset – I've got plenty of reasons!'

> 'I **realise** I need help; I just don't know where to turn.'

The words in **bold** help Carol to question herself, which will eventually lead to change. In this case, what Carol is admitting to herself is that she can't deal with life's challenges without support. If she gets the message and acts on it, her situation will become much less stressful and she'll have a lot less reason to constantly be on the verge of becoming angry. If she doesn't own up to herself, however, her emotional life will remain unchanged.

Writing until time is up

Give yourself sufficient time to do the exercise in a meaningful way. We recommend 15 to 20 minutes. Make it easy on yourself by setting a kitchen timer (or some other type of time-keeping device) and writing until you hear the bell, which is your cue to stop what you're doing immediately. Stop writing even if you're in mid-sentence or haven't completed your thought.

Grammar, handwriting – how you write – is not important. What's important is that you write until the time is up.

If you do run out of things to write about before the end of the allotted time (not likely when you get started!), go back and read what you've already written and find something that you can expand on. Trust us: with a little prompting you'll quickly find those emotions that are just waiting for a chance to be expressed.

Preventing emotions from getting in the way of writing

It's most likely you'll feel relieved, content and far less tense when you finish with your anger journal for the day. That, after all, is the goal of the exercise. But sometimes – typically when you first start writing a journal – you're very likely to feel strong negative emotions such as sadness, apprehension and nervousness.

Look back at the example we give in the introduction to this chapter about the reactions of our colleague's students to their anger journaling – some were in tears, others felt like they would explode. Keep in mind that these feelings are natural – after all, you're facing uncomfortable emotions that you've kept hidden away – and they usually go away quickly.

If you become upset while you're writing in your journal, don't let the feelings stop you from completing your work. You can write and cry at the same time, can't you? After you finish, don't dwell on what you've found. Switch focus to something you find comforting or fun for at least 30 minutes, to allow yourself time to recover.

If the negative feelings you encounter after writing are too strong for you to handle, or if the feelings persist and interfere with your day-to-day life, stop the exercise and talk to a qualified therapist. Counselling or therapy provides a safe place and supportive person to whom you can admit your feelings. Accepting help is a sign of judgement, not weakness.

Suspending judgement

Human beings are, by definition, judgemental creatures. You make literally thousands of judgements each and every day of your life about one thing or another: what should you wear today? What should you have for breakfast? Which route should you to take to work? Which emotions should you express and which ones should you keep to yourself?

Unfortunately, anger is one of those emotions that people tend to judge harshly. You may think of anger as one of the 'bad' feelings, and you may assume that no one around you wants to hear about your anger. You probably think it's all right to tell another person you feel wonderful, happy or blessed if he asks how you are, but you won't be as honest if the answer is instead, 'Touchy, irrational and angry!'

You're telling yourself that the world around you doesn't really want hear the bad news about your emotional life – it only wants the good news. If no good news exists, then the best course of action is to keep quiet or lie – 'I'm fine.' You may be right occasionally, but constant daily judgements like this cause you to store up negative feelings like irritation, sadness and hopelessness – feelings that you need to own up to later on.

Read back over your journal, looking for times when you're judgemental. When you can, see the confusion between your judgements ('He's so stupid; he's always losing his glasses') and what you're angry about ('Every time he loses his glasses we're late leaving and I feel embarrassed getting to work late').

As far as the rest of your world is concerned, your journal is anonymous. What you write is for your eyes only. No one else is going to see it, so they can't judge it – and you shouldn't either. This may be harder for you to do than you think. You may be so used to having a critical running commentary of your emotions as – or before – you experience them, that letting the feelings flow freely may be difficult at first. That's okay. In fact, that's also part of the goal – helping you become a less emotionally constricted person.

Sticking to pen and pencil

You're probably asking yourself, 'Can't I own up on the computer? That's how I communicate with the rest of the world.' Well, of course, you can. But we encourage you instead to stick to some old-fashioned technology for this exercise – pen and paper. The reasoning behind this is simply that writing by hand is a much more intimate mode of expression. There's something much more personal about hand-written messages than those that you type or email.

If writing isn't your thing and you tend to be more fluent (and comfortable) speaking, then you may want to find a tape recorder and use that. But don't change anything else – talk for your ears only, speak in the first person, continue the conversation for 15 to 20 minutes, suspend judgement and so on.

Finding a quiet place

You need to find a quiet place to write in your anger journal, a place where you can be alone (and uninterrupted) with your thoughts and feelings. Writing a journal isn't a public activity. If you can't allow yourself any personal time until you've taken care of everyone else's needs and done all the chores, then make writing in your journal the last thing you do – after everyone else is in bed. Another good time (though sometimes a bit tricky to engineer) is right after you come home from a day at work but before you jump headfirst into the demands and challenges of the evening. In fact, if you get rid of the unwanted emotions of the day, you're much more likely to enjoy better relationships with your loved ones.

 If you have the kind of job where you find yourself more and more fed up as the day progresses, you may want to use your lunch break to write your journal. It may make the rest of the work day go a little smoother and help you to avoid any outbursts along the way.

 You probably don't want to write in your anger journal over a cup of coffee in a cafe: that's not a good place to access strong emotions and start crying. If there's a place of worship (like a church or synagogue) nearby, a quiet corner in a library, or an open space or park bench, that would do the trick.

Chapter 12

Balancing the Effects of Your Temperament

*I*deas about temperament – your character, typical characteristics, personality style, make-up – have been around for many centuries and in many cultures. Temperament concerns your inborn traits and characteristics, rather than those you learn from life. Theories of temperament (or personality) all attempt to explain typical characteristics of people and the differences between these types of people. So how do these qualities affect your adjustment to each stage of life? For example, why does one person in a car accident walk away unaffected yet their friend in the passenger seat is mentally traumatised and unable to drive afterwards? Why do the same stresses affect people differently? Why are some people content to relax and let life go by, but others compete and are driven to be the best?

Anyone who has – or knows – more than one child of the same parents will confirm that, from early days or weeks, obvious differences exist between them. The children's alertness, usual mood, emotional stability, reaction to fear, sociability with people, and the level of curiosity and interest they show in new experiences all differ.

In this chapter we ask, what's typical of your character? What do those who know and meet you expect you to be like, whether at home, school or study, at work, in friendships or wider life? And how does your character influence your response to angry feelings, and your ability to deal with them in a healthy way?

Recognising Your Style: Temperament and Anger

Psychologists and academics can't agree on a single theory of temperament or personality. So instead, we introduce you to some of the knowledge and ideas that you need to consider as you work towards your goal of better anger management.

Aggressive styles

So what kinds of characteristics or personality traits make healthy anger management more difficult? It's likely that you know people in your everyday life who:

- ✔ Always appear serious about life – are more likely to interpret events without seeing a light side and less likely to believe there's a purpose to relaxing.

- ✔ Are often very self-absorbed in conversation – preoccupied with what they're doing, what they have, what they need to do right now, what they've achieved, without actually telling you much about themselves at all.

- ✔ Bully others with threats, physical violence, put-downs; use their position to be oppressive, abusive or to discriminate against others.

- ✔ Can't become involved in something without wanting to run it; prefer to work alone, feeling that they'll do the job quicker and more efficiently than a team.

- ✔ Destroy possessions, mistreat or hurt animals, drive dangerously, use physical violence to make a point or get something, take risks without thinking of others.

- ✔ Even when talking to someone, constantly scan the room while speaking.

- ✔ Find it hard to let others finish a sentence, are always hurrying to 'get on' – rushing around, driving fast, eating quickly, pushing others to do more or do better.

- ✔ Get more and more impatient (and irritated) when facing a deadline that may not be met.

- ✔ Show emotions as soon as they feel them, with no disguise or delay.

> ✔ Use physical strength or size to stand over or intimidate, or use other non-verbal behaviour like pointing, slamming the door, fist shaking, displaying hate symbols and forcing others aside on the road.
>
> ✔ Work all the time, never spending time with family or friends, or having fun without being competitive.

Having a high number of these traits and behaviours adds up to a pattern associated with an aggressive approach to life – competitive, ambitious, with a greater potential for anger and a tendency to find it difficult to manage anger without showing aggression. In some areas of life, these characteristics can be the foundation of success, but at the same time, such people can be difficult to be around, can have an edge to them and may not have many friends or admirers.

If you recognise yourself, you may be thinking that you can't win: with many of these characteristics, expressing your anger can push others away, but as we explain in Chapter 3, suppressing anger may shorten life expectancy and affect your health. Don't worry – it's possible to make changes that help you to move beyond your inherited nature towards a style in which problematic anger is much less likely to happen. Whatever you've heard, it *is* possible to moderate your temperament!

Passive styles

Although fewer studies, anger-management books and classes deal with passive anger, in recent decades psychologists have better recognised the negative effects of passive anger on health and on others. If your temperament is to be avoidant of conflict, anxious and with limited coping strategies, or obsessional, perfectionist and controlling of your world, you may be particularly likely to mismanage your anger using passive aggression.

It's likely that you know people in your everyday life who:

> ✔ Carry grudges – every time they see the people they're angry with (and with this style there'll be more than one), their energy is on defeating that person, 'paying her back' (getting revenge) or making her look foolish.
>
> ✔ Give help constantly while settling for second best, refuse help but give off signs of feeling martyred or taken advantage of, say 'It doesn't matter' when asked what's troubling them.

✔ Manipulate situations – to trigger anger in others and then patronise them or to stand back and look blameless – like pretending to be ill, passing messages through others or breaking up a relationship.

✔ Sabotage by refusal, avoidance, missing deadlines or being careless, treating others dismissively, show hostile indifference or sulk, constantly blame themselves (secretly demanding reassurance).

✔ Use hidden or devious behaviour – gossip behind someone's back, tell lies or exaggerate, secretly damage possessions.

✔ Use non-verbal signals instead of communicating with words: sigh, tut, avoid eye contact, mutter inaudibly, turn away or withdraw, smile falsely, raise eyebrows, smirk at others to encourage them to choose sides.

Having a high number of these traits and behaviours adds up to a pattern associated with a passive-aggressive approach to dealing with others. A passive-aggressive person's expectations and 'rules' about how people should behave aren't discussed or obvious, but her anger is!

This kind of behaviour and interaction affects others through loss of trust – they're more likely to avoid you in return. If you're passive-aggressive then dealing with you is likely to be difficult: you don't say what you mean, are always looking for reassurance, can't tolerate not getting your way and show little sign of important human qualities like sympathy and empathy (the ability to see things from another's perspective and to feel parallel emotions). Again, it's within your grasp to change how you interact.

Moving Beyond Your Temperament

You're probably thinking, 'Change my ways, my personality? That can't be easy. I've been this way all my life!' Well, it may be easier than you imagine – but you won't know unless you try. Like changing anything, it takes determination and practice.

Becoming assertive

So, if aggression and passive-aggression are both potentially unhealthy for good anger management, what are you aiming for? *Assertiveness* is the ability to deal with and interact with other people, while being able to put across your point of view and maintain your rights. Assertiveness isn't a style of temperament or personality, but a life skill used to manage your actions and feelings, whatever your temperament. Being assertive means:

- ✔ Recognising your emotions accurately.

- ✔ Using your emotions to guide you in what you want, without them overwhelming you.

- ✔ Being able to say what you feel in words, with your body language, tone and expression, showing calm confidence, rather than hostility, defensiveness or withdrawal.

- ✔ Linking your emotions with information. For example, 'I feel sad when you walk out while I'm talking. I feel as though you don't care what I have to say.'

- ✔ Being able to say what you'd like to happen. For example, 'I'd appreciate it if you'd stay and take a moment to listen.'

- ✔ Remaining calm and accepting if the other person chooses not to do as you want. After all, you're free to assert your view, and everyone else is free to assert theirs.

Not excusing yourself ('It's just the way I am')

Temperament is inherited and you can't do much about it – or can you? People with obsessive personalities or a shy temperament come up against problems that mean they're at a disadvantage in life, unhappy or not able to reach their full potential. Those who have a naturally 'sunny' nature, good looks or a gifted talent rarely complain. We don't hear those clients saying 'I was born like it, I'm stuck with it' – they've come to talk through ways to change. If you have a fiery temperament, chances are you're also passionate, motivated, energetic – all qualities for success. But you need to be willing to make an effort to find ways that work for you and for others around you.

Anything you want to achieve in life can be yours, without using anger to get it. Being in control – managing your anger well – gives you more choices, more positive feelings, better relationships and fewer obstacles in life.

Focusing on who you are, rather than what you do

Often, the first question a stranger asks you when you meet is, 'What do you do?' Questions like this can be a way to open up a topic of conversation with a stranger (since many people spend a large amount of time working). But these questions can also be a way of measuring a person's social and economic status compared with your own (for example, she's more powerful, I'm richer). The answer allows you to make a fast judgement about the other person, without really getting to know her.

The 'So, what do you do?' question allows quick judgements, but it's not really an accurate way of finding out who someone is. Telling someone that you're a surgeon only tells her that you're well educated, disciplined and earn good money. It doesn't necessarily follow, though, that you're a decent human being: generous, kind, a trustworthy friend, a good parent, interested in others or honourable. In fact, you may be none of these, even though you're a talented surgeon.

If you want to move beyond your temperament, start by sharing with others as much about who you *are* as what you *do*. Try the following exercises to help you move towards that goal.

Taking the remembrance test

No matter how old you are, you can start thinking right now about how you want to be remembered. Take a look at all the epitaphs in Table 12-1 and, as honestly as possible, choose the one that you think the people in your life would say is accurate about you.

Table 12-1	The Remembrance Test
Epitaphs about What You Did	*Epitaphs about Who You Were*
Here lies a person who made a fortune.	Here lies a person who was a friend to everyone.
Here lies a person who was feared but respected by all.	Here lies a person who was intelligent.
Here lies a person who hated to be late for anything.	Here lies a person who could be trusted.
Here lies a person who was a go-getter.	Here lies a person who was a team player.
Here lies a person who fought through life and wasn't afraid to be angry.	Here lies a person who had a constant curiosity about life.
Here lies a person who was a great provider.	Here lies a person who loved passionately.
Here lies a person who succeeded alone.	Here lies a person who knew contentment in her life.

After you've chosen, ask yourself if that's how you *want* to be remembered? What would those who know you well prefer to choose for you? Is it time for a change? For example, if the epitaph that most accurately describes you is 'Here lies a person who made a fortune,' you can start by looking for new friendships among people who don't have, or want, great wealth.

Writing about your life

Sit down for just 15 minutes. Write the word *I*, and follow this by writing about your life so far; include anything and everything you think is relevant and important. Stop at the end of 15 minutes (set a timer, if necessary) and read what you've written. Try to be as objective as you can – pretend you're reading about someone else's life.

After you've finished reading, answer the following questions:

- ✔ How much of your life is about *you*, rather than other people?

- ✔ How much of your life is taken up with your work?

- ✔ How much of your writing is about financial success or failure?

- ✔ Does it sound like a life story in which the person is satisfied and content?

- ✔ Would you say that this essay is about someone who has a sense of purpose or meaning in life?

- ✔ How much of the essay is about what you're content with and how much is about difficulties?

- ✔ If this was another person's life story, would you want to swap places?

If your essay has a healthy balance between references to yourself versus references to others, if work and financial success (or failure) aren't the sole focus, if your essay portrays a reasonably content person whose life is full of purpose, if you can see a balance between *getting* and *giving*; and if you'd actually want to live that person's life, you can be fairly sure that you're assertive and managing your temperament well.

If you answered otherwise, take a long, hard look at yourself and think of ways that you can change your story. Repeat this exercise once a week for the next six weeks, each time asking yourself those same questions afterwards, and see whether you're beginning to move beyond aggressive and competitive traits in yourself. If you work at changing the focus of your life, the focus of your essay should change as well.

Looking at your own competitive streak

Competition is at the heart of a great deal of aggression – the need for dominance, admiration or having things your own way. Competition can be healthy, but when out of balance, the need (some would say *obsession*) to compete is insatiable. People with this style compete over *everything* – and when they're in competition, they take no prisoners. For example, a friend's father was talking about Christmas with his kids and the games they'd played. Dr Gentry asked him, 'Would you let your child win a game you were playing just to make her feel good?' His cheerful reply was, 'You must be joking. If she wants to win, she has to beat me. That's what life is like.' Now that's an aggressive style! For this man, it's better to crush the child's interest than to lose the game.

Passive people compete too – they're just more secretive about it. The winning for them may be manipulating a situation, or getting rid of their anger through sabotage or revenge.

The following is a list of ways in which you can modify your competitive nature and engage in *healthy* competition. This is often competition with different goals in mind:

- ✔ **Try playing a game without keeping score.** Do you play golf, football, board games, and not only keep your own score, but other players' scores as well (so there's no cheating, mistakes or altering the rules)?

- ✔ **Let your children win at family games at least half the time.** You're aiming for your kids to learn the pleasure of being together, having fun or developing a skill. They're not going to come back for a second go and improve if you're still crowing about your win last time.

- ✔ **If you feel like you have to compete with your partner about ideas and decisions, be sure to let your spouse win half the time.** If you do, you'll stay together longer!

- ✔ **Never ask others how much they get paid, how much their car costs or how much time they spend advising the boss.** Just do your job, pursue your own goals (rather than comparing yourself with theirs) and you'll be fine.

- ✔ **If you're going somewhere, don't try to see how fast you can get there.** Drive within the speed limit and enjoy the view. Life isn't meant to be a race.

✔ **Practise meditation.** If you've never meditated, or you don't really know where to start, pick up *Meditation For Dummies,* 2nd Edition, by Stephan Bodian or *Mindfulness For Dummies* by Shamash Alidina (Wiley). Both come with a CD of guided meditations that you can use to get started.

✔ **Alternate between competitive activities and non-competitive activities.** For example, one Saturday afternoon play cards with your friend (and allow yourself to keep score), and the next Saturday kick a ball around the garden.

Try to come up with your own creative ways to relax your competitive nature. If you're less competitive, you're less likely to get angry, and that's definitely a good thing.

Taking off your watch

Aggressive people are often obsessed with time – 'This is taking too long', 'It's getting late; I'll never get finished on time', 'I wish they'd hurry up'. They have an accelerated sense of time. They feel time 'slipping away' more and more as the day goes by. This leads to an increased feeling of time anxiety or *hurry sickness.* That explains why these people get so irritated when circumstances and others slow them down.

Of course, the perception that time is passing too quickly is false. Time passes at the same rate for aggressive, passive and well-balanced people!

 To test how aware you are of time, have someone you know pick a time, anywhere from 5 to 15 minutes, then ask her to chat with you for that length of time. When she stops, try estimating how many minutes have passed. If you have strong aggressive traits, you'll most likely *over*estimate the actual time. If you're more relaxed, you're more likely to either be right on the mark or *under*estimate how much time has gone by.

One of the best ways to reduce your aggression is to stop wearing a watch for a while. If your aggressive and competitive traits are strong, your first thought as you read this is probably, 'I can't do that – how would I know what time it is, how would I keep up with my hectic schedule, how would I get all this stuff done?' The answer is that you wouldn't. But guess what? The world wouldn't end. On the other hand, the quality of your work might improve; in fact, people are much more creative in their thinking and problem solving when they aren't bound by deadlines.

Here are some helpful hints on how to wean yourself from your watch:

✔ **Think about which parts of the day or week you'd find it easier not to wear a watch.** Then see whether you can take the watch off for an hour or two during those times.

✔ **When you're at work, put your watch in your pocket or bag and rely on a wall clock to keep track of time.** Only put your watch on when you leave the office.

✔ **Wear an old-fashioned pocket watch or turn the face underneath your wrist.** You still have a way of keeping time but it's not as obvious, staring you in the face all the time.

✔ **Set a timer on your watch to let you know when it's time to move on.** For example, when you're having lunch with a friend, set the alarm for when you need to leave. Then put the watch out of sight.

Acquiring Wisdom

Evidence shows that people who develop their assertiveness and use the calm and steady aspects of their temperament live longer and have greater satisfaction (as well as less anger) simply because they're wiser when it comes to navigating their way through life's twists and turns. We offer some tactics and ideas in the following sections.

Seeking diversity in relationships

Wisdom is something you acquire from your own life experience, but also from those around you. You can also acquire wisdom from all kinds of people: younger than you or older, children, friends, family or colleagues.

In order to become wiser, try to make new relationships with people whose personality isn't similar to yours. This takes effort if your life is heavily influenced by the hours you spend with your high-achieving colleagues, your drinking mates or your sports team. Look for things to involve yourself in that bring you into contact with new people, and set out to leave your old ways behind.

Developing better social skills

Learning to talk to others is *definitely* something we're not born doing! Many people overlook this – it's not until your fifth year of life and beyond that you really start to develop the language and personal skills to put across to others how you feel, what you need or want, and what you're thinking.

If you have a passive temperament and style in dealing with your anger, you're likely to be quieter, less forthcoming, less extrovert and less sociable than others. Over the years, your tendency to stay on the edges or to stop talking when you feel lost for words means that you've missed out on a lot of practice! These are life skills – information and behaviour patterns that should help you to deal with your experiences and emotions. Like any other skills, they need plenty of practice.

Whatever you've been told or believe, it's not lack of intelligence, lack of interest or lack of ability that cause you to struggle now to express your feelings in healthy ways – it's lack of practice. This is something you can begin to change today.

Pay attention to how those you like and admire communicate – particularly those who manage anger without being underhand or aggressive. How do they appear when they're being critical? How do they manage to bring the mistake in their wage slip up without being artificially 'nice' or getting someone else to do it for them? How do they bring a conversation to an end, and how do they manage situations with others before they get out of control? Don't feel embarrassed about imitating people – that's how humans learn to speak and to communicate. You'll develop your own ways and ideas as you make progress and find communication easier.

Letting yourself be curious

Passive-aggressive (and aggressive) personalities often lack curiosity about others. Encourage yourself to be curious about life in general, and the people you consider you know well. But do you? It's a tendency of passive-aggressive people to be sure that you know what others think and what motivates their behaviour, and to assume that they know how you're feeling (or to feel resentful if they don't). People with a curious and enquiring temperament (with traits such as motivation to learn, willingness to have new experiences and tolerance for differences in people) tend to gravitate towards a wide variety of new situations and people that catch their attention. Some of their curiosity is satisfied through reading or talking with someone; in other instances, it comes from hands-on involvement.

To develop your sense of curiosity, you might try one or more of the following:

✔ Check the news each weekend for interesting events locally. You never go to those things? Too busy? You won't know what happens if you don't go along (and no, you don't know already if you haven't been!).

✔ Join a club or group that covers a diversity of topics and has discussion regularly.

✔ Once a month, go to your local bookshop or online, and buy a book on a topic you know absolutely nothing about.

✔ Spend some time now and then with friends who have unique hobbies and skills. Ask them to show or tell you more.

✔ Watch educational television, take an evening class (but not for the exam), travel or find at least one experience a year that takes you out of your 'comfort zone'.

Chapter 13

Using Anger Constructively

*A*nger has a bad reputation! Typically, you associate anger with aggressive behaviour or some other type of destructive result in your life. This is true only because no one has shown you how to use anger constructively. In this chapter we illustrate the *positive* side of anger – the side that you can harness to resolve problems of everyday life, understand the other person's point of view and reduce your chances of future conflict.

Emotions aren't essentially good or bad. People feel tense and sometimes unwell during a happy event, like being promoted or moving house – just as they do if they hear the unexpected news of a loved one's death. Does this mean that you should avoid happiness, change and surprise at all costs? Of course not – just as you shouldn't try to avoid anger because of some mistaken belief that it only causes hurt and damage. It's what you *do* with anger – how you express it – that makes it good or bad.

Everyone gets angry: how do *you* show it?

A colleague asked 20 students he was teaching to write down what they did when they got angry. The following table summarises their answers:

Positive Expressions	*Negative Expressions*
Go to the gym	Be self-critical
Go for a walk and think	Complain, complain, complain
Talk about it with a friend	Cry
	Explode
	Feel depressed
	Feel guilty
	Feel sick
	Get a headache
	Get into arguments or fights
	Grind my teeth
	Ignore the person I'm angry with
	Lie awake all night
	Not speak to anyone
	Play the anger over and over in my head
	Say things I don't mean
	Scream
	Snap at people
	Stamp my feet
	Storm off
	Throw things
	Withdraw from everyone

The ratio of negative-to-positive expressions of anger in this group of intelligent students was a huge 13-to-1. If this is how people deal with anger, no wonder so many think of it as a bad thing!

Making Anger Your Friend

If you choose to use anger positively, you can compare yourself with some well known people! Martin Luther King, Gandhi and Nelson Mandela are just a few people who were angry – about poverty, racial injustice and occupation of their countries – but who turned their anger into constructive action that changed the world for the better.

In the following sections we cover a few reasons why you should consider making anger your friend, to build a healthier, happier and more productive life.

Anger is a built-in capacity

Everyone is born capable of anger. Mothers recognise anger in babies as young as three months of age. Anger isn't something that you have to learn or earn, like money or friendship. It's yours to experience as the need arises. You have a right to all of your feelings.

Ask yourself: do I want to use this inner ability to reconstruct my life?

Anger is invigorating

The *e* in *emotion* stands for 'energy'. Anger produces an instantaneous surge of adrenaline that causes your pupils to dilate, your heart to race, your blood pressure to elevate and your muscles to tense. If you're really angry, even the hairs on the back of your neck stand up! Your liver responds by releasing sugar, and blood shifts from your internal organs to muscles, causing a generalised state of tension. You're energised and ready for action. Remember, though, that emotions are short lived – they come and go. So, it's imperative that you strike while the iron is hot and use the energy from anger to your benefit before it evaporates.

Ask yourself: do I want to stop wasting energy on destructive anger?

Feeling alive through anger

Some years ago a colleague was conducting a workshop on anger management for mental-health professionals. He started off by asking the audience to define anger. Some people offered the usual, easy definitions: 'It's an emotion', 'It's a feeling' and 'It's something that feels bad'.

But then one young woman came up with the most intriguing definition of all: 'Anger is one way I know I'm alive.' She went on to say how refreshing emotions are because they disrupt the otherwise humdrum nature of daily life and for brief periods leave you feeling energised, full of vitality, alive.

Anger serves as a starting point for new behaviour

The *motion* part of *emotion* has to do with motivating behaviour. No doubt there're things you want to change in your life. But change makes you nervous, and you're afraid. You're uncertain about what will happen if you let go of what you know and move your life in some new direction – maybe a new relationship, a new career, a new place to live or a new, healthier lifestyle (joining a gym, starting a diet, giving up alcohol). So you do nothing – that is, until you get angry enough about the way things are that you spring into action.

Ask yourself: how can I change my life through constructive anger?

Anger communicates

Anger tells the world just how miserable you are – how *un*happy, *un*fulfilled, *un*satisfied, *un*excited and *un*loved you feel. Anger speaks the *un*speakable! Think about the last time you verbally expressed anger. Do you remember what you said? Was it something like, 'Get off *my* back', 'You don't care about *me*', '*I'm* tired of living hand to mouth' or '*I* give, give, give and *I* get nothing in return'. I'm sure others heard what you said, but did *you*? Did you listen to your anger – listen to what it's telling you about what's wrong with your life and what you need to do to begin correcting it?

Turning anger into action

Sometimes you just need a kick. Charlie was having lunch with a friend and was telling her about the new, exciting venture he was planning to begin shortly to turn around his failing business. 'I'm going to start the new business in about two months and I'm counting on you sending me some clients,' he said. Her reply, without a moment's hesitation, was, 'No, you're not.'

Charlie was shocked and irritated. 'Why do you say that?' he asked. His friend explained, 'Because you've been talking about this new business for over a year now, and every time we have lunch it's always going to start sometime in the next few months – but it never does. I think it's a wonderful idea and of course I'd send you clients, but honestly, Charlie, you're never going to do it. It's just talk.'

Now Charlie was angry. He paid the bill, mumbled some pleasantry and went back to work. But the more he thought about it, the more he realised his friend was right. A year of talk hadn't turned into action. Charlie decided right then and there – while he was still angry – that he would begin his new business within the next 30 days. The rest, as they say, is history. His new venture got off to a great start, and over the next ten years he made a lot of money – all thanks to his good friend who made him angry that day.

The most helpful emotional dialogue you have is the one you have with yourself.

Ask yourself: what is my anger telling me about me?

Anger protects you from harm

Anger is a vital part of that built-in 'fight-or-flight' response that helps you adapt to and survive life's challenges. Anger is the fight component – the part that drives you to take active measures to defend yourself against real or perceived threats.

Do you ever get angry enough to stand up for your rights? Do you ever use anger to set limits on other people's rude or inconsiderate behaviour? Do you ever get angry and say to someone, 'Hey, that's uncalled for!', 'Just stop right there – I'm not going to sit here and take any more abuse' or 'You may bully other people in this office, but you're not going to bully me'. We hope so, because otherwise you may be well on your way to becoming a victim!

Ask yourself: how can I use my anger to defend myself in a positive way?

Telling it like it is

Edward loved to bully his employees. He had a daily ritual of calling someone into his office without warning, usually just as most people were leaving for the day so there were fewer witnesses. Edward would tell his 'victim' to have a seat and then immediately proceed to get red in the face with rage, come charging across the office and stand with his imposing figure over his helpless prey. Then he'd harangue him about all sorts of things he was displeased with for what seemed like an eternity. Everyone dreaded the day when their name would be called.

Then, one day, while several employees were preparing to leave, Edward summoned Sophie, one of the secretaries, to his office. Everyone felt bad for Sophie, anticipating what was to come. But before even five minutes had passed, she returned looking unperturbed. 'What happened?' her colleagues asked, 'Why are you back so soon?'

Sophie said, 'Well, it was just like everybody said it would be. As soon as I sat down, he came charging across the room and started shouting at me. So I stood up and started walking out the door, at which point he said, "Where do you think you're going?" I simply told him that no one had ever spoken to me like that in my entire life and I didn't know how to respond, so I thought it best to leave until he calmed down. And here I am.'

Two days later Edward called Jack, another employee, to his office. As soon as Edward started bullying, Jack thought about Sophie's experience and started to walk out. Edward asked him where he thought he was going, and Jack repeated Sophie's answer. At that, Edward stopped his ranting and calmly asked Jack to sit back down because he needed to talk with him about something important. Jack said, 'Okay, as long as you don't start shouting again.' The two had a civil discussion after that.

Anger is an antidote to impotence

Impotence, lacking in power and ability, feels lousy. And we're not just talking about sexual impotence. We mean being powerless in how you deal with the world around you – your relationships, your job, your finances, your health, your weight, the loss of loved ones and so on. You feel weak and inadequate, not up to the task at hand.

Then you get angry – and suddenly you're infused with a sense of empowerment, a feeling of strength, confidence and competence. You're standing up straight to the frustrations and conflicts you've been avoiding. Anger is a can-do emotion: 'I can fix this problem', 'I can make a difference here', 'I can be successful if I try'.

Pay attention to your posture the next time you feel down, dejected and impotent about some important thing in your life. Then notice how your posture changes when you get fired up and begin to take charge of the situation. We promise you'll be amazed at the difference.

Ask yourself: how often do I give in to impotent anger?

Exploring the Motives Behind Your Anger

Before you can use anger constructively, you have to examine the motives behind it. Ask yourself, when you get angry:

- ✔ What do you really want to achieve?
- ✔ What do you want to happen?
- ✔ What are you after?
- ✔ What would satisfy you?

The most frequently cited type of anger is constructive anger (63 per cent of those surveyed), followed by vengeful anger (57 per cent) and finally anger that's aimed simply at letting off steam (37 per cent). We cover each of these motives for anger in the following sections.

Bringing about a positive change

You use *constructive anger* to show authority, to achieve independence and to get another person to do something that's good for them. If you're a parent, have you ever got angry with your child when you were just trying to show him to behave safely (for example, not stepping into the road without looking, or not staying out until three o'clock in the morning)? Probably. At work, have you ever been angry with your subordinates and said, 'Enough messing around. We've got work to do here; let's get on with it.' Most likely. As a young married person, have you ever expressed irritation with your in-laws because they're always telling you what's best for you ('You need to give up that job', 'That house is too big for you', 'Don't you think it's time you started a family?') instead of letting you make your own decisions? Have you put your foot down, firmly saying 'We feel those things are a private matter between us. I'm sure all parents worry, but we're happy with our plans?' Well then, you've used anger constructively.

Liz was a student at university, studying sports science and enjoying her second year. She'd settled in to a new city and made some good friends. Coming home late from birthday celebrations at the pub one evening, Liz was attacked, kicked to the ground and her mobile and purse stolen. The three lads threatened to hurt her more badly if she looked at them, so Liz kept her eyes shut until they'd run off. She was furious that, despite her fitness and confidence, she hadn't fought back, run or looked at her attackers so that she might identify them.

Liz made an appointment with her sports trainer to plan a programme while she recovered from the bruising, spent the last of her birthday money on a new phone that she'd wanted, and spoke to the local victim support group. One year on, she volunteers each week for victim support, determined to use her shock at how vulnerable she'd felt in a useful way – for herself and others. Instead of seeing herself as weak, angry and hurt, Liz made the most of a traumatic event, converting her anger to motivation almost straight away.

Ask yourself: am I satisfied that I'm using my anger in a way that benefits me more than it hurts me?

Seeking revenge

Is anger your way of getting revenge for a wrong that has been done to you? Is the goal to hurt someone or destroy something – to hurt their feelings, to physically attack them or to break something when you're frustrated? Is your anger designed to intentionally inflict suffering and do you experience pleasure in the harm you do to others? If the answer is yes, then your anger is, by its very nature, destructive not constructive – this kind of anger is called *vengeful anger.*

David was constantly in trouble. His father, a successful businessman, often told David he'd have to do things his way to make it in life. Feeling constantly put down, David started to feel suspicious of everyone around him, seeing insults where they didn't exist. He saw someone from school days driving a good car – much better than his – and felt angry, so he scraped his key down their paintwork and was charged with criminal damage. He felt so angry that when he was released, he returned and covered the car with graffiti. When he calmed down, he was back in police custody. Sadly for David, this was just one of the many episodes of vengeful anger in his life. He says, 'I can't remember all the times I've ended up with my head in my hands, worse off than before, and my dad just has another reason to put me down.'

Ask yourself: do I want to go through life like David, destroying something every time I get angry? Am I willing to take the cost of my vengeful anger?

Letting off steam

Have you ever felt like you were just going to explode – and then you did? Anger is one way a lot of people – normal people, not crazy or vengeful people – let off steam. Their anger isn't tied to any specific issue or person; it's sort of generic. It reflects a good bit of pent-up frustration and stress that seeks relief. Think of a pressure cooker and you get the idea. Even though it feels good, this type of anger isn't constructive. Rather, it's anger that, to quote *Macbeth*, is 'full of sound and fury, signifying nothing'.

Matt had just about finished putting in the new kitchen cabinets. He was putting up the moulding around the cabinet tops when he realised he'd cut a piece too short. He flew into a rage and proceeded – much to his wife's horror – to take a crowbar and rip out all the cabinets and throw them one by one into the garden until his anger subsided. He destroyed months of hard work in a matter of a few seconds. After he cooled down, he headed off to the local hardware shop to buy materials to rebuild the cabinets. Sadly for Matt, his anger frequently burst out in this way. He says, 'I can't tell you how many things I've had to rebuild in my life because of my anger. It's cost me a fortune.'

Ask yourself: is it enough to just 'feel good' after I express my anger or would I rather use anger to benefit my life in some meaningful way?

Using Anger to Understand Yourself

Anger is like a mirror – it doesn't build character, and it doesn't destroy it. It simply reveals character. Anger tells you and the world what kind of person you are, what you expect from life, what you're passionate about, how much alcohol you've had to drink, how stressed you are and much more.

Close your eyes and imagine the last time you got angry at someone. Get that situation fixed in your mind's eye for a minute or two, as though you're a camera observing without feelings. What did you say or do in that moment of anger? Try to be as detailed as possible. Stay with the scene until you feel comfortable that you can honestly answer the question 'What does my anger say about me in that situation?'

Here are some possible answers:

- ✔ My anger says that I'm a selfish person whose needs always come before others.
- ✔ My anger says that I'm a moral person who believes in fair play and justice.
- ✔ My anger says that I'm impatient – my needs have to be met *now*.

✔ My anger says that my life is in chaos – nothing is working right.

✔ My anger says that I care enough about you to get upset when you put yourself in harm's way.

✔ My anger says that I'm greedy – I always expect to have more than others and I get angry when I don't.

✔ My anger says that I feel I'm not being treated with respect.

✔ My anger says that I need to dominate others in all kinds of life situations.

✔ My anger says that I feel I'm a 'special' person and so always entitled to have my way.

✔ My anger says that I can feel another person's pain.

✔ My anger says that I'm a pessimist, always expecting that things won't work out and getting angry when they don't.

✔ My anger says that there's far too much stress in my life – I'm overloaded!

✔ My anger says that it's high time to make some positive changes in my life – there has to be a better way to live.

Do you like what you see in the mirror? If not, then it's time to make some changes.

Moving Towards Constructive Anger

Constructive anger involves two things:

✔ Deciding where it is you want your anger to take you

✔ Arriving at that goal through a step-by-step process (which we outline in this section)

Before you begin, try saying the following statements to yourself – and believe them. Even if you don't believe that all these statements are true, try this anyway.

✔ I need to understand and think about my anger.

✔ I need to put my anger into perspective.

✔ I can't change the trigger to my anger this time.

✔ I need to find a way to sort out the situation that made me angry.

✔ I need to find other ways to express my anger.

Step 1: Decide how you want to feel after you get angry

How you use anger is a choice, and with that choice comes consequences. If you choose to use anger constructively – so that it has a positive outcome – you'll generally expect that, after you finish expressing your anger, you *will;*

- ✔ Have a better understanding of the person with whom you had the angry exchange.
- ✔ Feel better about that other person.
- ✔ Feel closer to resolving issues between you and the other person.
- ✔ Realise that things were never as bad as you first thought they were when you became angry.
- ✔ Feel that you and the other person both came away feeling that something good happened.
- ✔ Have less conflict in the future.

And if you choose to use anger constructively, you *won't;*

- ✔ Continue to hold a grudge against the other person.
- ✔ Feel totally justified in continuing to be angry with the other person.
- ✔ Feel tense and agitated around the other person.
- ✔ Dwell on your angry feelings.
- ✔ Feel that you must go over your angry feelings (and the reasons for them) with anyone and everyone who'll listen.
- ✔ Be defensive in social situations involving the other person.
- ✔ Feel that you can't ever resolve the problem between you and that person.
- ✔ Feel victimised by the other person.
- ✔ Feel impotent and unable to deal with the problem that caused your anger.
- ✔ Feel as though you're going to explode any minute.

On the other hand, if you choose to use your anger *destructively*, you should expect the opposite outcomes – more conflict in the future, more tension between you and the other person and so on.

Step 2: Acknowledge your anger

A simple statement such as 'I don't know about you, but I find I'm getting irritated about what just happened and I thought you should know that' will do. What you want to do is let the other person know that emotions are in play here and that the emotion you're feeling is anger.

It's not enough just to acknowledge to *yourself* that you're angry – you have to describe or name that feeling to the person you're angry with.

Step 3: Focus your anger on the problem, not the person

Taking a line from the film *The Godfather*, when you engage in constructive anger you need to start with the idea that 'it's business – it's not personal'. In other words, focus on the issue that triggered your anger, not the person on the other side of that issue. When you describe what you feel, use words – not your expression, the tone or volume of your voice or your behaviour – to make your point.

Concentrate on the *what* not the *who*. When you begin to personalise anger (for example, saying something like, 'That stupid woman . . .') your anger invariably turns destructive. The person you're angry with can't hear your point, just the insult you use.

Step 4: Identify the source of the problem

This step is an easy one. Why? Because the source of all your anger is *you*! Before you slam this book shut and throw it across the room, give us a chance to explain what we mean.

All your emotions are a reflection of yourself. If you're angry with one of your employees when he regularly comes to work late, the source of your anger lies in the fact that *you* believe you aren't getting a fair day's work for a fair day's pay. Similarly, if you're angry with your husband because he continues to read the paper while you're trying to tell him about your day at work, the source of your anger is *your* belief that you aren't getting the attention that you want from him. If you didn't have those beliefs, the actions of the other people would be of no consequence.

CASE STUDY

Finding new solutions

Dr Gentry's client, Ted, called to say he was in a dilemma. He started by telling him how angry he was with his son-in-law, who often verbally attacked him when he visited the family. That anger had, on more than one occasion, led to hostile and unpleasant situations, including Ted saying some things he regretted later on, as well as some pushing and shoving. Now Ted's daughter had called and invited Ted to his granddaughter's birthday party. His question was: should he go and risk further abuse or not? Ted saw it as a lose–lose situation – he was damned if he did and damned if he didn't! He told Dr Gentry that he had tried talking to his son-in-law, but this only provoked further rage on the son-in-law's part. He felt the situation was hopeless.

First, Dr Gentry encouraged Ted not to have a general rule about attending family functions involving his son-in-law – in other words, Ted should decide what to do on an event by event basis. Dr Gentry reminded him that he was under no obligation to attend family gatherings and that his family wasn't entitled to have him show up regardless of the consequences.

Dr Gentry also encouraged Ted not to let his anger at his son-in-law totally shut down any possibility of future relationships with his daughter and granddaughter. He suggested that Ted look for opportunities to visit his daughter and granddaughter without the son-in-law present (for example, meet them for lunch, take his granddaughter for a visit to the zoo and so on).

Dr Gentry told Ted that he should be prepared to exit politely from any family situation at the very first sign that his son-in-law was intent on verbally attacking him. The expectation shouldn't be 'If I go, I have to stay no matter what'. (In combat, all good generals have an exit strategy.)

Finally, Dr Gentry advised Ted to share the responsibility for solving this family problem with his daughter – after all, it was she who had brought this angry man into the family. Dr Gentry advised Ted to ask his daughter what she was prepared to do to make things better, if anything.

These were all things Ted hadn't considered before and that might work. All Ted could do was try.

TIP

Right away, as you recognise the source of your anger (taking responsibility for how you feel – see Chapter 7 for a complete discussion on this), you begin to feel more in control of your anger. Now, the question is: do I change my expectations of the other person or do I make it clear for them what I expect and what will happen if my expectations aren't met? (Of course, this depends on the situation. Are your expectations realistic or selfish?)

Step 5: Accept that you can solve the problem

Fixing *problems* is much easier than fixing *people*. What you have is a problem situation. Try to remain optimistic that you'll solve this problem. Be open-minded – a closed mind goes nowhere; it just defends itself. Don't be afraid to try new solutions when the old ones don't work.

Think about some anger-provoking situation you've been involved in that seems unsolvable. Write down all the things you tried to correct the situation. Now, think about some things you *haven't* tried. If nothing comes to mind, talk to someone else about it and see what that person suggests. Two minds are always better than one! After you come up with a new strategy, use it the next time you're in this situation.

Step 6: Try to see things from the other person's perspective

Anger is so personal that it's hard to see past it, to put yourself in the other person's shoes. But seeing the situation from the other person's perspective is one of the most essential steps in using anger constructively.

The easiest way to understand why the other person thinks, feels or acts the way he does is to ask for his view. For example, Ted (described in the nearby sidebar) could say to his hostile son-in-law, 'Whenever we get into a discussion, I feel insulted when you call me names. I may be wrong, but it seems like you're really angry with me, and I'd like to talk with you about how you're feeling and why.' If you don't give the other person an opportunity to tell you where he's coming from, you're left to speculate – and odds are, you'll guess incorrectly.

Reverse roles. Think of yourself as the other person and ask yourself:

- ✔ How (if I'm them) am I feeling right now?
- ✔ What am I thinking?
- ✔ How would I explain my actions to another person, if asked?
- ✔ What could I tell someone that would perhaps make him less upset with me?
- ✔ What is it that other people don't know about that they should?
- ✔ Am I giving them the wrong impression of who I really am and what's on my mind?
- ✔ Is my behaviour justified in my mind and if so, why?

Learning from mistakes

For several years now the author Dr Gentry has been conducting anger-management classes in schools and, unfortunately, he's found out a lot about the things that *don't* work with angry, alienated children. What *doesn't* work is making them feel bad for being angry. Another thing that doesn't work is assuming they're all angry for the same reasons. Assuming that they want to stop being so angry just because the school wants them to doesn't work either.

What does work, Dr Gentry has found, is to engage young people in a dialogue that accepts their anger, doesn't judge it and puts it in a big-picture perspective that fits their unique life story. In other words, stop trying so hard to change people and instead work just as hard to understand their point of view.

So instead of telling the students how they should feel, Dr Gentry asks them a lot of questions: what was it about the teacher asking you to be quiet that made you angry? What did you hope to accomplish by punching the other kid on the bus? Do you see any relationship between you leaving the house angry with your dad and the fact that you verbally attacked the teacher as soon as you came in the classroom? Did you ever think of any other way of handling that situation without resorting to violence?

You guessed it: these questions are the kind you can ask yourself if you want to understand your anger and deal with it more constructively.

Step 7: Get the other person involved

Another key step in constructive anger expression is to get the co-operation of the person you're angry with in resolving the problem. The question here is not 'What am *I* going to do about this problem?' but 'What can *we* do about finding a solution that works for both of us?' The minute you begin to share the responsibility (or burden) of resolving an anger-producing problem, the intensity of your anger decreases.

Step 8: Keep a civil tone throughout

What you say in anger isn't what causes problems – it's how you say it. If you can keep a calm, civil tone to your conversation, you'll find that really listening to the person you're angry with is easier, and it's also easier to get your message across to that person. Lowering your voice in turn causes the other person to lower his. Civility doesn't require that you stop being angry – it just helps you use the anger more constructively.

Step 9: Avoid disrespectful behaviour

Clearly, you need to avoid some things – gestures, behaviours – if you're going to use anger constructively.

Try not to:

- ✔ Roll your eyes or show disrespect when the other person is speaking.
- ✔ Sigh or use other distractions while the other person is talking.
- ✔ Point your finger.
- ✔ Lecture the other person when it's your turn to speak.
- ✔ Use critical language (words like *stupid*, *idiot*, *crazy*, *ignorant* or *ridiculous*).
- ✔ Repeatedly interrupt or talk over the other person.
- ✔ Personalise your message (for example, 'What a fool you are!').

Step 10: Don't be afraid to take time out and resume the discussion later

It's okay to say to the other person, 'I think we've gone as far as we can with this right now, but I really think we should continue our discussion later.' Some issues take longer to solve than others – just as some destinations are farther away than others.

This strategy only works if you actually do resume the discussion later. Otherwise, all your constructive efforts were in vain! If the other person is too angry to want to stop, that's all the more reason to step back.

Step 11: Make it a two-way conversation

Solving conflict – which is a big part of anger management – takes a two-way conversation. The point here is that when it comes to addressing your anger in a constructive way you have to let the other person have a turn too. Vengeful anger and simply 'letting off steam' don't involve the other party, except as the object of your rage. Are you trying to do something different this time?

No wonder I have low blood pressure

Recent studies have shown that adults who express their anger constructively tend to have lower resting blood pressure even after you account for other known risk factors – age, smoking, obesity, family history. Studies have also shown that adults can learn constructive anger expression and, when they do, they experience less hostility and decreased blood pressure. This is an example of when *anger management* translates into *medical management.*

Step 12: Acknowledge that you've made progress

Old bad habits like destructive anger die hard. So if you're trying to use anger more constructively, it's important to acknowledge when you make progress. Tell the other person, 'You know, it's helped to talk about it. I understand better where you're coming from, and I'm not nearly as upset as when we first started talking about this.' Then ask him, 'Do you feel the same way? Do you feel that I heard what you were saying? Do you feel we're closer to sorting this out now than we were before?'

You hope, of course, that the other person says yes. But if he says, 'No, not at all,' that's okay. Maybe he'll change his mind in the future. (Most importantly, don't get angry just because he doesn't agree with you!)

What Goes Around Comes Around

Dr Charles Spielberger, at the University of South Florida, once wrote a paper with a great title: 'Rage boomerangs'. His message was simple: people tend to 'respond in kind' when they're confronted with anger. Anger causes anger, just like kindness causes kindness.

If you engage in destructive anger towards others, they'll most likely respond with destructive anger towards you. On the other hand, if you're constructive in how you express your anger, then a much greater chance exists that the other person will respond in a similar manner.

If you're caught up in this cycle of mutual anger, this is your chance to break out. Make your next move based on how you want the person you're angry with to respond. If you want him to notch down the intensity of his anger, start by toning down your end of the conversation. If you want him to understand why you're angry, start by asking him to help you understand why he's angry with you. If you don't want him to treat your anger with disrespect (see the previous section), then don't act disrespectfully towards him. Believe it or not, you'll find that you have more of a positive influence on 'what comes around next' than you imagined.

Part IV
Lifestyle Changes That Improve Your Anger and Health

'Well, that's not a very good start, Norman.'

In this part . . .

We argue that emotions, like anger, don't occur in a vacuum. To the contrary, your emotions say a lot about how you live your life – how much sleep you get, what kinds of chemicals (like nicotine or caffeine) you ingest throughout the day, how well you're handling stress, whether you have a balanced lifestyle, how spiritual you are, and your prevailing mood. The techniques we offer in this part are intended to make you a happier, healthier person, not just someone who's less angry.

Chapter 14

Managing Daily Stresses

. . . .

In This Chapter

▶ Defining stress

▶ Understanding that stress can be catching

▶ Identifying which types of stress are most dangerous

▶ Finding out which stress-busting techniques work and which don't

▶ Thriving on stress

. . . .

Does your anger sound like this?

'Get lost – I've had all I can take!'

'Give me a break for God's sake! How much do you think I can take?'

'I'm not going to tell you again – leave me alone!'

If so, your problem isn't anger – your problem is stress. You either have too much stress or the wrong kinds of stress, but either way, you're stressed. Anger is just your way of expressing it. Some people withdraw and go quiet under fire; others lash out. Unfortunately, neither strategy works well and both strategies end up a danger to your health (see how in Chapter 3).

This chapter shows you what to do when your plate gets too full and you see the warning signs of anger. We talk you through how to spot people who are stress carriers – if you aren't feeling irritated before you encounter these people, you will afterwards. We tell you how to avoid stress burnout and why it's the little hassles of everyday life that can do you the most harm. And most importantly, we show you how to thrive under stress – how to be a robust personality. It's easier than you think!

Distinguishing Stress from Strain

Believe it or not, your great-grandparents didn't get stressed out. Well, maybe they *felt* stress, but they didn't call it that. *Stress* and *strain* are engineering terms that people first applied to human beings in the 1930s.

Stress is a normal part of daily life. It's what fuels that built-in fight-or-flight response that you have to help you to defend yourself against things – people, circumstances, events – that threaten your survival. Stress isn't a choice – it's a gift (even though it doesn't feel like one!).

Here are some of the changes that occur in your body every time you feel stressed:

- ✔ Your pituitary gland is activated.

- ✔ Your hypothalamus gland is activated.

- ✔ Your blood cortisol level rises. (*Cortisol* is a stress hormone that enhances and prolongs your body's fight-or-flight reaction.)

- ✔ Adrenaline flows freely.

- ✔ Your pupils dilate.

- ✔ Your blood sugar rises.

- ✔ Your blood pressure increases.

- ✔ Your blood clots faster.

- ✔ The muscles throughout your body tighten.

- ✔ You breathe more rapidly.

- ✔ Your heart rate increases.

- ✔ Your palms become sweaty.

- ✔ Fat is released into your bloodstream.

- ✔ Your liver converts fat into cholesterol.

Strain, on the other hand, is what happens to your body when you become *over*stressed – that is, when you experience too much of a good thing. Think of a bridge (we told you this comes from engineering!) that has cars constantly crossing it year after year. Because of their weight, the cars stress the bridge; the more cars that pass over, the greater the stress. Now imagine that after a few years cracks begin to appear under the bridge – small at first, but larger as time goes by. These cracks threaten the reliability of the bridge. The cracks represent the strain that inevitably occurs from too much stress. The bridge is you – your body, your health.

Now imagine the bridge creaking and groaning as it begins to show signs of strain. You can see the role that anger plays in communicating to the world just how much strain you're under. Anger is simply your way of creaking (showing your irritation) and groaning (flying into a rage).

Why is my fuse getting shorter?

People ask us all the time, 'I've always had a short fuse, but it seems to be getting shorter all the time. Why is that?' In most cases, the answer is that these people are experiencing more and more strain as they struggle through life, first with one thing and then another. As the stresses accumulate, so does the strain. Life begins to weigh heavily on them. Their tolerance decreases and their reactivity increases, as indicated by the length of their fuse. Bear in mind, this doesn't happen under conditions of normal stress – only when stress becomes extreme.

Staying Away from Stress Carriers

Do you know someone who, when she walks into the room, seems to disrupt everything around her? Before that person arrives, people are in a good mood – laughing, talking, getting their work done, enjoying life – and this person changes all that. The laughter stops, moods change and tension suddenly permeates the air. That lovely person is a *stress carrier*. This is as true for sulking and passive aggression (see Chapter 10) as it is for obvious aggression.

You can tell a stress carrier by the person's:

- Body posture, signalling aggression (for example, hands waving) or defensiveness (for example, arms crossed in front of chest)
- Finger tapping
- Fist clenching
- Fixed, angry opinions
- Jerky body movements
- Rapid eye-blinks
- Sighing
- Tendency to frequently check what time it is
- Tendency to hurry up the speech of others by interjecting comments such as 'Yeah', 'Uh-huh', 'Right' and 'I know'
- Tendency to talk or listen to you while continually scanning the room
- Tendency to talk over other people in a conversation
- Tense facial expression (clenched jaw, frown or narrowing around the eyes)
- Tone of voice (pressured and tense, or sullen)
- Use of obscenities

Who's stressing me out?

Julia worked in a busy office, handling large and complex orders and dealing with transport companies. All kinds of daily hassles – weather, traffic, breakdowns, people problems – came up in an ordinary day. Julia came to see author Gill for help with her anger management, saying, 'I don't know why, but I just feel so wound up. I feel like screaming at people. I snapped at my manager, and now I'm in trouble.' Gill asked her whether anything had changed recently. She became upset and angry, saying, 'But that's just it. Maggie started working with me six weeks ago, and I've waited a year to have some help. But now I have it, I just feel like I'm cracking up.'

Gill asked Julia to describe Maggie. 'She's always busy, rushing around. Her desk is covered in reminder notes. She came off the phone yesterday cursing our head office – I know they can seem slow but they don't make many mistakes.' As Julia talked it became clear that Maggie's manner, the rush she was in and the constant, irritated way she talked about the small details she was dealing with were bringing a huge cloud of stress into Julia's previously calm office. It wasn't Julia who had difficulties with anger management – it was Maggie.

Limit the time you spend around stress carriers. Their stress is catching – if you're around someone like this for long, you'll feel stressed too. If a stress carrier's stress spills over into anger, guess what'll happen to you? You'll find yourself angry, and you won't know why.

You may be a stress carrier yourself. Check out the list and see whether you have any of those stress-carrier characteristics. If you're really brave, ask someone who knows you well to examine the list and tell you what she thinks. You may not be the best judge of your true self!

Identifying the Sources of Your Stress

Stressors – those people, events and circumstances that cause you stress – come in all sorts of sizes and shapes. Some are physical (noise, traffic, pollution), some social (noisy neighbours, spiteful in-laws), some emotional (death of a loved one), some legal (divorce, crime), some financial (bankruptcy) and so on. Some are even positive – getting a new job, getting married, graduating from university – and they excite your nervous system no less than the negative experiences do.

Psychologists tend to group stressors into two primary categories: minor irritants (or daily hassles) and major, critical life events.

Minor day-to-day stressors that you're likely to experience and that can eventually set the stage for anger include the following:

- Being interrupted while talking
- Caring for a sick child
- Developing a cold
- Driving in heavy traffic
- Finding that someone has borrowed something without asking your permission
- Having an appointment with someone who arrives late
- Having to deal with car repairs
- Having too *much* time on your hands (you read that right: people with too much time on their hands get bored – scientists call it *underutilisation* when it occurs at work)
- Having unexpected company
- Hearing a rude remark that's directed at you
- Hurrying to meet a deadline
- Misplacing something important
- Seeing that someone has pushed in ahead of you in a queue

Major stressors – which can have a much more significant impact on your life – include the following:

- Being behind on your rent or mortgage
- Being fired or made redundant
- Being promoted at work
- Being sentenced to prison
- Breaking up with your spouse or partner
- Experiencing the death of a close friend or relative
- Experiencing your children leaving home
- Getting pregnant
- Having a chronic or life-threatening illness
- Moving house
- Starting a new job
- Winning the lottery

How are you faring with major stressors?

A psychological test measures the amount of major stress a person has experienced in the past year. It lists 42 different stresses and gives each one a score, or *impact value*. The total score, it turns out, is a fairly good predictor of future illness – everything from a common cold to cancer or a heart attack. The cut-off score for serious stress is 300. Anything less than that is probably not going to be a risk to your health. Dr Gentry gave it to a client who came in saying, 'I'm not sure why I'm here, but I just don't feel good.' Her score was 2,292 – unbelievable! Oh, and by the way, she was a *very* angry woman.

Which type of stressors – minor or major – would you guess are the unhealthiest? If you're like most people, you said the major ones. But the reality is that you're much more likely to be undone by the small things in life. Why? Precisely because they're small and they occur on a daily basis. You come across minor stressors so often that you often don't take them seriously – and that's a mistake! The good news about major stressors – the ones that can affect your life in some critical way – is that they don't occur that frequently and you tend to make a real effort to deal with them well. In other words, you take the major stressors more seriously, so they're far less harmful and you handle them better.

Knowing Which Types of Stress Are Toxic

Each person has a finite *carrying capacity* for stress – that is, the amount of stress she can accommodate without showing signs of strain. Even the most resilient people can find themselves overloaded from time to time. That's when you need to take stock of what's going on around you and work to restore some semblance of balance in your life.

Being stressed out can become an addiction. You can consider yourself a stress addict if you:

✔ Can't remember the last time you didn't feel overwhelmed and rushed off your feet

✔ Enjoy the adrenaline rush or high that goes with meeting one challenge after another

✔ Find yourself restless and bored when things are too quiet

✔ Seem to invite and sometimes create stress where none exists

If you're a stress addict, you need to start weaning yourself off stress, with small steps. You can start by setting aside one otherwise busy evening a week to spend time with a close friend who isn't competitive and who doesn't require a lot of conversation. Try taking off your watch in the evenings and for portions of your weekend – say, Saturday afternoon from 12 until 6 p.m. (and build up to longer periods over time). Sign up for a yoga class or spend a few minutes in a hot tub three or four times a week.

Some types of stresses – regardless of their magnitude – are more poisonous to your life than others. We like to refer to these as the Four Deadly C's.

Cumulative stress

Cumulative stress is stress that – you guessed it! – accumulates or collects over time. It's one thing adding to another, and another, and another, until you can't take any more.

That's how Henry feels. Recently retired, Henry thought he was beginning to live out his golden years. He had a secure income and a paid-for home, and both he and his wife were in good health – or so it seemed. Now Henry is concerned. His wife of many years is starting to forget where she puts things, occasionally gets disorientated, is unable to master simple tasks and has to have things repeated over and over so she won't forget. Henry told her a week ago, for example, that he'd be out one evening at a volunteer meeting. The very next morning, she asked, 'When is it that you'll be out for the evening?' Henry told her again, giving her the benefit of the doubt. The next morning, she again asked, 'And when is it that you're going to that meeting?' Now clearly frustrated, Henry told her for the third time. The same thing happened again the next day. Finally, after six consecutive days of having to repeat himself, Henry finally erupted in a state of rage. He shouted, she ran to her room in tears and both were left feeling bad afterwards. Henry wasn't stressed because his wife asked when his meeting was – he was stressed because she kept asking over and over. One or two times, fine; six times, no.

Chronic stress

Have you ever found yourself confronted with stress that just won't go away? You wake up to it every morning and go to bed with it every night. That's *chronic stress* – it's with you all the time. Many of our clients deal with chronic stress in the form of disadvantages – poverty, bad housing, unemployment or illness. Trying to get by, they find themselves in a state of constant struggle, trying to just survive from day to day. No wonder these people stay in such an irritable state and are quick to get angry when confronted with any little problem that arises!

Catastrophic stress

Events such as terrorist attacks, tsunamis or hurricanes devastate people – particularly if you're one of those most immediately affected. They represent the most horrific, life-altering kind of stress – *catastrophic stress*. Some people never recover from catastrophic stress (for example, military veterans who 20 years later are still reliving a war as part of Post-traumatic Stress Disorder); those who do recover from catastrophic stress usually take a long time to heal.

Cultural beliefs and traditions in the UK and US restrict how much grief you show in public. We lost count years ago of the number of clients, friends and others we've heard suggest that most people are 'over the worst' within 12 months. It takes a *minimum* of five years to reach a steadier place.

Control stress

Human beings love to control things. People feel safer, stronger and more competent when they have a handle on their lives. The problem is, life doesn't always give you that opportunity.

Losing the love of your life

Most mental-health professionals agree that the death of the love of your life is a catastrophic loss, a disaster. This is particularly true if you've been together for 20 years or more. Those kinds of strong attachments, once broken, cause great personal pain.

Grief isn't something that always comes quickly or ends quickly. For example, men widowed after a long and loving marriage are most vulnerable to stress-related illness (heart attack) between 6 and 12 months after the loss of their wives. Women, on the other hand, appear fine for the first two years, before finally showing signs of illness that can be traced back to the death of their husbands.

Grief over the loss of a loved one is one type of stress where professional counselling or a community support group can make a big difference in relieving suffering. Reach out and get some help after you suffer such a loss – even if you don't feel like you need it.

Take Michelle, for instance. She's a bright young woman who had a great head start in a promising career in marketing before the company she worked for went through a major reorganisation. Michelle found herself with no immediate boss, twice the workload (with no additional compensation) and too few resources to meet the demands of her job. Worst of all, she no longer had time to devote to the activities she did best. Normally, Michelle was an energetic, positive, dynamic personality, but since her company's reorganisation she found herself exhausted all the time, dreading going to work, irritable, and suffering from migraine headaches and stomach pains. Michelle's life was out of her control, and she was experiencing control stress.

Avoiding Burnout

Burnout is a form of strain that inevitably results from prolonged, intense and unresolved stress. The dictionary defines burnout as 'the point at which missile fuel is burned up and the missile enters free flight'. Guess who the missile is? You. The fuel is your physical and psychological energy. And the free flight is all the disorganised, erratic and inefficient behaviour that leads you to chaos. Do you recognise this?

The best way to avoid burnout is to see it coming. How many of the following symptoms do you have? If the answer is five or more, you're well on your way to burnout.

- ✔ Agitation

- ✔ Anxiety

- ✔ Being accident-prone

- ✔ Bursting into tears

- ✔ Chronic fatigue

- ✔ Confusion about routine things both at work and at home

- ✔ Cynicism

- ✔ Depression

- ✔ Drinking alcohol most days

- ✔ Feeling bored and unmotivated

- ✔ Feeling just as tired on Monday morning as you did on Friday night

- ✔ Feeling up one minute, down the next

- ✔ Headaches

✔ Heartburn, acid stomach or indigestion

✔ Hopelessness

✔ Hostility and resentment

✔ Insomnia

✔ Loss of appetite

✔ Loss of passion for your work or life in general

✔ Missing work

✔ Poor concentration

✔ Sudden bursts of temper

✔ Suicidal thoughts

Here's a bit of irony: the people most likely to burn out in any walk of life are the ones most likely to succeed – people who are most passionate about their work, are most liked by superiors and co-workers, and are seen as being the friendliest, most energetic, most motivated, most conscientious, most confident and most assertive.

This book offers several strategies that can help to buffer you from the full brunt of the stresses you're currently under, including: moderating your use of stimulants (Chapter 15), relying on friends and co-workers for support (Chapter 20), getting enough sleep (Chapter 16) and participating in spiritual activities (Chapter 17).

But you can do other things as well. Find a solution to your chronic stress. For instance, Michelle (see the 'Control stress' section, earlier in this chapter) needs a new job. She's fighting a no-win battle. All she can conceivably do is continue to lose ground, spinning her wheels but getting nowhere.

Taking stress breaks throughout the day also helps. Stress breaks don't typically solve the problem, but they do eliminate the *chronic* aspects of stress. We're amazed at how few people we know who steal a few minutes here and there for themselves just to relax away some of the built-up tension. We can hear you shout, 'But, I don't have time to relax!' The answer: make time. You're making a choice to have control of your life and health.

If you want to avoid burnout, try to be more realistic about what you can expect from the situation you find yourself in, as well as your own abilities. Burnout usually occurs when there's too big a gap between those two. Forget how things 'should' be and deal with them as they really are. Stop demanding more of yourself than is reasonable. Believe us, whatever your job is, you're not going to save the world (or the company you work for) single-handedly. Try backing off a little and setting some limits to protect yourself.

Discovering How to Be Hardy

Dr Gentry's aunt, Lillian, was a hardy soul. She grew up in an orphanage after her parents both died suddenly in a flu epidemic. Vivacious and athletic, she was almost killed in a head-on collision with a drunk driver in her early 20s – an accident that left her with a mangled knee and stiff leg for the remainder of her life. An attractive woman, she had few boyfriends due to her injury, and she ended up marrying a much older man. She wanted children but couldn't have any, so she became the patron aunt of a host of nieces and nephews. She worked full time all her adult life. She and her husband managed a modest living, although money was always tight. Following a severe stroke, she spent the last ten years of her life in a nursing home, paralysed on one side of her body and strapped to a wheelchair. She died quietly in her sleep aged 88.

The remarkable thing was that Lillian never complained about life being unfair or about her physical limitations. She refused to adopt the role of a disabled individual. To Dr Gentry's recollection, she never – not once – displayed any anger towards anyone, even if the person deserved it. Instead, she was legendary for her forbearance, her good humour, her forgiving ways and her optimistic, anything-is-possible outlook.

Psychologist Salvadore Maddi made a career studying people like Dr Gentry's aunt, who he described as having a *hardy personality*. According to Maddi, hardiness is an amalgam of three separate traits:

 ✔ Control over your own life

 ✔ Commitment to the things and people that matter to you

 ✔ Your ability to face a challenge with a positive attitude

These traits, when combined, cut a highly stressed person's likelihood of becoming physically ill by half – even more when combined with other healthy behaviours like regular exercise.

Hardy personalities are more likely to use *transformational coping strategies* (transforming a situation into an opportunity for personal growth and societal benefit) when faced with stress. They're also less likely to try to deny, avoid or escape the difficulties at hand. In older people, being hardy also reduces the risk of stress-related illnesses – colds, flu, headaches, upset stomach and nervousness.

People who lack hardiness tend to feel alienated from the world around them. They feel alone and on guard. They don't have the support and feeling of being socially connected that hardy people enjoy, the connectedness that goes a long way towards reducing the impact of stress in daily lives. Because they don't belong to any group with helpful life values, their lives lack purpose and a code of behaviour, and they have no real drive to solve their problems – it's just easier to be angry.

There appears to be no gene for hardiness – it's a style of dealing with stressful life circumstances that's a by-product of life experience. In other words, you learn to be hardy – and if you haven't done so already, it's not too late!

Being the master of your own destiny

In order to have the kind of hardy personality that'll help you cope with stress, you need to believe in your own ability to deal with difficult times. Call it self-esteem or self-confidence – it comes down to being the master of your own destiny.

What do you do when you're on the wrong end of some major stress? Do you run and hide, avoiding even thinking about the problem or how you can resolve it? Do you let everyone know (silently) by your mood and disapproval that your way – avoidance – is the only way? Do you distract yourself with a cigarette, a beer or some serious shopping? Or, like Lillian, do you ask yourself 'What can I do to make things better for myself?' and then do it? One of the three critical elements of a hardy personality – a sense of *you* having some control – is a skill you can develop by turning your mind to it.

Practise thinking like a hardy personality by repeating to yourself statements such as the following:

- ✔ People get the respect they earn in life.
- ✔ Good marks in school are no accident – they're the result of hard work.
- ✔ Luck has little or no effect on how my life turns out.
- ✔ People achieve their goals because they take advantage of opportunities that come their way.
- ✔ I can influence what happens to me.
- ✔ People only take advantage of me if I let them.
- ✔ If I believe in myself, I am much more likely to try and to reach my goal.

To choose or not to choose

Maybe you like to choose your own destiny. You want to decide how to deal with problems, conflicts, challenges and stresses. Good for you! You're what psychologists call a *self-directed personality.* The more options you allow yourself (or others allow you), the better.

But, believe it or not, not everyone wants choice. In fact, you might get confused, upset or paralysed with indecision if you're forced to decide how best to cope with some major life stress. You're an *other-directed personality* – which means you need help from outside sources (family, professionals) to decide what you should do. So ask!

Being a player, not a spectator

Hardy people have a deep sense of involvement and purpose in their lives – the commitment component of a hardy personality. In life, you have to decide whether you want to be a player or spectator.

People who aren't hardy wait for life to improve (that is, become less stressful), but hardy personalities get stuck in. To be hardy, you can try the following:

- ✔ Enjoy the closeness of being involved in family activities.
- ✔ Find meaning in the smallest things.
- ✔ Find something interesting in everyone you meet.
- ✔ Get regular exercise, even when you don't feel like it.
- ✔ Have a willingness to make mistakes in order to develop new skills.
- ✔ Look after your health and go to medical appointments.
- ✔ Pray for yourself and others.
- ✔ Remember what you've achieved before.
- ✔ Remind yourself that life isn't fair, but can be improved.
- ✔ Seek out new relationships and friends.
- ✔ Tackle projects at work that nobody else wants.
- ✔ Take classes just for the fun of it.
- ✔ Take on new responsibilities.
- ✔ Volunteer or become involved in your community.

Transforming catastrophes into challenges

Life is always changing. Sometimes these changes are in your favour, other times they're not. Either way, change is often stressful. What matters is whether you see these changes as catastrophes or challenges. People either take on the change (respond actively to a challenge) or retreat from it (hide from a catastrophe).

Here's an example. Two people unexpectedly lose their jobs. One thinks of this as the end of the world. He goes home, gets drunk, loses his temper with his family and spends the next two weeks sleeping and watching TV. The other man tells himself, 'Well, now I can look for something that has more security and pays better,' and then he develops a plan (with his family's support) for what to do next.

When you're hit with some major stress in your life, which person are you?

The next time you have to deal with a major stress, and you start thinking it's the end of the world and wanting to retreat, try taking these steps:

1. **Clearly define the problem.**

   Did you lose your job? Did your youngest just leave home, leaving you with an empty nest? Is your spouse gravely ill?

2. **Ask yourself: what's the challenge?**

   If you've lost your job, you have to go and find another one. If your house is soon to be empty of children, you'll have to find other things you're passionate about. If a loved one has just been diagnosed with a fatal disease, you'll have to be with her to support her, prepare to grieve over that loss and to handle life more on your own in the future.

3. **Work out whether you have enough support to meet the challenge.**

   Support is all-important in dealing with major challenges in life. Work out how much support you have on your side. Ask yourself: 'Who can I count on to help?', ' How can she help – give moral support, lend a hand, tell me I'm okay?', 'Is her support nearby or long-distance?' and 'Do I need to find new sources of support – for example, legal assistance, a group to belong to or counselling?'

4. **Develop an action plan.**

   Ask yourself: 'What exact steps do I need to take to meet this challenge?', 'Where do I start?', 'Where do I want to end up – what's my goal?' and 'How will I know when I've met the challenge?' Set some deadlines for each of the individual steps.

Laughter eases the pain

Before being subjected to mild pain in an experiment, men and women were allowed to listen to one of three audio tapes – one that made them laugh, one that relaxed them and one that was on an educational topic. Pain tolerance, it turns out, was greatest in those who shared a good laugh. The next time you're feeling pained (challenged) by some stressful event or circumstance, find someone or something to make you laugh – it's good medicine!

Reward yourself along the way as you complete each step. Celebrate when you've completely met the challenge – when your life becomes less stressful.

These steps work whether you've experienced a true catastrophe (a hurricane has destroyed everything you own, your family has died in a plane crash) or you're facing something more common. What matters isn't the size of the catastrophe – what matters is that it *feels* like a catastrophe to you, and you can transform the catastrophe into a challenge. The more traumatic the event, the more help you'll need in meeting the challenge. But you *can* get through it, no matter what you're facing.

Coping with Stress: What Works and What Doesn't

Everything you do to get through the day – every thought, every action – is an act of coping with stress. Going to work, getting drunk, paying off debts, laughing, crying – all are acts of coping. Some ways of coping with stress help you through and past it; others only temporarily make you feel that you're coping (or help you not to care).

Here are some examples of coping strategies that feel good and provide some temporary relief from stress, but that *don't* resolve the problems that do you the most harm:

- ✔ **Acting on impulse.** When stressed, people can be tempted to do whatever comes to mind first. They don't think – they just act.

- ✔ **Avoiding.** Avoidance basically means you deal with stress by *not* dealing with it (for example, by eating, smoking or drinking alcohol).

> ✔ **Blaming.** If you cope with your stress by assigning blame, you either point the finger at other people or you beat yourself up.
>
> ✔ **Wishing.** Some people sit around and wish their problems away, but don't turn wishing into wanting and wanting into plans.

Here are some *effective* coping strategies for dealing with stress:

✔ Accept that you'll feel uncertain while you work towards a solution.

✔ Be optimistic.

✔ Be patient – don't look for a quick fix.

✔ Be willing to compromise.

✔ Develop several options in your problem solving.

✔ Draw on past experiences, remembering how you coped before.

✔ Focus on the problem, not your emotional reaction.

✔ Keep talking things over.

✔ Persist – keep trying no matter how long it takes to reach a solution.

✔ Pray for guidance or strength.

✔ Seek professional assistance (from a doctor, lawyer or therapist).

✔ Take things one step at a time.

✔ Talk with a spouse, relative or friend about what's bothering you.

✔ Try to find out more about the situation.

✔ Try to see the positive side.

The happiest time of your life

As part of Gill's assessment of difficulties when she first meets a client, she always asks, 'When have you been happiest in your life?' She's usually met with surprise, or silence, before the client offers an answer. The most common theme in the answers is a time when life is satisfying, pleasurable, often with little stress or burden, or where the client has balanced effort and gains. People tend to talk about goals they reached – not the times that were changing fast, but later, when change had settled.

Some clients don't fit this picture. Gill has great respect for the many people who've told her their stories, and the hardiest stand out. Many people who've survived terrible times or events talk about working towards their goals – times of constant change – as the happiest times for them. They're talking about believing in themselves, self-confidence from inside at a time when the world around them seems hostile and difficult. And afterwards, these people can look back and know just how well they did. They don't just cope during adversity, they make headway.

Chapter 15

Managing Your Body Chemistry

. . . .

In This Chapter

▶ Understanding how 'legal' substances can affect your anger

▶ Assessing your substance use

▶ Reducing your intake of caffeine, nicotine and alcohol

▶ Combating urges

. . . .

*Y*ou want to control your anger. Well, the good news is, doing so isn't all about the way you think. To give yourself a head start, we have three prescriptions:

✔ Stop smoking.

✔ Lay off the caffeine.

✔ Cut back on alcohol.

Otherwise, you're only fuelling the fire.

In this chapter we show you how to manage your anger by creating a less anger-friendly *internal* environment – the environment within your body. We show you how common chemical substances such as nicotine, caffeine and alcohol affect your body (and your anger). And we help you understand the connection between impulsive behaviour, anger and substance use.

Just Because It's Legal Doesn't Make It Healthy

If something is legal you probably tell yourself it can't harm you much, even when you have evidence to contradict your wishful thinking!

For example, cigarettes are legal, but everyone knows that nicotine is an addictive drug and that smoking leads to the illness and early death of millions of people. Alcohol is legal, but heavy drinking contributes to everything from domestic abuse, fatal road accidents and violent crime, to heart attacks and liver disease. And caffeine – perhaps the most popular drug of all – is certainly legal, but it interferes with brain chemicals that promote good sleep (see Chapter 16), raises blood pressure and increases the risk of miscarriage, stillbirth and low birth-weight babies in pregnant women.

We suspect the big problem is that most people don't think of common-use chemicals as 'real' drugs – certainly not in the same way they think of heroine, cocaine, amphetamines and marijuana. Maybe you consider chemicals like caffeine 'safe' drugs that have no ill effects on your health and wellbeing. Most people don't really know the connection between what we call the 'chemistry of everyday life' and emotions such as anger.

These so-called 'harmless' chemicals, as it turns out, can lower your threshold for anger arousal in a number of ways:

- **Caffeine and nicotine stimulate the central nervous system, making it more reactive to provocation.** *Translation:* If your nervous system is fired up, you'll have a harder time staying calm when that driver cuts you up.

- **Alcohol, even in small quantities, can cloud or distort a person's perceptions, causing an intoxicated person to misread the actions and intentions of others.** *Translation:* If you've had too much to drink, you may think your girlfriend is flirting with that bartender when she's really just asking where the toilet is.

- **Alcohol tends to make a person less inhibited (emotionally and behaviourally), allowing him to feel and act in ways he wouldn't if he were sober.** *Translation:* When you're sloshed, you're much more likely to lash out or throw a punch at someone you're upset with. (Bars have bouncers for a reason.)

- **Caffeine and alcohol disrupt sleep patterns and lead to increased irritability (see Chapter 16).** *Translation:* All that coffee may help you stay up late cramming for a final exam, and the alcohol you drink to celebrate when finals are over may feel good at the time, but there's a reason why you're tired the next morning.

- **Alcohol can affect a person's mood because it's a depressant. This then affects other emotions, such as sadness and anger (more about this in Chapter 18).** *Translation:* If you've ever ended up crying into your beer only moments after you were toasting your friends, it may be because the alcohol has wreaked havoc with your mood.

Raise your hand if you use drugs

Some years ago – when Dr Gentry still had school-age children – he was asked to address a group of middle-school parents about why kids take drugs. To his great surprise, the auditorium was filled to capacity, full of mums and dads hoping to hear something that would reassure them that drugs would never be a problem in their families.

To start what he hoped would be a lively, back-and-forth discussion, Dr Gentry asked the parents to raise their hands if they were drug users. Needless to say, not one person raised his hand. In fact, most people looked rather startled.

Then he asked how many had smoked a cigarette that day. Lots of hands went up. Next, he asked how many had had a cup of coffee, tea or some type of soft drink. Almost everyone's hand went up. Lastly, he asked how many had drunk some alcohol the night before. More hands went up.

Dr Gentry reminded the parents that caffeine, alcohol and nicotine are all drugs – legal drugs but drugs nevertheless. Then he asked his original question – how many of you are drug users? – and every hand in the auditorium was raised.

Why this exercise? Because illegal drug use among children is highly influenced by the drug use – legal or illegal – of their parents and by the fact that British and American cultures sanction the use of drugs as an integral part of what's called the 'good life'.

Keeping Track of Your Substance Use

Three good reasons exist for keeping track of your daily use of chemicals such as nicotine, caffeine and alcohol:

✔ You may not have the faintest idea of exactly how much you use on a regular basis. This means you're also unaware of the potential influences such substances have on your emotional life.

✔ Just by paying closer attention to your substance use patterns, you may find that you choose to cut back. (Psychologists call this the *self-monitoring effect.*)

✔ It helps you begin to appreciate how the substances you take in may be linked to the likelihood of you losing your temper.

Try keeping a daily record of all the cigarettes you smoke, as well as all the caffeine and alcohol you have, for one week. Be sure to include all three. Take a note of the time of day you had any of these, and also indicate whether you were irritated, angry or in a rage before or after you smoked a cigarette, drank a cup of coffee or had a beer. Table 15-1 illustrates a hypothetical record of one person's daily use.

Table 15-1	Substance Use Diary		
Time of Day	**Substance**	**Feeling Before**	**Feeling After**
7:30 a.m.	Coffee (240ml)	No anger	No anger
7:45 a.m.	Coffee (240ml)	No anger	No anger
9:30 a.m.	Coffee (240ml) and cigarette	Irritated	No anger
12:00 p.m.	Cigarette	Irritated	No anger
1:45 p.m.	Coffee (240ml) and cigarette	Irritated	Angry
3:00 p.m.	Cigarette	Angry	Irritated
6:00 p.m.	Beer (330ml)	Irritated	No anger
6:45 p.m.	Beer (330ml)	No anger	No anger
7:30 p.m.	Beer (330ml) and cigarette	Angry	Angry

Two things are apparent from this record:

✔ The person uses substances to self-medicate anger – that is, when he's angry, he usually has a cigarette, a cup of coffee or a beer.

✔ His approach appears to work. He's usually less angry or completely anger-free immediately afterwards.

The problem is that appearances can be deceiving. This diary shows that self-medicating anger may work in the short term, but that doesn't necessarily mean that it works in the long run. These substances may provide an immediate benefit to you when you're angry, but over time you may find yourself needing more alcohol, more cigarettes and more caffeine to have the same effect. First you're hooked on anger, and then you become hooked on substances. In addition, caffeine and nicotine are stimulants that have the capacity to over-stimulate your nervous system, thus making it easier for you to get angry the next time you get frustrated or provoked. In effect, you end up in a vicious cycle where anger leads to chemicals and chemicals lead to anger.

CASE STUDY

Self-medicating anger

Margo, a 43-year-old divorcee, has struggled with a drinking problem and intermittent depression for years. Every time she thinks she has loosened the grip that alcohol has on her life, something upsets her and she instantly falls off the wagon.

'I was doing fine – no alcohol for months – and then my boyfriend really hurt my feelings over the weekend. I'm so depressed,' she said, crying. 'Now all I can think of is getting drunk.'

Margo's core problem is suppressed anger. She's furious at her boyfriend – she says he's insensitive, uncaring and unsupportive – but she feels hurt instead. Alcohol – her drug of choice – is her way of medicating the emotional pain she feels. Its appeal, of course, is its anaesthetic quality. Where Margo needs help is in recognising and dealing with her deep-seated, unexpressed anger, not only towards her current boyfriend but also towards all those men in her life (and there have been many!) who have similarly mistreated her. Until she accomplishes that, Margo has no chance of remaining sober for any significant length of time.

Counting Your Caffeine

On average, adults can have approximately 250 milligrams of caffeine a day without experiencing negative physical, emotional and behavioural effects. Table 15-2 illustrates some common sources of caffeine and the concentration levels of each.

Table 15-2	Sources of Caffeine
Source	*Amount of Caffeine*
Ground coffee, 240ml	85mg
Instant coffee, 240ml	60mg
Decaffeinated coffee, 240ml	3mg
Tea, 240ml	50mg
Soft drink, 330ml	32–65mg
Cocoa, 240ml	6–142mg

This means that just three cups of ground coffee, or five cups of tea, takes you to your maximum! And that's without taking caffeine in any other products on that day. Caffeine is also present in chocolate, fizzy drinks, prescription and over-the-counter medications (including painkillers, cold remedies and hangover cures), and energy tablets. Read the label or check with your pharmacist to find out how much caffeine medications contain.

The length of time caffeine remains active in the nervous system is between three and seven hours (that's why you should avoid caffeine in the evenings to ensure a good night's sleep; see Chapter 16). Because of its lingering effects, concentrations can build up to harmful levels throughout the course of the day.

Try the following to reduce your caffeine intake:

- ✔ Switch from coffee to tea as your drink of choice. (Both have caffeine, but tea has less.)
- ✔ Alternate between caffeinated and decaf coffee.
- ✔ Try drinking 'half-and-half' coffee – half caffeine, half decaf.
- ✔ Cut back on your use of over-the-counter medications, such as flu remedies and painkillers.
- ✔ Drink water or juice – good for your health and caffeine free!
- ✔ Limit yourself to no more than two caffeine-containing soft drinks a day.
- ✔ Go through the day counting caffeine just as you count calories.
- ✔ Limit yourself to two units (cups of coffee, glasses of iced tea, soft drinks) at one sitting – anything more you can think of as a 'caffeine binge'.

Caffeine should come with a warning label – evidence suggests that it can become addictive even at low dosages. If you're a heavy consumer, you can expect physical withdrawal symptoms – headaches, fatigue, irritability – when you lay off the caffeine. If you're thinking, 'Oh come on, how bad can the consequences of too much caffeine really be?', consider the following list of potential side-effects:

- ✔ Headaches
- ✔ Increased anxiety and agitation
- ✔ Insomnia (trouble sleeping)
- ✔ Irritability
- ✔ Light-headedness
- ✔ Muscle cramps
- ✔ Palpitations (irregular heart beats)
- ✔ Raised blood pressure
- ✔ Restlessness
- ✔ Tachycardia (abnormally fast heartbeat)

Sudden withdrawal can cause these unpleasant effects. To avoid these, start by reducing your intake by a third per day. If you drink coffee or tea just because it's there, replace every second cup with a non-caffeine drink. Small, gradual changes are all you need.

Eliminating Your Favourite Cigarette

The best way to stop (or cut back on) smoking is to start by eliminating your favourite cigarette of the day. For most people, this is the after-dinner cigarette. The second most-favourite cigarette is the one first thing in the morning. (Interestingly, the latter is more typical of smokers who are nicotine addicted – their body is craving nicotine after several hours without while they sleep.)

Smoking is a *habit* (a predictable behaviour learned by repetition, which becomes automatic – without any conscious, deliberate thought or intent on the part of the smoker). Smokers light up basically because they have the urge to do so and that urge is stronger at certain times of the day than others. The logic here is simple: if you can eliminate the strongest urge in your day, it makes all the other weaker urges throughout the day easier to overcome.

When you decide which is your favourite cigarette of the day, develop a plan of action for outlasting the urge. As part of your plan, you may want to:

- ✔ **Spend the time you normally allocate to smoking a cigarette on some alternative form of pleasure. You could talk to someone, take a walk or spend what you save from not smoking cigarettes.** What you're looking for here is a substitute.

- ✔ **Talk yourself through the urge.** Find a saying or words of encouragement to use as your personal mantra. Use a simple relaxation technique – relaxation is incompatible with anger.

- ✔ **Rely on a higher power to help you find the strength to resist the urge to smoke.** Do you have sufficient faith in yourself to overcome the urge to smoke? Use this together with any form of other faith you hold to give you help.

- ✔ **Close your eyes and engage in some positive imagery.** Give your mind something to do other than focus on smoking a cigarette. Picture yourself doing something you enjoy where you don't usually smoke. Really focus – bring the picture to life in your mind.

- ✔ **Have a piece of chewing gum or a sweet, rather than a cigarette.** This strategy works with anger, why not smoking? (See Chapter 4 for details.)

The smokers who are the most successful in stopping (or cutting back) are those who create their own self-help programme. So if you're committed to this as part of your overall anger-management programme, then the odds are in your favour. Don't be afraid to be creative! Think outside the box – you never know what might work.

Adopting a New Drinking Style

The rules of safe, responsible alcohol consumption are simple:

- ✔ Women should have no more than two alcoholic drinks per day (14 is the weekly maximum recommended limit).

- ✔ Men should have no more than three alcoholic drinks per day (21 is the weekly maximum recommended limit). Limits for women are lower than men due to differences in body mass.

- ✔ Don't consume more than four alcoholic drinks at one sitting (three if you're a woman). Many people 'binge' or drink heavily one or two nights a week, rather than drinking daily. However, the damage alcohol does to your health affects binge drinkers more than moderate regular drinkers. If you're a man and drink ten pints in an evening out, you've had more than your maximum healthy limit for a week in one evening! The strain this puts on your liver, brain and other organs is enormous, as alcohol is toxic to the body.

Note: By one drink we mean one standard measure – not a home poured one!

If you stay within these guidelines, your alcohol consumption shouldn't have a negative effect. Responsible drinking doesn't mean no drinking – in fact, medical science has suggested that people who have one drink daily enjoy better health over a lifetime and live longer than teetotallers. Drinking in moderation isn't always easy – but what do you have to lose?

To find out more about safe alcohol consumption, visit: `http://units.nhs.uk/howMany.html`.

Unless you have a definite drinking problem, a few common-sense rules about how to drink responsibly will hold you in good stead. Here's our 12-step programme:

- ✔ **Avoid drinking alone.** Married people are less likely to smoke, drink and drink heavily than unmarried people. As crazy as this may sound, you're also less likely to abuse alcohol when you're in good company than when you're by yourself.

- ✔ **Eat plenty of food before you drink and while you're drinking.** Food absorbs alcohol and lessens its effect on your nervous system (especially high-protein foods such as meat and cheese).

Personality style and drink

Individuals with competitive, adrenaline-seeking personalities tend to drink alcohol more frequently than their steady, calm counterparts. Roughly half of those with competitive, aggressive personalities report drinking alcohol 'nearly every day' or 'every day'. One important reason for this lies in the fact that competitive people have more difficulty relaxing than laid-back people, and competitive people use alcohol to help them relax.

✔ **Alternate between alcoholic and non-alcoholic drinks.** That way, you'll cut your alcohol intake by half!

✔ **Drink slowly.** Aggressive drinkers drink everything faster and, as a result, end up having more drinks. Try to make each drink last one hour (the time it takes for your body to eliminate that same drink).

✔ **Volunteer to be the designated driver once in a while.** Your friends will love you and you'll feel much better than they do in the morning.

✔ **Always let someone else pour.** People are far more generous in the amount of alcohol they use per drink when they make it for themselves.

✔ **When you go out, decide in advance how much money you want to spend on alcohol.** With the price of a drink somewhere between £2 and £5, it won't take long to reach the limits of your credit card. (Better yet, pay cash – if you're like most people, you have less of that than you do credit!)

✔ **Never drink when you're in a bad mood.** Even though most people think of alcohol as a stimulant (it loosens you up and gets the social juices flowing), it's actually a depressant. The truth of the matter is that, after a brief period of euphoria, your mood takes a downturn. If you're suffering from clinical depression (see Chapter 18), you should think seriously – and we emphasise *seriously* – before you drink alcohol!

✔ **Let someone else in your group be the drunk.** Competing to see who can drink the most or get drunk the quickest is an immature game – and a dangerous one at that.

✔ **Don't drink before you drink.** Having a drink (or two) before you leave home, get on the road and head off to an evening of socialising (and more drinking!) only adds to the amount you're drinking.

✔ **Don't automatically drink the maximum.** The limits for men and women are just that – limits, not targets. Try drinking five, or even ten units less than the recommended maximum this week and allow your body some time to recover.

I'm no alcoholic!

You may be reluctant to consider the idea that you may be dependent on alcohol, as many people use 'alcoholic' as a negative term (rather than the description of a condition). Perhaps you think of an alcoholic as someone who drinks two bottles of spirits a day, or drinks in the morning. Gill uses a quick assessment when talking with anyone who's unsure of whether alcohol is a problem. Consider the following 'five Ls':

✔ **Liver.** Do you experience signs that your liver is struggling to deal with your alcohol intake? Do you have a hangover that lasts for hours (or all day)? Have you ever had pancreatitis, vitamin deficiency or any other health problems diagnosed by your doctor as linked to your drinking? This question can include your general health, for example, have you ever had an accident or injury after drinking?

✔ **Lover.** Does alcohol cause arguments in your relationship or in your family if you have no partner? Do others close to you worry about your drinking? Has anyone given you an ultimatum to cut down? Do you find yourself unable to get close to anyone because of your drinking?

✔ **Livelihood.** Have you ever missed work because of a hangover or 'heavy night'? Have you lost a job because of drink? Do you drink during the working day? Do you notice alcohol or its after-effects having a negative effect on how well you do your job or get on with your colleagues?

✔ **Loot.** Are you in debt because of the money you spend drinking? Have you ever been in debt because of alcohol (this may be a combination of your spending, loss of a job or loss of a relationship)? Do you have a poorly paid job because alcohol takes your focus away from other opportunities you may have had?

✔ **Law.** Have you ever been spoken to, cautioned or charged with an alcohol-related offence by the police? Have you ever been thrown out or barred from drinking venues because of your consumption? Are you an 'ugly drunk' – violent, suspicious, touchy or foul-mouthed, when you only meant to relax and enjoy yourself?

Try not to feel defensive – you're reading this for yourself and need to know if your alcohol use has crept up and had more of an impact on your life than you realised.

If you follow all these suggestions and you still drink too much, consider seeking professional help. You can get help for the treatment of alcohol dependence and addiction through your GP, or you can search online or contact a credible organisation such as Alcoholics Anonymous for local help near you.

Letting the Impulse Pass

Call it an urge, a craving, a hunger – whatever. You take most substances because of impulse. An impulse is your body's way of signalling to you that it wants (or needs) something, and your job is to satisfy that impulse. The whole process is mindless!

Some people have too many impulses to eat, and they end up obese. Some have too many urges to consume alcohol, and they end up alcoholics. Some have too many urges to smoke cigarettes, and they end up with lung cancer. Some have too many urges to buy things, and they end up broke.

The number of urges you have throughout the day to do something reflects just how big a part of your life is devoted to that want or need. For example, in Chapter 2 we talk about the difference between people who only occasionally get irritated versus those who fit the profile for chronic rage. The same distinction can be made between a 'social smoker' (smoking when with friends, only on an evening out) and a two-packs-a-day smoker. So, here's our question: do you want your life to be controlled by chemicals of this sort?

The good news about impulses is that they're brief – they come and go, passing through your nervous system if you let them. Each time you experience the impulse, but don't act on it, the strength of the impulse (or the habit) weakens. If you're a smoker, think of your favourite cigarette. Each time you don't smoke that cigarette, it becomes a little less important, until one day it's not your favourite cigarette at all. The same tactics work when you're trying to drink less – each time you put yourself in a situation where you always drank in the past, and don't drink, the connection between that place and alcohol weakens until you can go there with no urge to have a drink at all.

Why do I have a hangover?

How bad your head hurts the next morning may well be related to just how angry or distressed you were when you were drinking the night before. Dr Ernest Harburg at the University of Michigan found that 'angry drinkers' have far more hangover symptoms – stomach discomfort, tremors, diarrhoea, anxiety – than 'non-angry drinkers' do. Men were twice as likely to fit the profile of the angry drinker. Interestingly, the amount of alcohol they drank made little difference – more than the healthy limit tipped drinkers' behaviour. The bottom line is that anger and alcohol aren't a good mix! If you're angry, don't drink; if you drink, be cool.

Chapter 16

Getting a Good Night's Sleep

. . . .

In This Chapter

▶ Getting out of the right side of the bed

▶ Knowing how much sleep you need

▶ Monitoring your sleep patterns

▶ Creating positive sleep habits

. . . .

No doubt you've seen a child, out in public, screaming and thrashing about, totally at odds with everything going on around her. Or a child you know, at the end of her birthday party, suddenly in floods of tears. The child is tired and angry. Nothing her parents do suits her. As soon as she stops for a moment, in the car at last or in a parent's arms, she falls into a deep sleep, unlikely to wake for hours.

Fast-forward this scenario 20 or 30 years and you can see countless adults doing the same thing – irritable and snappy because they're exhausted and behind on their sleep. Too little sleep, and inadequate sleep, increases irritability and reduces the ability to balance emotions and to control impulses. Together, these are ingredients for a recipe for poor anger management.

In this chapter we talk about the vital role that rest and good sleep play in anger management. We tell you how to maintain good 'sleep hygiene' – and what that means. You discover how to listen to your body's signals when it's telling you it's time to give it a rest. With the information in this chapter, you're aiming to get out of the right side of the bed more of the time!

Understanding What Sleep Does for You

Contrary to what you may have always thought, sleep is *not* a waste of time.

A client came for help with anger at work. The foreman of a busy construction site, Callum took pride in how little sleep he needed. He'd work the hours a contract took to complete on time, priding himself on dealing with constant contractor questions and controlling a large workforce. He insisted that he did relax – out in the evenings drinking with his mates – and said, 'I can sleep when I'm dead. Right now I'm busy!' Irritated at even being asked to consider that lack of sleep might be a trigger for his anger, Callum took some weeks to become open-minded enough to hear some of the facts.

Sleep is an essential tool in the human nervous system's effort to survive. In an evolutionary sense, humans aren't well equipped to defend themselves or to hunt at night. Sleep also plays a restorative function, both physically and psychologically. The body requires sleep to process information and store memories, and for muscle recovery and physical revival after activity, regaining lost energy. It helps you to recover from the events of the previous day and prepares you to meet tomorrow's challenges. Importantly, sleep also plays a crucial role in physical development, especially in children and adolescents – the pituitary gland releases a growth hormone necessary for normal growth during sleep.

Perhaps the easiest way for you to appreciate what sleep does for you is to see what happens when you're sleep deprived. The following are just a few possible effects of chronic sleep deprivation:

- Dangerous driving
- Difficulty concentrating
- Difficulty with creative and imaginative tasks
- Emotional outbursts
- Greater risk of accidents
- Hallucinations (visual and auditory)
- Increased irritability
- Increased potential for violence
- Inefficiency at work or school
- Lower tolerance for stress
- Pessimism and sadness
- Problems with memory recall

- ✔ Reduced muscle strength

- ✔ Reduced problem-solving ability

- ✔ Rigid thought patterns (not being able to look at a situation in more than one way)

- ✔ Slower reaction times

- ✔ Slurred speech

- ✔ Suppressed immune system function and slow wound healing

To work out whether you're suffering from sleep deprivation, ask yourself the following eight questions. If you answer yes to three or more, you're definitely behind on your sleep.

- ✔ Is it a struggle for you to get out of bed in the morning?

- ✔ Do you have less than six hours of unbroken sleep a night?

- ✔ Do you miss out on sleep, and not pay the debt back to yourself?

- ✔ Do you nod off when you sit down to relax, watch TV or even in a meeting?

- ✔ Do you often catch up on sleep at the weekends or on your days off?

- ✔ Do you often need a nap to get through the day?

- ✔ Do you believe that determination can overcome tiredness?

- ✔ Do you take stimulants to keep going or give you a boost?

People who suffer from clinical depression or Attention Deficit/Hyperactivity Disorder (ADHD), are overweight and snore heavily or have sleep apnoea, those regularly taking drugs or drinking more than two alcoholic drinks per day, as well as shift workers and regular long-distance travellers, are some of those at high risk of sleep deprivation. Other people simply have the view that they don't have time to sleep. Unless you're busy fighting for your physical survival (as are those in areas of war or disaster) you may want to consider how true this really is.

Sleep deprivation is torture!

The Geneva Convention, the United Nations Convention on Torture and Amnesty International all consider sleep deprivation a form of torture that should be outlawed by all civilised societies. It has been a form of torture for centuries and across cultures. Yet millions of human beings torture themselves willingly day after day by not getting the proper amount of sleep. How can you start to protect yourself – from yourself? Why torture yourself?

Knowing How Much Is Enough

The amount of sleep you need depends in large part on how old you are. Table 16-1 shows you how much sleep, on average, different age groups require.

Table 16-1	Average Hours of Sleep Needed
Age Group	*Sleep Needed (in Hours)*
1–24 months	16–18
2–3 years	12–15
4–11 years	9–11
12–20 years	8–9
21 or older	6–8

In the early 1800s, at the start of the Industrial Revolution in Britain, machine and factory development brought much longer working hours and a huge change in lifestyle for many thousands of people. Social reformer Robert Owen (1771–1858) campaigned for a balance in the workers' lives (who often toiled for more than ten hours a day) with the goal of 'eight hours labour; eight hours recreation; eight hours rest'. Yet over the last few decades it's become common to hear claims that modern life is getting busier and that sleep deprivation, *insomnia* (trouble getting to sleep or staying asleep) and sleep disorders are increasingly common.

But how true is it that people, in general, are over-tired? Professor Jim Horne, director of the Sleep Research Centre at Loughborough University and author of *Sleepfaring: A Journey through the Science of Sleep* (OUP), has good news. Although you may believe you need more sleep than you're getting, research shows that the idea that people live in a faster and busier world and are getting too little sleep is a myth. Sleeping less than the seven or so hours that you need doesn't mean that you have a big 'sleep debt'. Regularly sleeping for less than seven hours isn't a problem if you're alert in the day, can concentrate and sleep without waking constantly.

However, Professor Horne does have evidence that young children are getting too little sleep, with a negative effect on their behaviour. Electronic and digital media – television, stereos, MP3 players, gaming consoles – are just some of the gadgets children have in their bedrooms now. Changes in parenting styles mean that many children don't have a regular bedtime or quiet time before sleeping in which to wind down. Poor sleep has a knock-on effect for the child. Difficulty concentrating can affect learning and how children manage at school, and irritability and mood can affect kids' ability to make and keep friends, which in turn affects self-esteem and confidence.

True sleep disorders affect humans 24 hours a day. Sufferers tend to spend their day stressed, have trouble concentrating, may use stimulants to keep them feeling alert and are still unable to sleep for long enough to go through the full sleep cycle. Specialist sleep clinics now exist to assess and treat these problems.

Rating the Quality of Your Sleep

Even more important than the number of hours of sleep you get is the quality of your sleep. Just because you spend eight hours in bed doesn't necessarily mean that you get a good night's sleep. Ask anyone who's slept off a big night of drinking whether she feels refreshed when she wakes up the next morning. Odds are, the answer's no!

To determine the quality of your sleep, all you have to do is rate how rested and refreshed you feel on a 10-point scale, where 1 is not at all and 10 is completely rested. Concentrate on how you feel when you first wake up in the morning (before you even head off to the bathroom!). Do that for a period of ten days and then work out your average (add up all ten numbers and divide by ten). This number tells you whether you're usually getting a good night's sleep. If your average sleep rating is 7 or above, you're in good shape. If your average rating is below 7, you might want to take some steps to help yourself.

The term *sleep hygiene* means healthy sleep habits. Keeping your sleeping time and place 'clean' of distractions, and adjusting your habits before bed, gives you the best possible chance of enough sound and restful sleep.

Sleep quality directly relates to sleep hygiene. Some examples of *poor* sleep hygiene include:

- ✔ Taking daytime naps lasting for two or more hours (except for the under 5s and over 60s).
- ✔ Going to bed and getting up at different times each day.
- ✔ Exercising just before bed.
- ✔ Drinking alcohol, smoking or having caffeine within four hours of bedtime.
- ✔ Doing something that boosts adrenaline (for example, playing or working on the computer, watching a violent film) just before bedtime.
- ✔ Going to bed angry, upset or stressed.
- ✔ Using the bed for things other than sleep and sex (like work, gaming or watching TV).
- ✔ Sleeping in an uncomfortable bed.
- ✔ Sleeping in an uncomfortable bedroom (one that's too bright, too warm or cold, or too noisy).

> ✔ Thinking hard, planning or other important mental activity while in bed (this isn't the time to rehearse the speech you're going to give at tomorrow morning's staff meeting, or rehash the argument you didn't win).

Improving the Quality of Your Sleep

Improving the quality of your sleep is one area where you can definitely make a difference. Rather than continuing to be a victim of poor sleep (and feeling exhausted and irritated) – and before considering the use of sleeping pills (see the later section on this) – begin practising some good sleep hygiene. In the following sections we show you how.

Listening to your body

Fatigue isn't in your mind – it's physical. Fatigue is your body's way of telling you – without words – that it's low on energy. Just like hunger tells you that your stomach is empty and thirst tells you that your body is dehydrated, tiredness is your body's way of saying, 'Get to bed!'

You have a fixed amount of energy to use each day to achieve whatever you need to. As long as the demands you face are within the limits of your energy supply, your mind and body don't show signs of strain. (In Chapter 14 we fill you in on the difference between stress and strain.) Think of tiredness (fatigue) as a warning sign that you're starting to run out of energy. Your body is letting you know it's time to begin conserving energy. Exhaustion – the most intense state of fatigue – is a sign that your tank is nearly empty. It's time to stop spending energy and begin the process of recovery.

Take a few moments every hour throughout your day to monitor your energy level. Rate your present level on a scale of 0 to 10 and keep a record. At the end of the day, plot the numbers on a piece of graph paper hour by hour. Do that for a week. Do you see any patterns? For example, does your energy seem to fall as the day goes on? At what point in the day does your energy level drop to a rating of 5 or less (fatigue)? Does it ever get as low as a rating of 1 or 2 (exhaustion)?

The lower your energy level, the more likely you'll begin to feel strained; one common indicator of strain is irritation, and the next step after irritation is anger! Improving your sleep is one of the ways you can manage your anger better, and feel better too.

Getting physical

Regular physical exercise is an essential part of good sleep hygiene. Exercise that benefits you, generally raises your heart rate for a steady 20 minutes a day. Many people looking for help with anger management or with insomnia protest that they don't have time to exercise, forgetting that it can easily be a part of their normal daily routine. The benefit of exercise on sleep comes when you;

✔ **Engage in moderate, non-strenuous exercise.** You want to tire your body out and relax it without over-stimulating it at the same time. Any type of prolonged or intense exercise – which makes you sweat and your heart pound – prior to going to bed won't be helpful. Consider doing 10 to 15 minutes of light weights, slow walking, slow cycling on an exercise bike, yoga or stretching exercises. Late afternoon or early evening is the optimal time to exercise if you want a good night's sleep, because your body rebounds (cools) a few hours later, which promotes good sleep.

✔ **Adjust your exercise to your age and overall fitness level.** When exercising, choose activities that don't place a sudden or extreme stress on your body, particularly if you aren't fit. Many people starting an exercise routine give up within the first few weeks. After throwing yourself into what you think you should be able to do, the muscle cramp, aches and failure to feel better put you off. If you don't build up to the right level for you, you'll stress your body and cause aches and pains that can trigger restlessness and keep you awake.

✔ **Make exercise part of your pre-sleep routine.** People who sleep well tend to have lifestyle habits friendly to their health and their body. Exercise is one important part of your pre-sleep routine. Together with controlling your intake of stimulants (see the following section), it's one of the most important things you can do to improve your sleep.

Avoiding stimulants

In Chapter 15 we explore the link between legal drugs like caffeine and nicotine and your anger. And these chemicals also have a big effect on your sleep. The two main stimulants that you should avoid for four hours before sleep are caffeine and nicotine. Both activate the central nervous system – your brain – and increase alertness, which isn't what you want to do when you're getting ready to go to sleep.

A word about alcohol

Although alcohol is a depressant rather than a stimulant on the nervous system, keep in mind the following:

✔ Smokers report that the most likely situation in which they smoke is when they're also using alcohol.

✔ Alcohol has been shown to increase anxiety and nervousness shortly after you drink it.

✔ Alcohol may lead to emotional outbursts (read: *anger or distress*), which in turn make it difficult for you to relax into sleep.

The bottom line? Drinking alcohol within four hours of bedtime isn't helpful for good sleep. Avoid hitting the bottle before hitting the hay!

Caffeine

When it comes to caffeine use, keep in mind:

✔ **Caffeine is available in many forms – coffee, tea, soft drinks, chocolate, over-the-counter drugs (for example, cold and allergy medication).** So just because you're turning down coffee after dinner doesn't mean that you're not getting caffeine in the form of that triple-chocolate cake you had for dessert.

✔ **The body can only handle about 250 milligrams of caffeine in a 24-hour period.** Exceeding that amount isn't difficult – three mugs of ground coffee alone contain your maximum caffeine intake for the day!

✔ **The half-life of caffeine (the time it takes your body to get rid of it) ranges between three and seven hours.** So the cup of coffee you drank at 8:00 p.m. can still be actively stimulating your nervous system when you fall into bed at 11:30 p.m.

✔ **Caffeine affects people differently.** If you're prone to anxiety and nervousness, you're very likely to become more so with caffeine use.

✔ **If you're a heavy caffeine user (by that, we mean you usually have more than 300 milligrams per day), caffeine withdrawal may be a problem when you abstain from caffeine for four hours or more before bedtime.** If you experience headaches, irritability and a sharp drop in energy when you cut back, see Chapter 15 for further help.

✔ **Evidence shows signs of sleep disturbance even in those people who claim that caffeine has no effect on their sleep.** Everyone can benefit from watching their caffeine consumption.

Nicotine

Nicotine, just like caffeine, stimulates the nervous system, leading to increased heart rate, raised blood pressure and generalised muscle tension – hardly helpful for good sleep. Smokers take longer to get to sleep, on average, and are much more likely to awaken repeatedly through the night. Interestingly, many smokers' first thought when they wake up is to smoke a cigarette. Smoking researchers attribute this to nicotine withdrawal – in other words, your brain wakes you up because it needs a fix.

Try not to let your favourite cigarette of the day – all smokers have one – be the one after dinner. Unfortunately, 40 per cent or more of heavy smokers, as well as lighter smokers (those who smoke fewer than five cigarettes a day), enjoy that after-dinner smoke the most, which means that you leave your body unprepared for sleep.

The stimulant effects of nicotine and caffeine combine together to cause poor sleep. A little bit of each adds up to too much when it comes to triggering the nervous system.

Setting up a pre-sleep routine

Your nervous system craves routine. It works best – and to your advantage when it comes to being healthy – when you carry on day to day in much the same way. *You* may find living a routine life boring, but your *body* loves it!

So, if you're after a better night's sleep – and you want to manage your anger – you need to have a pre-sleep routine. Develop sleep rituals that include quiet activities in the hour before bedtime. Babies and young children are generally lucky. Adults do this for them – a bath, a song, a story, a cuddle – before putting them to bed. Just like kids, adults need to unwind physically and mentally before sleep will come.

Your routine should begin four or more hours before you actually try to go to sleep. Finish exercising by now, eat your last big meal of the day (you want your body to complete the work of digestion before bedtime!), and from here on swap to caffeine-free drinks and snacks and put the wine bottle away.

Creating a positive sleep environment

When it comes to creating a sleep environment with reduced stimulation, it's not just a matter of what you eat, drink and smoke that counts. You also need to consider the room itself. Ideally, you want a place to sleep that doesn't just make getting a good night's sleep *possible*, but very likely.

Here are some tips on how to create a peaceful sleeping space:

- ✔ Use curtains and window shades to cut down on intrusive light from outside. Also, cover any LEDs or other small electrical lights.

- ✔ Avoid temperature extremes. The ideal temperature for sleeping is between 54°F (12°C) and 75°F (24°C).

- ✔ Relax your muscles and regulate your body temperature by taking a hot bath two hours before bedtime.

- ✔ Use earplugs if your room is noisy or the person sleeping next to you snores.

- ✔ Use background noise – a ceiling fan, a radio on low volume or your radio's white noise or nature settings – if you need to block out more disruptive sounds.

- ✔ Spend some money on a good mattress. You want one that fits your body size (you don't want your feet hanging off the end of the bed) and provides you with adequate support.

Eliminating competing cues

The human brain works on the principle of association – if two things occur in time and space often enough, your brain makes a connection. When your mind makes that connection, one part of that association triggers the other.

Your brain should have only one connection – one thought, one impulse, one craving – when it comes to the sleep environment and that is: 'Hooray, *finally*, I can get some sleep!' If you're saying, 'What about sex?', don't worry, sex is the one other activity that the brain can connect with the bedroom, but sleep is the primary reason for being there.

You may have a problem getting to sleep in your bedroom simply because your brain has too many connections to other activities that compete with sleep. For example, your bedroom may be the place where you:

- ✔ Argue with your partner
- ✔ Drink your last alcohol of the day
- ✔ Eat late at night
- ✔ Have late-night phone conversations
- ✔ Have your last, favourite cigarette of the day
- ✔ Listen to loud music
- ✔ Plan for tomorrow

✔ Play with your pets

✔ Watch television or play competitive digital or online games

✔ Work or study

If using your bedroom as a multipurpose room sounds familiar, no wonder you have trouble sleeping and are tired – and irritable – all the time. You can do all these activities elsewhere. Where? Anywhere but where you sleep. Your bedroom should be a place of peace – a place where your mind and body can rest and recover.

What if you live in a studio (one-room) flat or share a room with others? Try to separate your sleeping area from the rest of the room with bookshelves, a screen or a room divider, or something similar. Then plan to keep your non-sleep activities out of your sleeping space.

Distancing yourself from work

For many people, work has become the most important daily activity (maybe even an obsession!). If you're not actually at work, it's on your mind and in your home. In fact, the most likely competing cue (see the previous section) that interferes with your sleep is work.

If work is filling your every waking moment, you need sufficient time to disconnect or unplug your mind from work activities before you can have any hope of getting to sleep. We recommend starting to put down all things work related four hours prior to sleep. If four hours seem impossible, at least give yourself one hour of separation time between work and sleep – and increase it as you get more comfortable with your new routine.

Uncluttering your mind

Another reason you may have difficulty getting a good night's sleep is that your mind is too cluttered with emotional 'junk' at bedtime. The instant things go quiet and the room gets dark, your brain begins to focus on all the unsolved problems, grievances, anxieties, worries and frustrations that make up your psyche.

As part of your pre-sleep routine, make a list of things you have to do the next day. Keep a notebook handy by your bed, and if you wake up in the night, just write down what's on your mind and let yourself fall back to sleep. That way, the list will be there for you in the morning and you won't have to toss and turn all night, worrying that you'll forget to pick up your dry cleaning or de-flea the dog.

CASE STUDY

Always on the go

When author Gill first trained as a therapist she worked in a city well known for high levels of drug and alcohol use, as well as an unhealthy diet and lifestyle. A young man, Joe, came to the clinic, complaining of chronic insomnia. He'd apparently tried everything to solve this problem, and nothing worked. As Gill was interviewing Joe about his sleep environment, she quickly identified the problem: he was a musician and he worked in the hours most people associate with relaxation and sleep. Joe's music equipment, all around him in his room, was there when he fell asleep and within reach as soon as he opened his eyes. His daily routine was never the same. His life at work involved waiting around (drinking and smoking), alternating with intense physical activity and a rush of adrenaline. Joe came off stage dehydrated and hungry, hyped up and happy, but far from sleep.

To make matters worse, Joe wasn't allowing any time between the highly creative and stimulating activity of playing music and trying to go to sleep. His brain was still very much *on* when his head hit the pillow.

Gill suggested a few changes:

- Only sleep in his bedroom, a room separate from his studio

- Make changes to his drinking, smoking and diet that he could manage without depriving himself (see Chapter 15 for more)

- Build a small routine of at least an hour before he went to bed

Joe could accept that there was little point in being unhappy about something he wasn't prepared to do anything about, and agreed to try. When he returned for review two weeks later, he was amazed to describe the improvements in his sleep – and in his mood. He felt more positive and was less irritated by small daily hassles. He left with the comment, 'If I'd known it was so much to do with my body, and not my head, I'd have done this years ago.'

Getting into a good rhythm

For the best shut eye, get up and go to bed at the same time every day, and try not to change this at weekends. Develop a sleep habit. This allows your body's natural clock (known as your *circadian rhythm*) to help you to keep a healthy sleep pattern.

TIP

Try to avoid naps. The length of time that you're awake adds to something called 'sleep drive'. The longer you stay awake, the more you want to go to sleep. By taking a nap you can relieve this desire to sleep, but it also makes it less likely that you'll be able to easily go to sleep later. Adults should have a solid period of sleep at night. If you're still very sleepy in the day, this might suggest a sleep disorder and is worth discussing with your doctor.

Mind or medication?

During the Roman Empire and earlier, people used herbs to help or cure insomnia. Valarium was a herb in widespread use. Another several hundred years passed before people across Europe began using another sedative – laudanum (made of alcohol, opium and sugar). Gradually, the practice of medicine has eliminated opiates, cocaine and cannabis from non-prescription medicines and 'tonics'. More recent developments in the last few decades have produced other medicines, such as valium and diazepam. However, the same problem affects all of these remedies – their chemically addictive nature means that you have to take an increasingly higher dose just to get the same effect. Ultimately, the 'quick fix' route to better sleep isn't going to be the most healthy for your body, or the method that works best. Studies still show that good sleep hygiene and a healthy, balanced lifestyle give your body the help it needs to achieve good rest.

Sometimes your rhythm gets disturbed – perhaps due to a nap, a recent late night or a stressful day. If you're having trouble getting to sleep, don't lie there stressed or you'll make a link between your bed and not being able to sleep! As you do this night after night, you train yourself to associate your room with tension and frustration. If you're unable to get to sleep within 15 minutes, get up (keep warm) and sit somewhere comfortable. When you feel tired, try going back to bed. You may need to repeat this many times before you build up a good association between your bed and sleeping. While you're awake, distract your mind from negative thoughts such as, 'I'll never sleep' or 'I've got to get up in a few hours'. These may be true, but you're increasing your stress and adrenaline levels and so reducing your chances of nodding off.

Considering sleeping pills

Many people – frustrated from days, weeks, months or years of bad sleep – think that sleeping pills are a good option.

Using sleeping pills to get a good night's sleep, and reduce fatigue and irritability, isn't something you should do without consulting your doctor. Many types of sleeping pills produce negative side-effects (daytime drowsiness, anxiety, rebound insomnia or increased irritability when you stop taking them). Plus, using them may only reinforce the idea that you're a victim of a disorder over which you have no control – which is far from true. No evidence exists that over-the-counter sleep aids improve sleep.

Coping with sleepless children

If you're the parent of a young child, the complaint that you always have disturbed sleep because you have to get up in the night is something you know you can control. After the first few months, babies and toddlers benefit from learning to sleep through, just as you do. They may put up a fuss at first. Would it stop you taking them to school, or feeding them, if they made a fuss? Of course not. Your child may be protesting, but this is part of learning that she doesn't always choose what happens – an essential skill if you want her to find a happy place for herself in the world later on.

Your child's need is for healthy sleep, and the ideas outlined in this chapter (setting up a pre-sleep routine and creating a healthy sleep environment) apply to adults and children alike. However, teaching this to your new baby, as parents know, can take some time. Here we make some suggestions for helping your baby or toddler to develop healthy sleeping habits.

For babies:

- ✔ Many infants find monotonous or humming sounds very soothing – putting on a fan, driving your child in the car, even ordinary household objects such as vacuum cleaners used as the child prepares for bed can help. You can record the sound to play in the bedroom, or look for recordings specifically designed to help your baby sleep.

- ✔ Develop a routine with a tune, lullaby or music every night from an early age. Your child learns to recognise that it's time to sleep.

- ✔ In the winter, warm your baby's bed sheet a little to reduce the contrast in temperature from her clothes and avoid unsettling her.

- ✔ If she starts to fall asleep while feeding, but wakes if you put her down, try feeding your baby with a muslin or cloth under her head and transferring her to her cot with it to transfer your scent and warmth.

- ✔ Never tiptoe around sleeping babies. Normal household noise and conversation teaches your child not to be over-sensitive to her environment, and she will learn to sleep through most things!

- ✔ Don't try to decide for your child when she should transfer to a bed from her familiar cot. Instead, set up the new bed with some of her toys, and wait for her to show an interest.

For toddlers:

- ✔ Once you have your toddler in a sleeping routine, try not to change it for minor reasons. For example, one night allowed in your bed because she woke after a noise may mean days of difficulty getting her to sleep alone again.

✔ Try to use covers that won't fall off the bed and leave your child cold. Use a sheet under a duvet, which you can still tuck in.

✔ Set a timer switch for a regular time in the morning to encourage your child to stay in bed (before she can use a clock). Leave her story books or quiet play things to allow her to entertain herself.

✔ Reading a bedtime story helps your child to prepare to go to sleep, just as music or a song does for babies. Try to choose a story which ends calmly, or perhaps with the character having a nap if your child finds story time exciting rather than restful.

Many resources can help your baby develop healthy sleep habits. As well as speaking to staff at your well-baby clinic, or your Health Visitor, have a look at *Parenting For Dummies* by Helen Brown, which has plenty of useful information and tips. You can also find help and information on sites such as www.mumsnet.com and www.parentlifeline.org.uk.

Chapter 17

Looking After Your Spiritual Health

. . . .

In This Chapter

▶ Exploring the link between spirituality and emotional health

▶ Linking faith with anger management

▶ Trying hard to be humble

▶ Swapping contempt for compassion

. . . .

*M*any people find that the peace of mind that comes from a belief in a higher power is an antidote to anger. If you believe in something more powerful than yourself and act in keeping with that belief, you may feel less helpless about life's struggles, and less hopeless and more optimistic about your future. You can relax into your problems because you feel support from your faith, and your faith community.

In this chapter we look at why spirituality – which may or may not involve regular participation in religious activities – may lead to a more anger-free life. This chapter addresses traditional elements of spiritual belief such as faith, compassion, hope, values, gratitude and humility – common to all spiritualities – that you can also use in defusing anger.

Reaching Up Rather than Out

Social support and a sense of belonging are essential to human survival. For most people, that support comes from other human beings with whom they're closely connected – their spouse, family members, friends, children and members of their church or faith community.

But what if those usual sources of support aren't readily available for some reason? What do you do in situations where you've exhausted all the supportive resources you usually have available? What do you do if the people who typically support you are angry at you? In other words, what do you do when you can't reach out for help but may need it the most?

Spirituality: it's good for you

If you want to minimise the chance that you'll suffer from uncontrolled anger and the health problems in which it plays a significant role (see Chapter 2), consider exploring a spiritual path, making time to think about this at least once a week. Medical studies of Christian populations have repeatedly shown, for example, that churchgoers have about half the risk of coronary heart disease as do non-churchgoers. As a group, churchgoers also have lower blood pressure – regardless of their age, whether they smoke, their weight and their socio-economic circumstances. Apparently, participating in spiritual activities can be the remedy for what the great psychologist William James called the 'sick soul' of mankind.

Interestingly, studies also show a link between religious attendance and being a hardy personality. Hardiness involves a sense of inner control, an active commitment to life and the ability to view adversity as a challenge rather than a catastrophe. Does attending a religious service make you hardy or does it simply reinforce that which is already part and parcel of your personality? Who knows? As the two seem connected, why not give it a try?

You can explore new avenues. Consider turning your thoughts to a higher power. You pray. You take respite from the burdens of the world by turning your problems over to that unseen, invisible, spiritual entity in whose hands you now feel safe and secure. This may help you to relax. You no longer need to defend yourself against adversity or threat – which means you don't need to carry around all that fear and anger.

No evidence suggests that one religion or spiritual path – Christianity, Judaism, Islam, Hinduism, Buddhism or other world faiths – conveys more health protection than any other. Spirituality is a personal matter and it appears that any spiritual practice offers some benefit.

Seeing How Anger Can Choke Faith

In our work we've met many people who are incredibly angry because something terrible, a trauma or a tragedy, has happened in their life. They talk about how God, or their spiritual leader, has abandoned them, is cruel or is useless.

We know that they have real emotional pain and real anger. Their safety, their family or home, really has come under threat. They may be struggling to resolve the big gap between what they believe (or maybe feel they have a right to expect) their life should be like, and how it has become.

What concerns us is that this becomes an intense grievance, a separate thing from the tragedy that happened. Say someone is angry that their son died, and they're angry at their protector, holy figure or God for letting it happen. They've lost not one but two of the important, loved and stabilising things in their life. And more than a few lose their spiritual faith, because they believe they've been abandoned.

If anger is ruining your ability to have faith, it's time to tackle the root causes of your rage head on.

Using Faith to Help You Fight On

Faith can be a weapon – and just as powerful as anger. Faith can be an antidote to fear, isolation and depression. Faith can be comforting. And as long as you have faith in some higher power (spiritual or religious), you belong to a community that has solid beliefs about offering help and support – and that means for you too.

No one can make you have faith. It isn't something that you earn. Believing in something you can't prove and over which you have no control is a personal choice. For example, you need a lot of faith to believe that an angry, defiant teenager will actually grow up and amount to something in life. You need a lot of faith to work your way through some unexpected crisis in your life – a loving spouse who's suddenly diagnosed with cancer, a major hurricane that destroys everything you've worked hard for over your lifetime, the loss of a child to a drunk driver. Religious faith and spiritual belief can offer that things will get better, even when all the evidence contradicts it. Having faith is what keeps you from despair – and despair is often a trigger for anger.

Faith is a weapon that can help you deal with an uncertain future. Like most human beings, you probably find that uncertainty isn't great because it elicits fear – and fear, in turn, can lead to anger. Is anger your way of fighting off uncertainty ('Why can't things settle down and go well for a change?')? If so, look for positive ways to live with the uncertainty of the situation (see Chapter 14 for tips on how to become a hardy personality) and transform a crisis into a challenge.

For the most part, anger is about defending yourself from threat and has a partly biological basis. Faith, on the other hand, can offer a coping strategy. Anger is reactive; faith is proactive.

CASE STUDY

Keeping the faith

It was 2:30 a.m. and Arthur sat at his dining room table contemplating taking his own life. He did so while his wife of 25 years slept soundly in the other room. Arthur had suffered from chronic pain for almost 15 years, and he was tired of always hurting, being unemployed and being severely limited in his routine, day-to-day activities. He was angry – not angry because of anything that had happened in the last day or two, but angry about the endless struggle with pain. He felt totally alone with his suffering; even his wife, who loved him, couldn't understand why he couldn't get well.

The decision he had before him that morning was whether to end his suffering (he had the tablets on the table) or to begin a whole new approach to life that very day. At 54 years of age, Arthur's life was full of nothing but uncertainty – the only thing he was certain of was that he would experience pain every minute of the day ahead of him.

After hours of going back and forth, he finally decided to stay alive and explore faith as a possible source of hope. That was over a decade ago and Arthur remains in chronic pain, but is a reasonably happy man. He travels, works in his garden from time to time, even plays a little football with his grandchildren – all while in pain. And all it took to move from that old, despairing state of mind into this new one was a little faith!

Praying Prayers of Gratitude

Many forms of prayer exist. Some people pray for understanding, some for forgiveness, some pray to their God to 'fix' things in their lives that have gone wrong, some for pain relief, some for opportunity and so on. These all represent prayers of *supplication* – you want something! Such prayers always begin with the word *please*.

REMEMBER

Asking a higher being for something, or looking for a new spiritual path, is fine. But when you stop to think, prayer is often talked about as though it's simply asking for things. If you want to get something out of your prayer life, it can help to think in terms of *thank you*. It's hard to be angry when you're being thankful.

Anger has a lot to do with feeling that you're not getting what you want (or what you feel entitled to). You're not getting recognition at work or making the money you feel you should. Your children don't show you the respect you feel entitled to as a parent. Your dog doesn't come when you call him. So you get angry.

Gratitude, on the other hand, has to do with being thankful for what has already been given to you. Thinking back over your life so far, what have you been happy to have? What's keeping you from despair now? What makes you want to see another day? The act of saying 'thank you' reminds you what you can name that you're thankful for. And this can be a powerful antidote to being angry about what you don't have.

Start each day with thoughts of gratitude. Make a mental list of all your blessings – people, events, whatever – and recite them to yourself (silently or out loud). This way, you remember the good things that have been bestowed on you and that you're indeed thankful. Try this – and see whether you feel a sense of inner peace as you take on the challenges of the day.

Practising Compassion

All world religions, regardless of their differences, have one thing in common: they teach and preach *compassion* (consideration and sympathy), which moves you to help your fellow humans. For example, when the Bible talks about 'doing unto others as you'd have them do unto you', it's not talking about anger and violence – it's talking about love and respect for all humankind. Table 17-1 highlights some differences between two opposing ways of treating other human beings: compassion and revenge.

Table 17-1	Revenge versus Compassion
Revenge . . .	*Compassion . . .*
Is born out of anger or hatred	Is born out of love
Has the goal of hurting someone	Has the goal of helping another person
Heightens conflict	Eases conflict
Is judgemental	Is non-judgemental
Says, 'They're wrong.'	Says, 'They need help.'
Says, 'I'm against them.'	Says, 'I'm for them.'
Is destructive	Is constructive

Make a pact with yourself not to let a day go by without finding some way in which you can show compassion to others. You might be surprised at how small acts of compassion – a kind word at exactly the right time, patience, a smile – can salvage someone's day.

The apple doesn't fall far from the tree

The difference between revenge and compassion is illustrated by a wonderful story told by the legendary golfer Chi Chi Rodriguez. Chi Chi was born into a poor Puerto Rican family. Even though his father worked hard, he still had difficulty feeding his family.

One night his father heard someone prowling around in the back garden. When he went to investigate, machete in hand, Chi Chi's father discovered his neighbour – also very poor – picking up bananas off the ground. Instead of getting angry with his neighbour and attacking him for his theft, Chi Chi's father took the machete and cut off a big stalk of bananas, handed them to his neighbour and told him that if his family needed something to eat he shouldn't steal it but instead come and ask him for help.

That lesson in compassion set a standard for Chi Chi's whole life – and no doubt accounts for why he went on to share with those much less fortunate the wealth he gained from playing professional golf.

Being Humble – It Helps

Developing a sense of humility, another value held in most faiths and spiritual practices, is yet another antidote to harmful anger. Being humble is the opposite of

✔ Being arrogant

✔ Feeling entitled

✔ Seeing yourself as superior

✔ Adopting an attitude of contempt towards all those who you see as not as good as you are

All of these opposites of humility tend to cause anger.

We remember hearing about the world-renowned stress researcher Dr Hans Selye who, when asked why he wasn't stressed by the infirmities of his advanced age (hobbling up and down from a stage to lecture about stress), and the fact that not everyone in the medical profession agreed with the conclusions of his life's work, replied simply, 'Because I never took myself that seriously.' That's humility.

Humility can be born out of adversity or trouble. Few people grow more humble on the way up the ladder of life – humility is what you experience on the way down. Being in the business of human suffering, people ask us all the time, 'Why does God let bad things happen?' Not wanting to speak for God, we instead offer them our personal theory of why such things happen, and that is: 'Because that's the only way we learn to be humble – which is God's plan.' Who knows if we're right?

Each day, look for ways to be humble. It doesn't matter what you do with your time, how much you know or how rich you are, you're still human – just like everyone else! Contempt (looking down on others) is involved in a lot of anger, from sarcastic put-downs to violence. Instead, try to be modest. After all, if you're that good, people will notice without you telling them. Try getting involved in a community task without being the person in charge. Find some fairly basic ways to make the world a better place.

Having a Blessed Day

No matter how bad your day is, it can also be blessed.

For many years Dr Gentry ran treatment classes for pain sufferers. One of his most memorable chronic-pain classes included three women, all of whom had suffered from agonizing back and neck pain for many years. Now, the majority of pain clients respond to Dr Gentry's cheerful 'How are you doing this morning?' greeting as they walk through the door either with a silent shrug or a hostile retort – 'How do you think I'm doing?' But these ladies always came back with, 'I'm blessed – hope you are.' And when they left four hours later – sometimes after painful, strenuous fitness training – the last thing they said was, 'Have a blessed day!'

At first, Dr Gentry wasn't sure how to respond to their 'blessing'. Not only was it not a typical response for patients, it almost seemed out of place with the purpose of that setting – pain management. But he soon got used to it and began responding in kind ('I'm blessed – I hope you are.'). And he realised that this was why these three women weren't as angry, bitter, depressed and frightened by ongoing pain as most of his other clients. Rather than dwell on the painful part of their day-to-day lives, they were able to view pain and injury as only a part of an otherwise blessed life. They felt blessed to be alive, to have caring friends, to have supportive families, to still be mobile enough to attend church on Sunday – in effect, to have what it took to effectively live with their pain.

Start your day by saying to the first ten people you meet, 'Have a blessed day.' Watch how they respond. And see if they don't answer, 'You too!' every time. Along the same line, try ending conversations you have with particularly hostile people with a 'Have a blessed day!' and see how they respond. We bet it takes some of the steam (and sting) out of people's hostility. It's hard to be nasty to someone who just gave you his blessing!

The three black angels

At the end of the five-week chronic-pain class (see 'Having a Blessed Day' in this chapter), the same three ladies, all of whom are African American, surprised Dr Gentry with a gift. They wanted him to know how much they appreciated all his hard work in helping them find a way to continue having a meaningful life despite their chronic pain. Their gift was quite unique – three wooden black angels. 'We wanted you to know that no matter what comes your way in life – especially hard times – you always have three black angels looking out for you.'

Dr Gentry felt truly blessed. He keeps those angels prominently displayed in his office as cherished mementos. And, on days when he's down or irritated and fully prepared to snap someone's head off, he looks at them and instantly feels much better.

Chapter 18

Staying in a Good Mood

· ·

In This Chapter

▶ Finding ways to stay in a good mood

▶ Identifying a mood disorder

▶ Linking anger to depression

▶ Exploring effective treatment options

▶ Knowing when to seek professional help

· ·

A strong link exists between anger and a bad mood – you can't be angry and in a great mood at the same time. But sometimes this link goes beyond a bad mood: if you're depressed, anger comes all too easily. In this chapter we cover the reasons that depression and anger are so closely connected – including an alteration in brain chemistry, a pessimistic outlook and loss of meaningful relationships. Suppressing anger can also lead to depression – for example, when you fail to speak out in anger (Chapter 5) or harbour old grudges (Chapter 13). And, finally, just as with substance use or abuse – nicotine, alcohol, caffeine – anger can be a way of self-medicating a mood disorder, the term we use here for both depression and anxiety. This means not just feeling down, or being sad, or grieving, or a bit nervous, but having a recognised disorder of mood that needs treatment.

In this chapter we also consider the important role that prescription medication – antidepressants – can play in anger management. We also look at different talking therapies, and how exercise can lift your mood.

Eliminating the Negative: Maintaining a Positive Mood

Have you ever noticed how some people *always* seem to be in a good mood, no matter what's going on in their lives? Gill has a friend like that. Although from a poor family, one of five children in a house where there was never enough to go around – food, affection, time – and with a long-term illness, Simon left home to work, saved to go back to train for the job he wanted most, as an engineer, and married happily. The loss of his youngest child to cot death, his redundancy four times in a changing industry and some times of ill health never seemed to affect Simon's outlook. A believer in the good in people (but not a soft touch), he never complains, gossips, never raises his voice and has a smile for people every day. Simon's positive spirit is never threatened.

For years psychologists really didn't understand people like Simon. They were far too busy studying the *opposite* kind of people – those who seem to lack whatever qualities Simon has that allow him to transcend and overcome life's many difficulties. But that's all beginning to change with the advent of what's called *positive thinking*, which identifies and strengthens the assets a person has (things like optimism, resilience, wisdom and hardiness) to thrive in the face of adversity and achieve her potential and success in life.

In the following sections we tell you about some behaviours that promote and maintain a positive mood. Then we tell you what you can do to correct a bad mood – things like laughing, being optimistic, finding the bright side and creating an emotional climate in which you can do well.

Laughter really is the best medicine

Laughter is literally a painkiller. It can kill both physical and emotional pain. Studies comparing some type of neutral distraction, relaxation and laughter found laughter to be the most effective in raising a person's pain threshold.

The same is true for *anger sensitivity* – how touchy you are and how easily you can be provoked to anger. In other words, you're less likely to be annoyed by something if you're in good humour than if you're not. Humour also gives you an alternative reaction to choose – if you drop the birthday cake on the floor just as you go to cut it, you can throw a tantrum or laugh instead. Think of humour as a shield that protects you from the stinging impact of someone else's bad behaviour.

Some people seem to have been born with a great sense of humour. They don't have to *try* to be funny or make themselves and other people laugh – it just comes naturally. Other people have to look outside themselves to find something to make them laugh.

Here are some ways you can bring laughter into your life:

- ✔ Avoid the serious stuff on TV – especially the news – and watch things, such as comedy, that are light-hearted, even to the point of being silly.

- ✔ Close your eyes and remember a situation where you laughed until your sides hurt. Let yourself smile as you do it.

- ✔ Find films or programmes that make you laugh, and watch them repeatedly – think of it as therapy!

- ✔ Go and buy a joke book. It's a good partner to this book on anger management!

- ✔ Go out to places where people are openly having fun. Carnivals, football matches, live music and events where everyone takes part can bring instant mood improvement.

- ✔ Involve yourself in activities that provide good-natured company. Just being with others and hearing their laughter and banter can lift your mood enough to make you want to join in.

- ✔ Keep photos and reminders in your home and at work of fun times with friends and family.

- ✔ Spend time with people who have a good sense of humour as often as you can.

- ✔ Spend time with pets and animals. The effects can be calming as well as positive for your mood.

Adopting a light-hearted approach

Earlier in her life, Gill rarely laughed – she was too serious for her own good. Involving herself in sport brought her into contact with people far more playful than she'd ever been, and it was a revelation! These people laughed at frustrating little things like delayed trains. They laughed when they came off their bike into mud, when the only map they had was lost, when it started to rain so hard that they might as well have been planning to swim. Gill quickly realised that life has no rule saying that when you're adults you can't play any more. She also discovered that life is funny, sometimes ridiculous, and that it feels better to laugh along with it than to fight the inevitable.

Hanging around with optimists

A direct link exists between your attitude towards life and your mood. Generally, people are either positive or negative in their outlook:

- ✔ **Optimists** believe that things will generally turn out for the best, and tend to be in a positive mood. They see the best in people; both people they know, and people in general. Even when life seems to be conspiring against you, if you're an optimist you tend to believe in a more hopeful day somewhere in the future.

- ✔ **Pessimists** always expect things not to turn out well (just wait, you'll see!) and, as a result, they're more apt to find themselves anxious, worried and ready to be angry when their negative expectations are met. They're the people who, even when something goes well, say to themselves, 'It's all going so well, something's bound to go wrong.'

You form attitudes like optimism early in life, mostly as a result of experience. They may also partly be influences from inherited personality traits, handed down from one generation to the next. Regardless of their origin, however, these attitudes remain fairly stable from cradle to grave, unless you question them, and reconsider whether they're helpful to you.

Attitudes are contagious. Because they're largely learned, hanging around with people who have a positive outlook on life means that you're more likely to think and feel the same way. The reverse is true if you spend your time with a bunch of pessimists who see the worst in everything.

Letting optimism rub off on you

Gill worked with two staff teams based in very different locations. In one centre, staff saw themselves as trying to reach a standard they'd be proud of. Simply by taking part in training and putting their knowledge to good use, they overcame the reputation of the business as being out-of-date and old-fashioned. Despite working in a run-down building and with very little budget, they became the leading example of change in the area.

Their colleagues in the other centre, a much more modern building and with a steady source of funds, did not believe that training the team could set new standards. They found it hard to make time to attend training, wouldn't step in

and help if someone couldn't remember what he should do next, and would shrug off motivating feedback about improvements, saying, 'We're nowhere near as good as we should be.'

Only when staff started to rotate between the two centres did the positive 'can do' attitude of the first team begin to rub off and the two started to work to the same set of goals.

We've seen this pattern repeated time and time again, and we're convinced that one requisite to staying in a good mood is to surround yourself as much as possible with positive-thinking people. It's the next best thing to being a naturally optimistic person yourself!

Finding the good in the bad

Psychologists have a new name for finding something good in a bad situation – it's called *benefit-finding*. Studies of patients with a variety of catastrophic, disabling illnesses – heart disease, breast cancer, rheumatoid arthritis, multiple sclerosis – suggest that most people can identify at least *one* benefit they derive from being ill. The possibilities include:

- ✔ A greater appreciation for what life offers
- ✔ A heightened sense of compassion and sympathy for struggle
- ✔ An enhanced sense of spirituality (see Chapter 17)
- ✔ Closer, more meaningful interpersonal relationships
- ✔ Greater introspection (examining your inner self)
- ✔ Greater sense of mastery in dealing with day-to-day stress
- ✔ Greater willingness to openly express emotion
- ✔ Improved mood and determination
- ✔ Increased activity
- ✔ Less tension, anxiety and anger

Being able to find the silver lining was the key to Ann's ability to endure chronic neck and back pain. Ann, a divorced mother of three, was only 36 when she was permanently injured while employed as a nurse. Asked one day during group therapy by another pain client why she continued to be so upbeat despite intense pain, she said, 'Had I not been injured, I would just be another working mum who hardly got to spend time with her kids. At least now I'm part of their lives. That's a good thing.'

Calculating your positivity ratio

Supporters of positive psychology point out the crucial role that emotions like joy, love and contentment play in helping human beings flourish in everyday life. *Flourishing* is the opposite of *languishing*, which suggests that someone is in a rut, going nowhere and feeling bad. Working with adolescents with anger-management problems, we've seen many who are just drifting. These are young people who, in addition to being terribly angry and aggressive, aren't taking advantage of the positive activities available to them – scholarship, sports and organisations requiring co-operative behaviour to achieve something. To help them to move forward, the first step is to help these teenagers see that the future isn't exactly like the past. Every day life offers chances to do something new. Until they grasp the possibility of being involved in something that shows off their abilities, talents and interests, all these young people know is anger and negativity. And all humans tend to repeat what they know, rather than to risk what's new and unknown. If this is you, you have a reason to feel stuck, but not an excuse.

Psychologists believe a critical positivity ratio of roughly 3-to-1 (positive emotions over negative ones) is necessary if you're to flourish in your life. Think of it as a recipe – three parts laughter/love/surprise to one part irritation. Anything less than that is a recipe for languishing.

Once a week try recording your emotions for 24 hours – both positive and negative. Find a quiet time and place, preferably at the end of the day, to review Table 18-1. Circle any feelings or emotions you experienced that day. Now count up the positive feelings and divide by the number of negative ones. This is how you derive your positivity ratio. If the value is below 2.9, you're heading for trouble! If it's 2.9 or above, you're more than okay.

Table 18-1	Feelings You Experienced Today
Positive	*Negative*
Appreciated	Afraid
Contented	Angry
Curious	Annoyed
Excited	Anxious
Happy	Ashamed
Interested	Dejected
Jubilant	Disinterested
Loved	Frustrated
Respected	Guilty
Satisfied	Irritated
Surprised	Sad
Validated	Worried

If you're a little short on positive feelings, think of some activity, pastime or social situation that you can take part in. This isn't easy, but you need to get up (even if you're nervous or negative) and give it a go. Try saying to yourself, 'If I don't like it, I don't have to go back, but I'm not giving up before I try. Anything is better than sitting here feeling negative.'

Finding benefit now, and relief later

In a study of 96 women undergoing treatment for breast cancer – including radiation, chemotherapy and reconstructive surgery – those who could identify a potential benefit of their cancer experience were much less anxious, angry and depressed when reassessed seven years later. This is yet another good example of how what you do today may affect tomorrow's anger.

Realising When Your Mood Becomes a Problem

Mood becomes a problem when it's negative, when it persists and when it's severe enough to negatively affect your life. All three elements must be present. No one comes to a mental health professional complaining of a persistent, disabling case of joy or happiness. You don't seek professional help, nor is your life changed significantly, because of one bad day. It's also unlikely that your life will get worse because of one or two mood-related symptoms – a sleepless night or low energy level.

But, if you're like Lisa, mood is a problem. In her wildest dreams, Lisa would never have pictured herself feeling the way she does when she wakes up every morning. 'I just dread getting up. I wake up tired even after sleeping all night, and all I want to do is go back to sleep,' she says. 'I just want to run away, go somewhere where no one can find me. I just hate my life!' Describing how she feels is enough to make Lisa cry – which she does quite often lately. Lisa eats, but she has no appetite. And she can't relax.

When was the last time you felt good?

You can tell how long a person has been depressed by asking a simple question: when is the last time you really felt good – positive, happy, relaxed, satisfied – for a whole month (more of the time than not)? If the person says, 'I don't know – it's been so long', 'Oh, at least a year or more' or 'Before my father died, five years ago', that's how long the person's probably suffered from depression.

Lisa is suffering – and we do mean suffering! – from clinical depression, a condition so prevalent that it's known as the 'common cold of mental illness'. To determine whether you're depressed, think about how you've felt over the past two weeks and answer the following questions:

- Do you feel sad most of the time?

- Do you not enjoy things the way you used to?

- Are you feeling hopeless about your future?

- Do you find yourself less interested in other people than you used to be?

- Do you cry for no apparent reason?

- Do you wake up early and have trouble getting back to sleep?

- Have you lost your appetite?

- Are you more irritable and angry than usual?

- Does it take extra effort for you to get started doing something?

- Do you feel tired or exhausted most of the time?

- Do you ever think about harming yourself?

- Are you less interested in sex than you used to be?

If you answer yes to at least half of these questions, you may be suffering from a mood disorder. Talking to a doctor, finding a therapist or mental-health professional (www.nhs.uk), or seeking help from mental-health promotion charities such as Mind (www.mind.org.uk) or SANE (www.sane.org.uk) can help you to work out for yourself whether you have a problem for which you need to seek treatment.

In the normal course of life moods vary quite a bit, ranging from brief periods of exhilaration and joy to episodes of grief, despair and gloom. In between these extremes, you can also experience the everyday blues, mild excitement or feel neither positive nor negative. If you swing between all of these different mood states on a regular basis, the people who know, love and work with you probably describe you as 'moody'. And – as you may have guessed – moody people are more prone to anger.

Exploring the Anger–Depression Link

We use the word *depression* here to mean clinical depression, a mood state that you find yourself unable to lift without making some changes, usually with help from those around you and from professionals.

There's no shame in being depressed. One in four adults needs help for a mental-health problem in their lifetime. There's far better understanding than in the past that the mind – just like the body – can become unwell, and can recover.

Seeing how depression can make you angry

Almost all those who've experienced an episode of depression remember or know that anger seems to be far harder to manage – and happens much more easily – than when their mood is good. In addition to chemical changes identified in the brain that increase agitation and irritability during depression, negative thinking plays a part. Increasing levels of depression are linked closely to increasing levels of hopelessness, suspicion or over-inclusive negative thoughts, which can easily lead to anger (see the nearby sidebar 'Everything's a mess').

The more depressed you are, the more negative your view of the world. In fact, in extreme states of depression, people can become paranoid – harbouring a fixed belief that everyone, even those closest to them, is out to cause them harm. Depressed people are more likely to read malicious intent into the actions of others ('You did that on purpose!'). And because of lack of sleep, decreased energy and an increasingly self-critical attitude – all symptoms of depression – they struggle more in keeping up with the demands of their day and, thus, are more easily frustrated.

Everything's a mess

When Danielle came for help with anger, Dr Gentry quickly recognised the thinking style of someone severely depressed. She was difficult to talk with, asking snappily, 'Why do you need to know that?' to the simplest question. She seemed very sad, and told Dr Gentry several times in the first hour that there was probably nothing he could do for her because she made a mess of everything. During this appointment Dr Gentry asked Danielle whether she was eating meals. Danielle said tearfully, 'I made myself dinner yesterday, but it all went wrong.' Asked to tell more, she revealed that she'd cooked a fish pie, but had burnt the top and so thrown the whole meal in the bin untouched. This over-inclusive thinking – 'I've burnt the top of the pie so it's *all* ruined' is clear evidence of depression. Danielle's anger became unmanageable whenever she came up against a small problem or obstacle. Her increased irritability, together with her feelings of hopelessness ('nothing *ever* goes right'), cause her to behave in an instantly impatient way, throwing aside something that breaks, shouting at someone who makes a mistake and delays her and so on. Anger management and mood management go together in helping her to regain control of both.

All of these elements of depressed thinking can have a big impact on your anger. You may be more likely to take offence, less able to laugh off daily stresses and have trouble sleeping. As we explain in Chapter 16, lack of sleep makes you more vulnerable to irritability, less able to think clearly and more likely to become agitated – none of which are helpful to healthy anger control. It's amazing how, when you're no longer depressed, the things that used to set you off into a tirade now, at worst, only annoy you.

Anger and depression share a common chemical pathway in the brain – a neurotransmitter called *serotonin*. A wealth of psychiatric research shows that a chemical imbalance involving a shortfall in serotonin is a root cause of depression. A shortage of this important brain chemical is also associated with smoking, increased appetite and weight gain, and alcohol consumption – which are symptoms of both harmful anger and depression.

Separating depression and grief

Anger and depressed mood are often seen together in grief. Grief is another natural emotion which, like anger, can be harmful if dealt with through extreme behaviour or by complete denial or suppression. It's a feeling of deep, intense sorrow or mourning over the loss of a significant person or attachment. It can look the same as depression, but it isn't the same thing. If you suffer the loss of a loved one, you should grieve. It means you loved that person and you miss them – your life will take some readjusting because your loved one is gone. In fact, if you didn't grieve over someone you loved or were attached to, that would be unhealthy. In Western culture, obvious displays of grief aren't encouraged.

We have lost count of the number of people – and not just those seeking help – who tell us that they think a reasonable time for someone to overcome grief and move forwards with their life is a year. We find this incredible! If this is true, then within a year you're hoping to live through, and manage the memories of, the death and funeral of someone you loved, allow yourself to be sad at what you've lost and start to see ways in which your life goes forward without that person. The space that the loved one left is still there, together with a complex mix of anger because you've lost the person and that she left you behind, fear of life without her, disbelief that you can never see her again, and things unsaid or unfinished. Each of these things can then cause its own kind of sadness, which you need time to feel and express. That's fast work in just one year! Healthy grieving is a gradual process that takes years – our clients suggest that somewhere around three to five years after the loss they recognise a change for the better that lasts.

The most dramatic illustration of how long a mood problem can persist comes from a client, Anna, a woman in her mid-50s who came to see Gill in clinic. When she sat down, Gill asked her 'How are you today?' She began to sob uncontrollably and did so non-stop for the next 20 minutes. The second question Gill asked Anna was, 'How long have you felt this bad?' She replied, 'Twenty years!' and began to cry again. When she once again stopped, Gill asked her, 'Why did you wait so long to get some help?' With a look of despair, she said, 'I just kept telling myself that it would get better – but it never did.'

If you need help coping with bereavement, visit www.crusebereavementcare. org.uk. If you have lost a child, help and support are available at www. childdeathhelpline.org.uk and www.compassionatefriends.org.

Fixing the Problem

So, what do you do if you find yourself in a depressed mood? Simple: you get help. The good news is that successful psychiatric, psychological and mental-health treatments are available for depression, backed up by an increasing range of good self-help approaches (including online cognitive behavioural therapy, self-help books, groups, and private therapists and counsellors). (For a complete and comprehensive discussion of depression and its treatment, turn to *Overcoming Depression For Dummies,* and *Overcoming Anxiety,* by Laura L. Smith, Charles H. Elliott and Elaine Iljon Foreman (Wiley).)

No single method has been proven to be the single cure for depression. Research from large trials suggests that a combination of both medication and cognitive behavioural therapy (CBT; also called cognitive therapy, explained fully in *Cognitive Behavioural Therapy For Dummies,* by Rob Willson and Rhena Branch (Wiley)) provide the best treatment for depression and prevention against its return. This doesn't exclude other forms of psychological therapy, activity (such as sport) and complementary therapies, which can all be effective and helpful. Try hard not to become isolated; mood disorders aren't unusual and many other people also understand how you may be feeling. We suggest a range of therapies that, when used alone or in combination, enhance your mood – and thus reduce your anger. The more intense your depression, the more necessary it is to combine treatment strategies. Finally, no magic wand exists when it comes to treating depression – believe us, we wish there were! – so therapists, sufferers and their families all have to find ways to be patient with the process.

Taking antidepressants

More people rely on antidepressant drugs to 'fix' their mood than any of the other forms of therapy available. In part, this is because, in the modern world, a pill exists for almost everything and society tells us that pills can fix anything – cheaply and quickly. Taking a pill is also far easier than seeking other help – less time consuming, less effort and less exposing or embarrassing (according to our clients) than therapy or discussing problems with someone else.

Most of our clients are wary of antidepressants, or just not ready to consider taking *any* tablet regularly. They say 'I don't want to get addicted' and 'How will I know when I'm better?' and sometimes they offer scare stories about the side-effects of medication as reasons not to take such pills. It's true that antidepressants have side-effects – every medication does, and that's why only trained doctors prescribe them. It's not true that antidepressants are addictive, or that your mood doesn't stay steady once you stop taking them – you don't get another chest infection as soon as you stop antibiotics! We've always encouraged people seeking help to take medical advice alongside other treatment or therapy. If two treatments are better than one (medication and CBT) – and research tells us that this is so – why not give yourself the best chance of recovery?

We suggest that, before taking antidepressants, you see a mental-health professional for an accurate assessment of your mood. If you have a mild level of depression, you're much more likely to benefit from talking therapies. Many of our clients with mild mood disorder complain that they 'can't really feel any difference' on medication, which may suggest that the gap between healthy mood and their mood is too small to outweigh the side-effects of medication.

Depressed people make three big mistakes when they take antidepressant drugs:

- ✔ **They don't take the medication for long enough for it to work and achieve the desired pharmacological benefit.** Stopping prematurely may be for either of the following reasons:

    - **They don't like the side-effects.** All medication – even aspirin – has side-effects. If you're taking medication for depression, be sure to ask your doctor (or your pharmacist) what to expect – dry mouth, weight gain, hypersensitivity to the sun – when you take it. Often, if you persevere, side-effects settle and the positive effects of the drugs become increasingly noticeable. But don't be afraid to call the doctor if you think you're having some unusual side-effect – that's what doctors are there for!

- **They feel a little better.** So they stop taking their tablets, but all too soon they're back to square one. Typically, it takes three to four weeks before you begin to notice any type of sustained improvement in your mood and several months before you can obtain the full, lasting relief you hope for.

✔ **They don't take the drugs regularly.** Antidepressant medication only works if you follow your doctor's prescription about when and how to take the pills. Antidepressants aren't like most other types of medication – they aren't designed to be taken 'as needed'. To restore healthy and balanced brain chemistry you have to take the pills every day – regardless of how you feel. Otherwise, they don't have a chance to build up in your brain to the point where they do you some good.

✔ **They stop the medication suddenly.** You need to reduce your antidepressant dose gradually, with medical advice. The last thing you need when you feel depressed is to experience unnecessary rebound effects that are unpleasant and avoidable.

Levelling your mood

Joseph is a good example of the effects of using both antidepressants and all the other strategies for reducing harmful anger (all the ones we outline in this book). Joseph referred himself for treatment following an incident where he assaulted his wife. This was the third time he'd taken his anger out on her physically, but his temper had been an ongoing problem since his early childhood – as had depression. In addition to having difficulty controlling his anger, Joseph also reported having trouble concentrating, worrying constantly, bursting into tears, pessimistic thoughts and feeling 'blue' most of the time – all of which had progressively worsened in recent years.

At first, Joseph was very doubtful about taking medication – he thought that his problem with anger would go away. However, at assessment, Joseph scored within the 'severely depressed' range on a depression inventory. What he didn't count on was just how much better he'd feel when his antidepressant kicked in – approximately three weeks after he began taking it and well before he started to see benefits from therapy.

A great deal of research now shows that talking therapies are much less effective if you're moderately or severely depressed when you first attend. The mind cannot pay attention to the information you're trying to take in, and without attention, you won't be able to store memories of what you discover, or techniques to help you. For Joseph, the combination of medication and therapy was an important factor in his recovery.

Following treatment, Joseph reflected, 'I wasn't ever happy before – I am now. I wouldn't talk with my family when I got angry before – I do now. I couldn't get a good night's sleep before – I can now. I was always tense before – I'm not now.' All these changes had led to a reduction in the frequency of Joseph's angry outbursts, at home and at work. The levelling effect of the medication gave him an opportunity to think and to work on adopting a more positive thinking style and anger-control tactics. Without the feelings of physical agitation, anxiety and low mood, Joseph felt better about himself, more confident and able to sit down and face his wife's distress at his violence.

CASE STUDY

Tyler's turnaround

Tyler was a businessman, which meant that he was used to achieving results quickly. When Gill recommended he see a medical colleague as he was sufficiently depressed to consider a trial of medication, Tyler was doubtful but agreed to try anyway. He came in a week after he started the medication and the first thing he said was, 'I don't think the pills are helping me at all.' Gill reminded him that antidepressants typically take three to four weeks before you begin to notice any difference in your mood. The second week, he came in saying the same thing – 'They're not working!' Each week Tyler said the same thing, until the eighth week, when Tyler came in looking very upbeat and said, 'I don't know what happened, but all of a sudden I feel a lot better than I have in months. I'm sleeping better, laughing more, have more energy. I'm more my old self.' All of a sudden, Tyler was a believer. Because he hung in there and gave the medication a chance to work, he now had better concentration and greater optimism, which he put into his therapy. The antidepressants gave him the lift he needed to be able to confront with Gill the problems behind his depression. Tyler made the most of therapy and was ready to return to full-time work within five months.

Talking as a cure: Psychotherapy

Therapy works! We don't say that just because we've seen it for so many years in our clients and those of our colleagues, or because of the benefits we've gained ourselves.

When most people think about therapy, they conjure up a picture of lying on someone's couch, or regressing back to childhood in order to relive all the painful experiences of the past. In today's world, nothing could be further from the truth. Therapy is primarily about helping people in emotional or mental distress to make sense of their difficulties so that they can make changes for the better. It's not a mysterious process – the therapist can't read your mind – nor a magic cure, in which you just turn up and chat, and all's well again. Going to therapy takes effort, and willingness to feel emotions. The emphasis for both anger management and mood management is more likely to be on what you're doing *today* that's keeping you in a bad mood – not what you were thinking, feeling or doing 30 years ago.

Many types of therapy exist. They're different in the way they take place (how often, how long for, what happens in the sessions and whether you take away tasks to do).

✔ **Art psychotherapy** is an exploratory psychotherapy (see the later bullet on psychotherapy). It uses materials and images, so people who struggle to put feelings or experiences into words can find this therapy particularly helpful. The therapist helps you to understand through images and stories what's troubling you and where solutions might lie.

✔ **Behavioural therapies** are primarily for breaking behavioural habits – from smoking and phobias, to patterns of anger and violence. One central part of behavioural approaches is learning: you gain the understanding that you may have learned unhelpful habits, but this means that you're just as capable of learning new ones.

✔ **Cognitive therapy (also called cognitive behavioural therapy)** starts from the principle that humans interpret their world in different ways (because we're capable of language and thought). Your thinking style – the way you see things – affects your moods and behaviours. Attitudes and beliefs that are healthy and helpful at certain times in life aren't necessarily helpful many years later. Cognitive approaches give you the skills to reshape the way you interpret life. Thoughts like 'I have to be perfect in everything I do or else people won't love me' and 'It's wrong to ask people for help – that only lets them know that you're weak and incompetent' can slowly, but surely, lead you into a mood disorder. The use of the term 'behavioural' refers to the changes you make in your behaviour as you complete exercises (just like those in this book) and try new ways of dealing with your mood, anger or the difficulties you have sought help with.

✔ **Counselling** starts from the basis that each person has it within themselves to overcome problems, but may benefit from someone who is interested, non-judgemental and empathic to talk over experiences and feelings in order to find their way through.

✔ **Psychotherapy** has many forms, but is based on the understanding that it's early relationships and experiences with others that shape the way people feel and act as they grow older. Patterns of relating carry over into new situations and new relationships. Psychotherapy is often *exploratory*; in other words, people may go without a clear idea of what's troubling them.

By all means, if you've got the midweek blues or are having a terrible day, reach out to friends and loved ones for support and comfort. But if you're suffering from clinical depression, you probably need more help than friends can provide.

Have a look at online treatment now available, such as `www.beating theblues.co.uk`, an online self-help course of eight cognitive behavioural therapy sessions of around 50 minutes. You can pay for it yourself or, if your GP thinks it's suitable for you, access it for free via the NHS.

A shrinking network

Recent surveys indicate that the typical size of people's social support network – those people you can confide in, whose advice you trust and who love you no matter what – has shrunk drastically. For example, in 1985, Americans reported having an average of three close friends. By 2006 the number had dropped to two. Even more troubling is the fact that 25 per cent of those surveyed indicated that they had no one – not one living soul – whom they could turn to in a time of need. All of this happened in the same timeframe that rates of depression soared. Coincidence? We don't think so.

Healing through exercise

Extensive scientific evidence supports the fact that regular physical exercise improves mood in non-depressed people and, more important, can assist recovery in someone who's clinically depressed. What's also clear is that

- ✔ **It doesn't matter what type of exercise you choose.** Dr Gentry heard someone ask a friend of his who owns and operates a gym, 'What's the best kind of exercise?' The response was, 'The kind you'll agree to do!'

- ✔ **Exercise doesn't have to be strenuous to be effective.** The key seems to be that you include exercise in your lifestyle so that it's not just an add-on – doing it only when you have time to, or feel like it.

If you're depressed and you choose to exercise regularly (three times a week), you can expect to:

- ✔ Be better able to concentrate
- ✔ Be less irritable
- ✔ Be less obsessive
- ✔ Be less self-absorbed
- ✔ Be less tense
- ✔ Be more active
- ✔ Be more optimistic
- ✔ Complain less about minor physical ailments
- ✔ Enjoy life more in general

✔ Feel less alienated from those around you

✔ Find it easier to make decisions

✔ Have more energy

✔ Show a greater interest in sex

✔ Sleep better

✔ Think more clearly

Ironically, people who need to exercise because they're depressed are the ones most likely to stop sooner rather than later. One thing about depression is that it keeps people from being disciplined and persistent – sticking with things. Here's where having a trainer, a club or friend – someone who understands where you are emotionally – comes in handy; that person can help to motivate you. *Mind* and other mental-health organisations also run programmes of sport for wellbeing.

Depressed people tend to be more isolated and spend far too much time alone, which only makes their negative mood last longer. For that reason alone, we recommend that you do your exercise in a gym or club where you're in contact with lots of people. Even if you don't talk to anyone, just being around other human beings makes you feel better.

Finding hope

Depression often happens after a meaningful loss, and can be hard to tell apart from grief. Freud called it *melancholia* – a feeling of loss expressed through sadness. The more meaningful the loss – such as the death of a loved one, a child leaving home to go to university or get married, or the loss of the best job you ever had – the more severe and persistent the grief of loss (and resulting depression) can be.

Whether you feel low, anxious or are grieving, one strategy for coping with this type of unwanted, negative change in life circumstances is to look for hope. We're not suggesting that you replace that which you've lost (you probably can't – otherwise, you would). What we're suggesting is that you redirect the energy, sense of commitment and feeling of emotional connection you had in that past relationship, job or role as parent into something else that has a future. Otherwise, you'll spend each day mourning – as well as being angry over – what's not in your life, rather than appreciating what is.

One of Gill's clients, Fred, lost his teenage son to a tragic illness. He'd progressed from grief to a full-blown episode of depression by the time he finally took his family and friends' advice to get some professional help. Interestingly, one of the things he decided to do – after medication gave him more energy – was to use his skills as a photographer to take pictures of all the children who were in his son's class. He did this for free – as a gift to those who were healthy and had outlived his son. He felt connected again in a small way to his son, which helped reduce his feelings of loss. Fred knew he could never replace his son, but he came to understand – through therapy – that he could replace his love by helping other young people and make a difference in both his life and theirs.

Part V
Managing Anger in Relationships

'Hurry, Mum — he's about to boil over!'

In this part . . .

You'll see the effects of harmful anger on key relationships with your colleagues, family and loved ones. Is your workplace a battleground? Are you struggling when it comes to effective parenting? Are you locked into a loving, but angry relationship? This part of the book provides you with everything you need to know to avoid counter-productive work behaviour, improve your negotiating skills, create an anger-free family atmosphere, adapt to the changing role of a parent, avoid ending up being an angry couple, inoculate yourself from abusive anger and keep your cool when loved ones are losing theirs. In effect, this part is a guide to turning hostility into harmony with all the key players in your life.

Chapter 19

At Work

*I*n this chapter we highlight the role that anger management plays at work – the place where most people spend the majority of their waking hours. But before diving in, consider these questions:

   ✔ While you're at work, do you often find yourself daydreaming rather than doing your job?

   ✔ Have you ever come to work late without permission?

   ✔ Have you ever made fun of a co-worker's personal life?

   ✔ Have you ever told someone outside work what a useless boss or employer you have?

   ✔ Have you ever done something at work to make a fellow employee look bad?

If you answered yes to any of these questions – and don't worry, these situations are common – you're engaging in confrontational and unhelpful behaviour – unhelpful to you, your colleagues and workmates, and your employer! *Unhelpful behaviour* is any action by an employee that harms the organisation or its members, from idle workplace gossip to acts of physical violence. This may be hard to admit to yourself. How much harm does being 20 minutes late do? Surely everyone gossips? But the cost of confrontational and unhelpful behaviour to industry is billions a year, including direct costs (such as theft) as well as indirect costs (such as employee inefficiency from bullying, sabotage or disinterest). The number one cause of unhelpful behaviour? You've guessed it: anger!

CASE STUDY

Am I late? Sorry

Margaret, a 54-year-old PA to a company director, fully expected to be in her well-paid and high-status job until she retired. But a merger with a larger company meant that her boss chose to move on. Although the new company was keen to keep her, and moved her to work for the vice-president, Margaret was angry. She now had to answer to a more senior PA, and believed that she had been passed over for her boss's job. Margaret was trying hard not to let anyone know that she was furious. On the first day of her new role, she was due to take minutes of the board meeting. She came into the boardroom ten minutes late – without her, the chair had been unable to start. The delay was her way of protesting – 'You think you can do without me? You won't get far.'

Margaret came to see the author Gill, angry about work, but not seeing herself as having an anger-management problem at all. Only when she looked at the messages her behaviour was sending, and the gap between how she wanted to be seen and her actions, did she take steps to change things.

In this chapter we tell you how anger plays itself out in the workplace, which types of personalities are most prone to confrontational behaviour, how you can be competitive at work without being counterproductive, and how you can be more polite to workmates and colleagues – by having new anger-management skills.

Recognising Unhelpful Work Behaviour

Recognising unhelpful work behaviour – in yourself and in others – can be difficult. Partly, that's because you think of much of it as 'normal' at-work behaviour – coming to work late or taking a longer break than you're allowed. You tell yourself, 'Doesn't everyone?' In addition, the majority of anger at work is passive and non-violent in nature.

Here are some typical examples of unhelpful behaviour at work:

- ✔ Avoiding returning a phone call to someone you should speak to
- ✔ Failing to report a problem and allowing it to get worse
- ✔ Ignoring someone at work
- ✔ Intentionally coming late to a meeting
- ✔ Leaving work earlier than you're supposed to
- ✔ Purposely failing to do as you're asked or instructed

- Refusing to accept an assignment or job
- Refusing to help a workmate
- Staying off sick when you aren't
- Trying to look busy when you aren't
- Withholding needed information from a colleague
- Working slowly when things need to be done fast

Less often, anger triggers more actively destructive or dangerous behaviours such as:

- Being nasty or rude to a customer or client
- Deliberately damaging a piece of equipment
- Deliberately doing your work badly
- Hitting or pushing someone at work
- Insulting a workmate's ability to do his job
- Making an obscene gesture or swearing at others
- Playing a nasty trick on someone at work
- Purposely wasting supplies or materials
- Starting a harmful rumour about another colleague
- Starting an argument with a colleague
- Stealing something that belongs to your employer
- Threatening another employee with violence

Look at the lists of unhelpful work behaviours and make a note of which ones you've done lately – say, in the last three weeks. Do you do any of these things on a fairly regular basis – once or twice a week? Pick one of these and tell yourself, 'I'm not going to express my anger this way anymore.' Then use some of the anger-management strategies we outline later in this chapter instead.

Avoidance versus aggression

Employees typically adopt one of two response styles when they're angry: avoidance or aggression. *Avoidance* means you disengage in a variety of ways from getting the job done – coming in late or ignoring someone. *Aggression* means you attack the source of your anger – bullying a subordinate or insulting a customer. It's that old fight-or-flight pattern we talk about throughout this book (see Chapter 4, for example).

Sound familiar?

Researchers asked 74 employees at one work-site the following question: how often have you observed each of the following behaviours in your present job? Here are the respondents' top 15 responses, starting with the most common:

- ✔ Complaining about petty things at work
- ✔ Coming to work late without permission
- ✔ Taking longer breaks than allowed
- ✔ Ignoring someone at work
- ✔ Being nasty or rude to a client or co-worker
- ✔ Daydreaming rather than doing work
- ✔ Leaving work early without permission
- ✔ Pretending to look busy
- ✔ Making a big deal of others' mistakes
- ✔ Telling people outside work what a useless organisation it is
- ✔ Insulting colleagues about their job performance
- ✔ Refusing to help out at work
- ✔ Avoiding returning phone calls that are important
- ✔ Making fun of people
- ✔ Verbally abusing a workmate

Confrontational behaviour is an employee coping strategy. It's one of the ways you deal with work stress. The motivation behind confrontational behaviour at work is often retaliation. When you feel angry at work, confrontation is your way of paying people back. And each time you make someone else angry, you're giving that person an invitation to be angry back.

Most unhelpful work behaviour is the result of interpersonal conflict – between workmates, and between supervisors and employees. The more conflict exists, the more unhelpful behaviour you can expect. Conflict resolution and positive behaviour at work go hand in hand.

Person versus organisation

Employees also differ in terms of where they direct their anger at work. About 50 per cent of the time people are apt to retaliate against a *person* – for instance, insulting a fellow worker about his performance. The other 50 per cent of the time people take their anger out on the *organisation* – perhaps destroying property. Either way, the behaviour disrupts the workplace.

Understanding the aggressive personality at work

Some people have a more aggressive style of interacting or dealing with the world than others. By *aggressive,* we don't necessarily mean that you deliberately attack or try to hurt others, just that you seem to go against the world instead of going with the flow. Whether this is good or bad depends on which type of aggressive personality you are.

Katherine is a classic example of an achievement-driven personality. She goes well beyond just trying to succeed. She's *driven* – all her energies work towards achieving success in her career. Katherine is extremely task orientated, has a really competitive nature and is forceful when it comes to pursuing goals. She's direct in her communications – including how she expresses anger – leaving little doubt as to where she stands on issues. Those who work with her admire her determined spirit. She's not a talker – she's a doer! The only time she gets angry is when she becomes frustrated by obstacles that slow her down in her efforts to be efficient and

get the job done. If you can keep up with her, she's your best friend and easy to work with, and for.

Kelly, on the other hand, is more combative in how she approaches work. She, too, is highly competitive, but she tends to come across as confrontational in her dealings with others. If something goes wrong, she's in your face in a second! She's impatient, intense and can be quite demanding of those she works with – 'Get that report to me by the end of the day and no excuses!' Ask anyone in the office and he'll tell you what a dominant personality Kelly has. She's the type who has the first – and last – word on every subject. And yes, she's angry a lot. But her anger – unlike Katherine's – isn't linked to frustration; rather, it simply serves as fuel for satisfying her combative personality. Kelly's like the football coach who was once described as 'a bloke who could walk into an empty locker room and start a fight'!

Aggressive employees are three times more likely to retaliate against people they work with, whereas avoidant employees are more likely to satisfy their anger by directing it towards the organisation or boss they work for.

Which of these profiles do you fit? Do some self-examination and ask yourself why – 'Why do I always blame my team-mates when I get frustrated or irritated?' or 'Why do I always hide from my anger and the difficulties I have underneath?' Avoidance usually results from fear. What are you afraid of – losing your job, losing control of your temper after you get started, what? Attack typically implies that you're dealing with an enemy. Are your colleagues really your enemies? Is this work or is it war? Is it because you have a combative personality and, thus, everything inevitably becomes a war?

Knowing Who's Likely to Have Problems with Anger at Work

Not everyone is likely to engage in unhelpful work behaviour because of anger. But clearly, if you're experiencing harmful anger – that is, intense anger that occurs on a daily basis (see Chapter 2) – you're a prime candidate.

The fed-up employee

Employees likely to engage in destructive behaviour often exhibit one or more of the following signs of disguised anger:

- They seem disinterested in their work.
- They're generally disagreeable at work.
- They show clear signs of distress or stress.
- They're discouraged about how their careers or jobs are progressing.
- They keep their distance from other team members.
- They're highly distrustful of their superiors.
- They frequently appear distracted while completing a task.
- They show disrespect to those higher up in the organisation.
- They complain regularly about working hours, salary and promotion.
- They're pretty much disgruntled, disgusted and disheartened by everything that goes on during the working day.

Most people don't go around telling everyone within earshot that they're angry, fed up or even annoyed. Most people show their anger in more subtle, politically correct terminology – but it's anger nevertheless.

Aaron, a 58-year-old urban planner, was definitely a fed-up employee – and he made no bones about it. For 22 years he'd worked at a job he thoroughly enjoyed and that consistently rewarded him for his efforts. But then his company unexpectedly reorganised, and Aaron was made redundant. The only job he could find that fitted his experience paid him much less than he felt he was worth. He took the job, hoping that if he worked hard and gave his employer his usual 120 per cent, he'd eventually receive a substantial increase in pay. But as it turned out, that wasn't on the cards, because his educational background – working his way up without a degree – prevented him from moving up a grade. Aaron was stuck! Now all he did was spend his time complaining about almost everything – no matter how insignificant. His complaining, as you can imagine, didn't go down well with his employer, who finally told him to either stop complaining or leave.

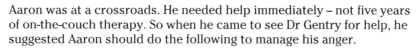

Aaron was at a crossroads. He needed help immediately – not five years of on-the-couch therapy. So when he came to see Dr Gentry for help, he suggested Aaron should do the following to manage his anger.

You can do the same in *your* life:

- ✔ **Accept the reality of the situation.** To a large extent, Aaron was fed up because he refused to accept that he was dealing with an 'immovable' object – company policy about qualifications. Complaining was his way of trying to push his employer to change that policy – to make an exception in his case.

- ✔ **Stop personalising the situation.** Aaron was angry because he believed the promotion policy was directed at him. Dr Gentry asked him, 'Do all the other employees have to abide by this policy?' Aaron's answer, without hesitation, was yes. So Dr Gentry reminded him, 'This really isn't about you at all. It's just the way they do business.' Aaron agreed.

- ✔ **Write down your feelings.** To defuse some of the anger that Aaron was carrying around – which was leaking out in the form of complaints – Dr Gentry recommended that he take 20 minutes a day and write about his anger (see Chapter 11).

- ✔ **Balance your effort level.** Aaron needed to stop giving 120 per cent to his employer, such as when he worked overtime without pay. His only reason for this was that it was a means to an end – the end being a pay rise. Dr Gentry reminded Aaron that his employer wasn't exploiting him, he was exploiting himself – and that's not healthy!

- ✔ **Engage in some positive thinking.** Aaron's anger was also the result of the fact that this whole situation was constantly on his mind. The psychological term for that process is *rumination* – chewing something over and over. Because Aaron admitted he had trouble distracting himself from this constant thinking, Dr Gentry suggested that instead he choose something else – something positive and something that he had some control over – to ruminate about. (Chapter 4 offers some possibilities.)

- ✔ **Find some benefit in what you do.** Dr Gentry advised Aaron to think about his current job and come up with something positive. In other words, 'What aren't you complaining about? Salary aside, what's good about your job?' Aaron needed a more balanced view of his work situation to let go of some of his angry feelings.

- ✔ **Get some exercise.** Regular exercise is a good way of 'exorcising' not only physical toxins in the body but also emotions like anger. Forty-five minutes in a gym three days a week can do wonders for your mood.

- ✔ **Forgive, forgive, forgive.** Aaron was carrying around yesterday's anger, and it was becoming a real burden both to him and his employer. The only way we know of unloading this burden is to forgive (see Chapter 8). Aaron needed to forgive his previous employer for making him redundant, and he needed to forgive his current employer for having what he considered an out-of-date promotion policy.

By following these suggestions Aaron got 'unstuck', not from the financial realities of his job but from the negative emotion – anger – that accompanied it. He still had to watch his pennies, but he was no longer a disgruntled man.

The self-centred employee

The link between big egos (the technical term for this is *narcissism*), anger and unhelpful work behaviour is a strong one. The more self-centred you are, the more easily angered you probably are at work. This means that you're also more likely to engage in confrontational behaviour. Although no one likes to be restricted at work – interrupted by others, inadequately trained, lacking the resources you need to do the job well – self-centred employees take these restrictions personally ('Why are you doing this to *me*?') and react with anger.

How do you know if you fall into this category? Here are some clues:

- ✔ You tend to be self-absorbed in your job and unaware of (and unconcerned about) what your colleagues are doing. You aren't a team player.

- ✔ You tend to feel entitled. For example, you might say things like 'You *owe* me respect' and feel 'I have a *right* to that pay rise or promotion'.

- ✔ You can't put yourself in the other person's shoes whenever there's a conflict of some sort, or difference of opinion. You just keep reiterating what *you* want, how *you* see things and why *your* solution is the right one.

- ✔ You tend to be *grandiose* – feeling as though you're somehow special when it comes to working with others or completing a project. You expect your colleagues to defer to you because of your energy, brilliant ideas and charismatic personality.

- ✔ You tend to exploit others at work – that is, always use others to get your own way, regardless of the cost to them. And to add insult to injury, you get angry if your co-workers don't *appreciate* the fact that you chose them to exploit!

What if you're tired of the come-back from being so self-centred? What do you do to change? Here are some strategies:

- ✔ When you find yourself thinking like a self-centred employee ('Why a re these people in *my* way?'), balance that by thinking instead, 'I'm sure these people have important things to do, just like I do. The problem is we're both trying to do them at the same time. Maybe if I help this person, he'll help me.'

- ✔ Stop *demanding* that your co-workers do what you want – this goes along with a sense of entitlement – and instead, *request* that they do what you want. You'll be surprised at how much more receptive and willing they are!

✔ Spend more time trying to look at things from other people's perspective. Pay more attention to the people around you – to what they're thinking and feeling. Try being curious about their point of view – 'What do you mean?', rather than 'What do you *mean*?' (in frustration).

✔ Remember that life is a two-way street. The more understanding and sympathetic you are to those you work with, the more they respond that way to you. Not a bad idea?

✔ Just as you were taught, always say 'please' and 'thank you' – yes, at work too!

Improving Your Negotiating Skills

Negotiating is a skill you use all the time at work. *Negotiation* is any effort between two or more workers aimed at getting the job done through co-operation, give and take, and talking problems through. Resolving a conflict of interests or opinions means you've been a successful negotiator.

We're always curious when we're approached by organisations that want us to work with managers to make sure 'everyone is on the same page'. Organisations seem to think that it's normal for their workers to be like-minded and are always surprised (and sometimes angry) when this doesn't happen. But the truth is, conflict, and therefore negotiation, is inevitable in the workplace.

Negotiations always involve emotions – because the negotiators are human! But that's only a problem if the emotions around are negative. If negotiators are in a positive emotional state – excited, optimistic – they tend to be co-operative and conciliatory. This more often leads to a win–win solution, where both parties come away feeling they've got something they wanted. If either or both negotiators, however, are in a negative emotional state – angry, pessimistic – things tend to be much more competitive and neither party wants to make concessions. If no one concedes, you're in a deadlock. No one walks away a winner!

Negotiators respond to their opponent's emotions. The best way to ensure a positive outcome is to start with a smile. That, believe it or not, sets the tone for everything that follows. Start with a look of irritation on your face and you'll have a hard job. Begin by talking about some point of possible agreement (hard to do if you're angry – but worth the effort). Doing this sets a positive tone before getting down to differences of opinion. Remind yourself that, even though the other person may be disagreeing, he's not the enemy (see more of the ten anger-freeing thoughts listed in Chapter 22). And finally, if you must be angry when you enter into some type of negotiation, try to express your anger constructively (details in Chapter 13).

Creating a Positive Work Climate

Anger at work isn't confined to one or two people, one particular conflict or situation, or one particular issue – for example, work overload. Your anger and other emotions happen in the overall work environment – not just within your job but within the whole organisation. That overall environment (or climate) can be very different from one work setting to another. Walk into any workplace – from a factory floor to a corporate boardroom – and after about five minutes of watching people at work you can tell whether the climate is hostile (people at each other's throats), sad (too many lost opportunities, too much turnover in personnel), tense (lots of uncertainty) or optimistic (it's great working here).

Psychologists have come up with a fascinating theory about how workplace emotions affect productivity. Instead of concentrating on one specific emotion – anger – they look at the balance between positive and negative emotions, which they refer to as the *positivity ratio*. So far the researchers have found that

✔ For employees to flourish in their work, the ratio of emotions expressed in the workforce overall must be approximately 3-to-1 in favour of positive feelings. If that 3-to-1 ratio isn't reached, workers tend to struggle – describing their work lives as empty and unsatisfying.

✔ Too many positive emotions can also be a problem – a small amount of negativity is necessary to stop work behaviour becoming rigid, boring and too routine. This kind of climate can lead to self-satisfied and less energetic work – a 'we've made it' atmosphere where people don't bother to push themselves any more. But having too positive a climate isn't something that most companies need to worry about!

✔ The negativity must be appropriate to stay healthy – that is, employees who express negativity as contempt, rage or violence are counterproductive (see Chapter 13 to find out how to use anger constructively).

✔ The expression of positive emotions needs to be genuine, not forced. Telling staff to smile doesn't mean they feel happy about it!

In the following minitable we list a number of emotions that you may have seen at work. Circle ten of those that you feel best and most accurately describe the emotional climate of your workplace *in the past week*. It doesn't matter which column you circle from – just choose ten emotions in total. Then calculate the positivity ratio by dividing the number of positive emotions by the number of negative emotions (for example, if you have three words circled in the 'Positive' column and seven words circled in the 'Negative' column, you do this simple calculation: $3 \div 7 = 0.43$). Is your positivity ratio above or below 2.9? If the ratio is 2.9 or below, you – and everyone else you work with – are much more likely to get angry at work. If the ratio is at least 3 (but less than 11 – this is an example of too much positivity), your workplace has a healthier environment.

Positive Emotions	_Negative Emotions_
Amazed	Afraid
Amused	Agitated
Appreciative	Alarmed
Cheerful	Angry
Content	Anxious
Curious	Ashamed
Delighted	Bitter
Enthusiastic	Bored
Excited	Depressed
Generous	Frustrated
Grateful	Guilty
Happy	Irritated
Hopeful	Petrified
Joyful	Regretful
Kind	Resentful
Loving	Sad
Optimistic	Sorrowful
Satisfied	Unhappy
Thrilled	Worried

If you're an employer or boss, here are some tips on how to create a more positive work setting:

- ✔ Award an 'Employee of the Month', based not on how much he does, but on how positively the person relates to customers, clients and colleagues.

- ✔ Offer small rewards for displaying a positive attitude at work.

- ✔ Celebrate every employee's birthday, and remember that a small treat (a lunch, cakes, time away as a group) doesn't cost the organisation much, in return for how appreciated your staff feel.

If you're an employee, try the following to make your work climate more positive:

✔ Begin each day at work by saying hello. Just because you work with people every day doesn't mean you don't need to bother being polite and friendly.

✔ Interject some humour into the workplace dialogue. Laughter lets your colleagues know that you're not a threat.

✔ Always apologise when you do something that you know offends someone. Not only will you feel better but, as it turns out, saying you're sorry also defuses the tension in the other person and makes it harder for him to hold a grudge.

Making Politeness the Norm

At work, manners count. Treating your fellow employees in a polite manner – fair, respectful, courteous, pleasant – sends the message that you want to be treated politely too. The reverse is also true – be rude and hostile to others and they'll act that way to you, or go out of their way to avoid you!

Anger is often the by-product of being on the receiving end of rudeness. And poorly managed anger often leads to some form of unhelpful work behaviour.

How big a problem is rudeness at work? Huge! Approximately 90 per cent of all working people believe a lack of courtesy at work is a serious problem – even though it doesn't rise to the level of physical violence. A negative emotional climate is a major reason for turnover. Approximately one in two employees on the receiving end of rudeness or other unhelpful work behaviour think about leaving their job, and one in eight actually leaves.

If you're an employer and you want to ensure that politeness is the norm, try these suggestions:

✔ Make it clear – from the top down – that rude and hostile behaviour won't be tolerated (no matter what was allowed in the past) and that no exceptions will be made in terms of job status.

✔ Introduce training in positive behaviour as an integral part of recruitment and orientation.

✔ Have written policies on what constitutes polite and rude behaviour, and what will happen to those who ignore the standards. Ask for the views of all your employees.

✔ Survey employees periodically on the climate and behaviour in your workplace.

✔ Emphasise *constructive* criticism, *constructive* anger expression and *constructive* competition.

If you're an employee and you want to make politeness the norm where you work, try the following:

- ✔ Make 'treat others as you want to be treated' your personal style at work.

- ✔ Be constructive in your criticism of other staff – tell them how they could do what they do better, not what they're doing wrong!

- ✔ If you think your workplace is too negative, initiate some positive change – don't wait for someone else to do it.

- ✔ Make it clear to all those you work with that you wish to be treated in a polite manner at all times and don't be afraid to provide corrective feedback when it's called for.

- ✔ Remind yourself and others at work that a positive climate isn't about who's in charge or who's right – it's about mutual respect.

- ✔ Always address any problems or criticisms with a colleague in private. It's less intimidating and embarrassing.

- ✔ Be optimistic. Always assume that others are trying their best. Give them the benefit of the doubt, unless you have proof to the contrary.

- ✔ If you have to be critical of a fellow employee, show him the courtesy of saying what you have to say face to face. If you can't say it to his face, don't say it at all! This is particularly important if you're prone to passive aggression, sulking or gossip.

Speaking Up, Not Out

Anger always speaks out – if not in actual words, then through your appearance and behaviour. Outward anger – passive or aggressive – is what unhelpful work behaviour is all about.

Better than speaking *out* is speaking *up* – saying what's on your mind and in your heart. Psychologists refer to this as *assertiveness*. The assertive person speaks face-to-face, one-on-one about what he needs ('I need you to speak to me politely'), owns up to his emotions ('Yes, I'm angry and I think I have a right to be'), acknowledges the positives as well as the negatives of the situation ('You know I like working here, but . . .') and assumes a positive outcome – all without being aggressive.

Assertiveness is about action and attitude. If you don't often stand up for yourself, and just expect others to know what you need, you end up being seen by those you work with and for as weak (a pushover, the proverbial doormat) and someone not to be respected or taken seriously. This invites others to treat you badly. You don't hear someone at work say, 'I really admire him – he's such a mouse!'

So how exactly are you supposed to speak up in an assertive manner? Follow these tips (and dip into Chapter 12 for even more info):

- ✔ **Take ownership – always start with the word *I*.** For example: 'I need to talk to you about something that's bothering me.' 'I need to give you some personal feedback about this morning's meeting.' 'I'm not sure you understand where I'm coming from.'

- ✔ **Open with a positive statement.** For example: 'I think you know how much I like working here, but . . .' 'I think it's fair to say that you've always been fair with me in the past, but . . .'

- ✔ **Stop bobbing and weaving and get to the point.** Be specific about what's bothering you – making you angry. Don't just say, 'I'm angry!' Tell the other person exactly why. What's happened, or not happened, that you dislike?

- ✔ **Appeal to the other person's empathy (his ability to 'stand in your shoes').** For example: 'I'm not sure you appreciate the impact your words earlier had on me.' 'I want to think you weren't intentionally trying to make me angry, but . . .' 'If I were to talk to you rudely, I'm not sure how you would feel, but it really upsets me.'

- ✔ **Avoid four-letter words.** No one likes to be sworn at, not even the person who swore at you. Besides, the message gets lost when surrounded by bad language.

- ✔ **Be persistent.** Don't expect one assertive act on your part to change the world. You need to make yourself clear, calmly and politely, focusing on the issues and not the emotions, until others start to recognise that the climate around you has changed!

Chapter 20

At Home and In Intimate Relationships

Can families have conflict without combat? Can you get on with your partner without blazing rows? Absolutely. In this chapter we look at what a healthy family or partnership does to minimise destructive anger – the kind that can end in division or, worse still, in domestic violence. Don't worry . . . it can be as simple as sitting down together at dinner every night.

Take the Smiths as an example. Mum, Dad, two teenaged sons and a daughter – they're a family in trouble. Anger is at the centre of almost every interaction the Smiths have throughout the day. They complain, they shout and they push (sometimes physically) to get whatever they need from each other. They're all just surviving the day and the week, but feel hopeless about their future as a family. Mum continues to wish for a peaceful solution to family conflict, but Dad has given up. He spends most of his time away from home and loses his temper when he's there. The daughter battles with both parents over almost everything.

Long ago the Smiths decided their daughter's anger was the problem that needed to be fixed. They took her to one mental-health professional after another, all without progress. What the family *didn't* do was look at their own patterns – the style with which they communicate and deal with one another. What this family needs is to see themselves as being in this together.

Anger within families involves power struggles; it's the antithesis of co-operation. It wastes family resources – energy, time, money – and can leave a residue of hostility and resentment. Family members become so concerned about winning battles that they lose sight of the fact that, together, they're losing the war. Relationships become fragmented – every woman for herself. They can no longer trust or count on each other for support. They've become a family in name only.

In this chapter we give you some practical tips on how *not* to end up like the Smiths. We talk about how families can use anger constructively and form more intimate, loving relationships. And we show you how to teach your children *how* to be angry, rather than *not* to be angry. There's nothing wrong with the natural emotion of anger. It only becomes a problem when you show it destructively or hide it so it festers.

It Takes Two: Avoiding Angry Dialogues

When an angry family member confronts you, the easiest thing to do is respond in kind – answer anger with anger.

If you don't want to dance the anger dance, you have two options:

- ✔ **Simply opt out – in effect saying, 'Thanks, but I'll pass.'** Teenagers, for example, often initiate an angry exchange with parents as a means of releasing pent-up tension, mostly relating to difficulties they're having with their peers. And what do most parents do? They jump right in with both feet – first, by telling their child, 'You shouldn't feel like that,' and when that doesn't work, by getting angry themselves. The best course of action is to be sympathetic but don't engage with the other person's anger. Let her anger be her anger – don't make it yours. It'll die down quicker that way.

- ✔ **Engage in another type of dance, one with less drama.** You can begin by accepting the person's emotion and then give her a chance to work through it. Consider the following example:

Parent: Hi. How was school?

Teenager: Leave me alone. God, every time I walk in the door, you're always asking me how I feel!

Parent: You sound like you're angry.

Teenager: I am. But I don't want to talk about it, okay?

Parent: That's fine. But if you do, I'm here. I feel that way myself sometimes – just want to work things out myself.

Never laugh at an angry loved one

Some people have a hard time expressing their anger out loud, so the last thing you want to do is laugh when someone does find the courage to say, 'I found that annoying.' When you laugh at someone who's expressing her feelings, you're being dismissive and showing contempt. This is the most destructive type of communication between family members. Having someone listen to you when you're angry is not only important, it's essential to good family relationships. If people listened to each other more when they're annoyed, maybe they wouldn't have to listen so much when they're in a full-blown rage.

Teenager: (voice louder) Well, I'm not you! Besides, you wouldn't understand. You never do.

Parent: (not raising voice) Of course you're not me – I wasn't suggesting that you were. You have your own way of dealing with your anger. I was just being sympathetic.

Teenager: It's that stupid Jen – she thinks she's so much better than me. I could just kill her; she makes me so angry.

Parent: So you're angry with Jen. What has she done this time?

Now the two are engaged in a dialogue about anger rather than an angry dialogue.

Managing Anger From the Top Down

Family members – parents and children alike – learn by example. If a child sees her parents rant and rave, swear or hit one another in anger, she'll learn to handle anger poorly herself. Similarly, if parents allow their daughter to throw an angry tantrum every time she doesn't get her way, and end up shouting at her, they're in turn acting the same way – they've learned to react to their child like a child.

Parents are the ones who set the tone at home, and they need to take responsibility for making sure that all family members express anger in a polite and constructive way. (You may make your children responsible for cleaning their rooms, but you can't make them responsible for the anger in your household.)

One of Gill's clients, Andy, is a typical example of how children pick up anger management from their parents. Unfortunately, Andy's parents were poor role models for reasonable anger – his mother was a shouter and his father was a hitter, and neither one could keep from bringing out the worst in the other. Not wanting to be like either of them, Andy ended up going to the other extreme and became a pouter and a sulker.

The home environment is a learning laboratory, a classroom where all the important lessons of life, and survival, are taught. Important among these is the lesson on how to survive – and even benefit from – conflict between family members. Conflict is present in all families simply because its members have different interests, personalities, temperaments, values, wants, likes, dislikes and anxieties – all of which have to be negotiated if the family is to operate in relative health. The major distinction between healthy and unhealthy families is how they choose to resolve these conflicts – not whether they have the conflicts in the first place.

So, as a parent, how do you set a healthy tone for your family's conflicts? Here are some tips for managing the anger that results from family conflict:

- ✔ **Be accepting of conflict and anger.** Don't disapprove of or dismiss conflicts between family members or try to distract people's attention away from problems. Anger is a signal that something's wrong and you need to resolve it. You *want* those signals – if you don't have them, or don't heed them, the anger only grows.

- ✔ **Distinguish between different levels of anger and conflict.** You want to help your family differentiate between being irritated, being angry and being in a rage (check out Chapter 2). The first two are okay – the third isn't.

- ✔ **Don't punish – instead, problem-solve.** Instead of being annoyed with each family member for being angry, ask two simple questions:

  - What are you angry about?

  - What would you like to do about it?

  The first question defines the problem; the second question defines the solution. If the other person knows what the problem is, but doesn't have a solution, help her find one – one that doesn't involve acting out her anger in some destructive or vengeful way.

- ✔ **Keep your cool.** You don't help children keep their cool by losing yours! You're the adult – even if you don't feel like you have much ability to keep your cool, you can bet that you're better able to keep calm than your children are.

Won't somebody listen?

When we work with angry clients it's very clear that one of the main factors in fuelling the anger fire is not being listened to. This is why we ask each client, 'How are you? How angry have you felt since we last spoke?' You aren't just asking how the other person feels, but listening and taking in their response. How does what the person is telling you affect your previous view of the problem? Have you jumped to conclusions? Is there something you didn't know about, which changes how you feel too?

Listening can be more complicated when you're talking to someone who finds it hard to put their feelings into words – children, adolescents, young men. But if you start trying to communicate about anger with little interest in the other person's view, how are you going to reach a win–win solution?

✔ **Seek win–win solutions.** No one likes to lose – certainly not someone who's already angry. She just gets angrier! You want to find a solution to family anger that leaves everyone feeling that they got something positive out of the exchange – if only the fact that they were actually *heard* for a change. Here's where a non-aggressive approach works best – an approach that's not competitive ('I win, you lose!') or confrontational, and where one person in the family doesn't try to dominate the others.

✔ **Talk about anger comfortably.** Don't make anger a taboo topic that becomes an 'elephant in the room' – something everyone knows is there but no one talks about.

✔ **View anger and conflict as an opportunity for new learning.** Step back, look at each other and find out something about the other person – the result is a greater sense of intimacy as you share your real self.

Choosing the Unfamiliar: Changing Your Family's Patterns

One of the hardest things about change is that you're choosing to behave and think in ways that aren't automatic. Benjamin Franklin said, 'Insanity is doing the same thing over and over again and expecting different results.' Humans are creatures of habit, and so are family units. Over time families develop certain predictable patterns of behaviour – family dynamics – that have a life of their own. Families have decision-making patterns, problem-solving patterns, patterns that define how you react to major changes in life circumstances and how you react to each other emotionally.

After these patterns are established, families and couples tend to follow them like a reflex, mindlessly – even if they don't work. In fact, we believe that at least *part* of the anger that flares up in families is the frustration of those previous difficulties in managing anger successfully together. Family members feel frustrated because they're already aware that their patterns don't work and that conflict tends to happen.

You can only change yourself. Even though you may be determined to manage your anger better, those close to you may not. If your family works by blaming you for problems with anger (or other things), they won't *want* you to change – you'd be taking away their excuse! This doesn't prevent you from changing what you do, but don't expect others around you to like it, or do the same.

Make a list of your own family's situations in which anger is most likely to occur. Think about how each member of your family reacts in that particular situation. What can you do to change how you react? The next time that situation occurs, take the initiative to choose the unfamiliar way. Maybe laugh instead of taking offence. Perhaps you can say, 'You seem very worked up. Let me know when you're calmer, and we'll talk.' Surprise the rest of the family by doing something unpredictable, and then watch how they respond – sometimes all it takes is one person changing the routine and everyone else follows suit. Pretend you're a scientist conducting an experiment on how to create family harmony. If one thing doesn't work, try something else – keep experimenting until you find what you're looking for.

This isn't just something that parents can do. As a child (especially a teenager), you know the dynamics of your family, you know what sets them off. Why not take the lead, try something different and see what happens?

Looking at Your Parenting Style

You have your own style of dressing or decorating your house or signing your name – and you have your own style of child rearing. How you raise your children doesn't just affect the intensity of conflict in your family – it affects your children's emotions, their learning in school, whether they start smoking and whether they engage in risky sexual behaviour, among other things.

Four main styles of parenting exist. See whether you can find yourself in one of these styles (and keep in mind that you may be a mix of more than one):

✔ **Authoritative style.** If you're an authoritative parent, you're highly involved in your children's lives and you're not afraid to exert control over their behaviour. You're aware of what your kids are doing and who they're doing it with, and also know their likes, dislikes and feelings. You're around them and encourage them to take part in activities that generate a sense of belonging and togetherness. Above all, you support a sense of *autonomy* (the ability and freedom to choose), which increases your children's independence with age. You present a clear message that with freedom comes responsibility. You rarely, if ever, use punishment – threats, arguments, ultimatums – to keep your children in line.

What can you hope for from your children? They're more likely to be co-operative, in a positive mood, do well in school, have high self-esteem, show self-control and persist at tasks.

✔ **Autocratic style.** Autocratic parents tend to be strict and demanding, and may have anger-management difficulties themselves. If you're autocratic, you make a lot of demands on your children. Either you shout, criticise and punish your kids when they fail to live up to your expectations, or you manage through an oppressive atmosphere: they learn to know when not to ask for or discuss something; they wouldn't dare. When it comes to talking with your children, no give-and-take exists between your ideas and needs, and theirs – your basic philosophy is 'It's my way or the highway!' You're definitely not a good listener or likely to know your children's true feelings. And independence is out of the question.

Your kids live with either fear or anxiety, and tend to suppress or aggressively display their negative emotions. Whether you realise it or not, they view you as harsh, cold and rejecting. Like you, your children often resort to force – sulking or aggression – to get their way. Boys, especially, show high levels of anger outside the home – at school and with peers.

✔ **Permissive style.** If you're a permissive parent there's no question that you love your children. There's also no question that you want to be their best friend. To ensure that, you put few demands on your kids, impose few limits on their social and emotional behaviour, and essentially leave the parenting up to them. You give them a lot of freedom and allow them to be autonomous (have free choice), even in areas where they're incapable of succeeding. You don't set curfews for your teenagers – you feel that they know when it's time to come home.

Permissiveness sounds good to some who believe that it offers the child the best chance of reaching their potential without a great deal of pressure from the people close to them and the world around them. But children raised in permissive homes tend to be impulsive, temperamental, defiant, rebellious and antisocial, and they show little evidence of self-control. Their relationships with parents tend to be hostile and dependent – they can be highly independent one minute and terribly demanding the next (don't tell me what time to be in, but why haven't you washed my shirt?).

✔ **Unengaged style.** Unengaged parents are parents in name only. They tend to be busy or more interested in their own lives than their children (this can be a particular issue if the children aren't their own by birth). If this is your parenting style, when asked where your children are and what they're doing your immediate response is, 'I don't know. I'm not sure.' And that's the sad truth of it. You tend to be *un*accepting of your children, *un*aware of what's going on in their lives, *un*available to them day and night, and *un*involved – whatever they're doing, they're doing with people other than you.

Children raised by unengaged parents are extremely alienated – they feel isolated and not closely connected to anyone, either adults or others their own age. They frequently use anger to keep others at a distance. They're emotionally volatile – prone to rage or sulking that may last for days. And they have very limited social and problem-solving skills. The truth is that children who raise themselves without love and parental involvement can't help but do a poor job of it – they've had no one to learn from.

When it comes to minimising anger in the home – both yours and that of your children – the best parenting style for good anger management is the authoritative one.

Take Ross and Jane, who have two teenage sons. The family chat about all sorts of topics each evening at the dinner table, and Ross and Jane invite their children to talk about their feelings, their problems and even difficult topics such as the recent suicide of a kid at their school. The boys are involved with lots of activities outside the home, with their parents' support. Ross and Jane argue with their children at times, but they're always respectful and their kids are respectful in return. As often as possible, decisions about family life are made as a family – even though Ross and Jane have the final say. Apparently, their children like their home environment – they're always bringing friends home and including them in family activities. Do Ross and Jane ever get angry with their kids? Of course. Do their kids ever get angry with them? Of course. But these times are few and far between and the anger never leads to disruption, disrespect or violence.

Josh, a friend of Ross and Jane's youngest son, has a very different relationship with his parents. Josh's parents have always been hard on him, demanding that he do well in school, disagreeing with him constantly over who his friends are, insisting that he participate in activities that interest them and restricting his movements as much as possible. (In other words, they're autocratic.) Josh ends up emotionally confused – he both loves and hates his parents. That's why he stays away from home as much as he can, but at the same time constantly talks to anyone who'll listen about his unreasonable parents. Josh is intelligent, but he does poorly in school – to get back at his parents. He smokes, drinks and has wrecked his car on more than one occasion. He and his parents are caught up in a vicious cycle of anger with no end in sight.

Parenting isn't a fixed way of doing things. As soon as you feel you've found a way that works, your child is older and you need to adjust again. Early on, of course, children need a lot of direct control, for no other reason than to keep them safe. You can't expect a four-year-old child to make good decisions about what to have for tea – she doesn't know about healthy eating. You can't explain to a two-year-old why she shouldn't run out into the road. She can't remember and doesn't have those instincts yet – you just have to say 'No!'

Later on, as children grow up and can watch out for themselves a bit, it makes sense for you to relax rules – using more indirect control or influence over they way they think, feel and behave, through discussion and through your example. Teenagers, for example, should be part of the family discussion about curfews, sex, drugs, alcohol, smoking, the difference between right and wrong and so on. As a parent, you want to encourage your children to have an opinion about what goes on in the world around them and what part they want to play in that world. Giving your child this practice at working out her choices and making ones that bring her good results while she's still at home gives her the best chance of success when she moves on in life.

If you don't progressively allow your children to make important decisions, they'll be indecisive or make poor decisions the rest of their lives. We have seen this often in work with students in distress. Raised by autocratic, unengaged or permissive parents, they spend their first term or year at university doing all the things they were never allowed to do (or discuss), sometimes with disastrous results. Or they try to feel more in control (when everything is new and suddenly no parental rules exist) through risk taking, isolating themselves or failing to meet deadlines.

Of course, when your children become adults, you make another adjustment in your parenting. After all, your 33-year-old daughter isn't likely to thank you for trying to make her choices for her. Continue to be interested in her welfare, but be available as a consultant or listening ear, and supportive of her efforts to succeed in life. When it comes to telling your 'child' what to do – forget about it!

The most effective parents are the ones who know when and how to move from one parenting style to another and adapt as their children grow up.

Try getting together as a couple or family. Ask each person to write down the style she believes fits each parent (including yourself as a parent). Is there agreement or not? Let each person give examples of why they rated each parent the way they did. Don't comment until everyone has had her say, and then open the floor for general discussion. Remember not to get defensive – that defeats the whole purpose of the exercise. You may be surprised by what you discover.

Electronic games and anger

Social psychologists demonstrated as early as the 1960s that children who witness someone being violent to another human (or objects) are more likely to copy and learn this behaviour. One thing families can do to minimise angry, aggressive behaviour in their children is to restrict the amount of time they see or play with violent or destructive video or computer games. This is now an increasing and serious problem as computer and online gaming becomes the norm for most children. The numbers of those – particularly adolescents and young adults – needing help with obsessive or addictive behaviour patterns linked to gaming are increasing fast. This problem isn't just a myth! These same children and young adults have poorer people skills, few close relationships, difficulties with motivation or time management, and physical effects of lack of exercise, sunlight and sleep disturbance.

The Power of One Small Step

When you want to make important changes in your life, think small. Beginning today, commit yourself to doing one – and only one – thing to manage anger better at home. It really doesn't matter what that one thing is, as long as it has some potential for creating family happiness and harmony and you're willing to stick with it long enough to see some change. In the following sections we give you some places to start.

One meal a day

Psychologists repeatedly find that families who share one meal a day together get along better than families who don't. Granted, getting everyone in the family together in one spot, at one time, can be hard work – but there's no mistaking the fact that it's a key to family unity and a feeling of connectedness between family members.

Sharing a meal together isn't just about food – it's about community. It's a time when the family members or couple can:

- ✔ Express ideas and emotions
- ✔ Get things off their chest
- ✔ Have spiritual time together
- ✔ Learn about family history
- ✔ Negotiate changes in family rules

✔ Plan future events

✔ Praise each other for achievements

✔ See things from the other person's perspective

✔ Share a positive moment

✔ Talk about current events

Family members won't be likely to drift away and become isolated – and thus become strangers – when they interact with one another in this intimate for-members-only way on a daily basis. And there's less likelihood of harmful anger happening where people know one another in the way that daily meal sharing allows.

One evening a week

Try sharing one evening a week with your partner. You can accomplish the same things you do by eating one meal a day together – only in more depth. You can use this time to address unresolved worries or problems – or just enjoy each other's company.

CASE STUDY

Opening up with family meetings

Rudy came to see Dr Gentry for anger-management support because he was being abusive to his family. He has started having family meetings once a week to talk about his anger and its impact on everyone else in his family. These evenings are difficult for Rudy because for many years he denied that he had a problem with anger. It's also hard for him because he has inflicted so much emotional harm on his wife and kids.

Rudy began the first family meeting by admitting to everyone that he has a problem with anger and by sharing what he's learning about himself in treatment. His teenage son opened up about how afraid he has been of Rudy his whole life and how that has forced him to connect only with his mother. The son went on to say how he

and his sister are constantly on guard whenever Rudy is around and how tense and frightened they become when they realise their dad will be coming home soon. Finally, his wife shared how she has hidden things from her husband all of their married life – important things, personal things – for fear that he'd erupt in rage.

After two hours of intense family discussion, Rudy was reduced to tears and had a profound sense of remorse. 'Good,' Dr Gentry told him. 'You *should* feel sad about using your anger all these years to hurt the people you love – and that's your reason to stick with the anger-management programme.' Facing up to his problem and allowing his family to speak out is probably the greatest gift Rudy has ever given his family – or himself.

One day a month

Spending one day a month together as a family isn't a lot to ask, in return for a healthier family climate – it's only three per cent of the year! This day can be the time when the family gets out and ventures off into some new area of interest or experience – for example, river rafting, visiting a local museum, hiking, taking a cycling trip or going to watch a match.

Take it in turns to choose what the family will do – remember, enjoying time together doesn't have to be expensive (you can look on the Web for local free events) and should be something that everyone can take part in.

Alternatively, you could just make time to stop doing what you usually get caught up in. Try having a day without phones, computers or other interruptions. How can you hope for a good atmosphere if you don't all spend time making it?

Enjoy the time together, because happiness is the emotional opposite of anger!

One week a year

Families who holiday together benefit from the time to revive family ties, cement relationships, reconnect to their biological roots and remember all the many good times they've had over the years. Holiday time reminds you that, no matter how busy your life throughout the remainder of the year, you're never really alone – your family is there to support you. One week a year may be a holiday away together, or spending time at Christmas, public holidays or festivals meeting up and catching up. It's a time when the past, present and future come together, offering you the chance to appreciate the closeness that family has brought to your life.

Making it work

What can you do if poor anger management is causing you difficulties with someone you love? Your partner or spouse is probably no happier than you are about this.

Here we give you some ideas for ways to get started:

✔ **Don't devalue your partner's point of view.** Being scornful, judgemental or dismissive doesn't help you both to make any progress. Healthy anger management in families and couples is about valuing the differences between people. If you were both identical, how interesting would life *really* be? The views and ideas of the person you love and are closest to can change your life, bringing new ideas and experiences and offering something you've never had before.

Closeness as a couple

Many people who haven't struggled with anger management over their life suddenly find themselves in difficulties when they start a relationship with a partner, move in together or get married. Many of the clients we see with anger-management problems describe intense irritation with a partner, or repetitive arguments, or physical fights. This level of threat — inside your home — can be a recipe for raised adrenaline levels and physical tension that's fuel to any daily stresses or big differences of opinion between you and your partner.

This problem may relate to the styles of parenting each of the partners experienced as a child —

if one partner comes from a high-conflict home, the other can find herself 'pulled in' to behaviour patterns she doesn't recognise and doesn't like. Equally, it can relate to an unsolvable issue (one partner wants children and the other doesn't) that, perhaps, needed more discussion and agreement before the couple made a commitment. Most often, however, it seems to us that both people forget, amid all the other demands on them, that starting a new family unit (even just two people) takes time, discussion and compromise. Closeness, time together and talking strengthened the bond each felt when they met.

✔ **Give your partner time to speak.** Arguing, shouting and violence aren't okay. Even if you rule out the relationship at home, this behaviour is very likely to be unpopular with the world at large, and may even get you into trouble with the law. You may feel that you need to take control, and this is your way of doing so, but the truth is, you feel out of control of your relationship when these problems keep on cropping up.

Rather than both trying to make your point over the top of the other, take it in turns. Use an egg timer to give you each a turn to speak. You can speak for as long as you have the timer and there's still time left. Whatever you're saying when it runs out, and however important it is to you, pass the timer over and listen. Learning to take turns stops the build-up of anger and helps you to focus on listening and replying to what's said. You don't have enough time to rage about the situation – you're trying to get your point across! When you get used to this exercise, you can continue to use it while you talk through and plan how to solve the trigger to your argument.

✔ **Make a plan together.** With a sense of common goals, a couple can start to pay attention to how they can overcome problems in the way of those goals. Arguing about the same things over and over? You're using energy having the first part of an exchange of views, but not following it through to reach an answer you can both live with. Getting involved in terrible rows that leave you exhausted and upset? There's probably very little listening going on. The secret is to make a decision to find a way you can solve problems, before they come up. Then try sticking to the formula or blueprint you made together. For example, if you need time away to calm down, take it, but tell your partner how long you need. Agree before any tension starts how you'll handle it, and start to make the changes you're working on.

✔ **Make time to talk.** No one knows what other people are thinking. You may tell yourself that you do, but it's nonsense. How can you know someone's thoughts, feelings and beliefs? You can make assumptions, and many people (particularly those from homes where there was disinterest in feelings or suppression of negative emotions) do this. But assumptions are almost always faulty. Try spending time with a person somewhere quiet, and being curious. Ask, but don't react. You aren't trying to sort out the problem at this stage, you're just getting a clear picture of how the person feels and why. Knowing what she'd like may give you both a way forward that you couldn't see before.

✔ **Say only what you mean.** People who hurl insults or say things they don't mean (in other words, things they wouldn't say if they weren't angry and uncontrolled) find that they can be left with two problems, rather than just the original one. You can't solve the cause, or trigger, for the anger this way. And now your partner feels hurt, uncertain or angry too at what you said. How does your partner know that you 'don't mean it'? Your words are a major part of how you communicate with the world. They're how others know what you think and what you want. If you really don't mean something, how does the person you're speaking to know what else you mean and what you don't? This is a recipe for constant tension and argument.

✔ **Ask yourself what you liked about your partner when you first became a couple.** Very often this is the same thing that causes tension for a couple later on! Perhaps you liked your partner's carefree, easygoing attitude to life. Now you battle with her lack of interest in looking for a better job with more pay, or perhaps she spends all her money on her favourite hobby and doesn't think about sharing the costs of living as a family. As you spend time together, try to remember that you value this quality in your partner, but work out together how she can keep this spirit in balance with the changes in responsibility in her life.

For more guidance, ideas and tips, take a look at Paula Hall's *Improving Your Relationship For Dummies* (Wiley).

Part VI
The Part of Tens

'And then, suddenly, the Easter Islanders
discovered anger management.'

In this part . . .

We offer ten ways to empower your children to effectively manage their angry feelings without resorting to punishment. We provide ten simple thoughts you can keep in mind at all times to eliminate harmful anger and help you find inner peace. We also give you ten anger-freeing actions you can try today.

Chapter 21

Ten Ways to Raise a Child to Have Healthy Anger Control

In This Chapter
▶ Being a positive role model
▶ Becoming a successful parent
▶ Teaching children to share the world
▶ Understanding tough love

*B*eing a parent is no easy job, especially when it comes to your child's emotional development. All children start out life angry. If you're a parent, you know all too well the angry cry that your baby lets out when he's hungry, lonely or in pain. Anger is his way of telling you, without using words, 'I need something!' The louder the cry, obviously, the stronger and more urgent the need. Your job – at least as your baby sees it – is to satisfy that need, whatever it is. You are – like it or not – the key to managing your baby's anger. But if you try the techniques in this chapter, that won't always be the case.

In this chapter we show you ten ways to give that responsibility for managing anger to your child – much the same as you teach him to ride a bike, play football or read. You discover how to be his emotional coach – showing him the rules for expressing his anger healthily and teaching him the skills he needs to be successful in this important area of his life. Think of it this way: if you help your child manage his anger while he's still a kid, he won't need this book when he's a grown-up!

This book is all about anger *management*. If you're looking to stop your child from being angry or showing anger, you're trying to stop a natural human emotion that has benefits as well as drawbacks for your health, relationships and life (see Chapters 1 and 3 for more).

Being an Emotional Coach

You love your child, you care about his wellbeing and you want him to be successful in life. Unfortunately, just loving your child doesn't mean you're feeling ready to be an emotional coach. Don't worry: you can be a great coach for him. Try keeping the following tips in mind:

✔ **Make raising a healthily angry child, who will grow into an emotionally balanced and wise adult, a primary goal.** Most parents have goals for their kids, but these goals tend to have more to do with education, success, sports or being popular than they do with personal qualities or emotional balance. Many parents assume the last two will come naturally – unfortunately, that's wrong. Make raising a healthily angry child a part of your job as a parent from day one. Keep it in mind at all times – even when you're frustrated and ready to tear your hair out!

✔ **Be active and get involved when you're with your child.** Can you imagine a football coach who sits quietly and lets his players work out how to play the game all by themselves, without any instruction or practice? Of course you can't. So how in the world can your child learn to manage complex emotions like anger on his own? He can't and he won't! Coaching requires active involvement from you. Your child needs your support, your guidance, your wisdom, your knowledge, your patience, your acceptance and your skills. Coaching is not about being hands-off (overindulgent and inattentive) or indifferent (emotionally detached).

Talk openly with your child about feelings – including anger – and help him understand that emotions are a normal part of being human. This helps your child to learn words for feelings, something he'll need all his life. You can use the information in Chapter 2 to help your child appreciate different levels of anger (irritation versus anger or rage). Find ways to show your child the difference between *being* hurt (an emotion) and *doing* hurt or harm (a behaviour) to himself or others. And then make it absolutely clear that the first is okay, but the second is not.

✔ **Be proactive.** Typically, parents wait for children to misbehave – for example, throwing a temper tantrum in a shop – and then they punish them afterwards. This style of parenting is about reacting: 'You were terrible in the shop, go to your room for the rest of the day.' Coaching is proactive; it's all about thinking ahead. For example, when you're about to enter a shop, you remind your child, 'We're about to go into the shop. Remember the rules we've talked about? Make sure I can always see where you are, don't run off and if I say you can't have something and you get upset you can tell me how you feel instead of kicking and screaming. If you don't follow the rules, we'll go straight home. But if you behave yourself, we'll go to the park afterwards and play on the swings! Okay?' That's being proactive.

✔ **Accentuate the positive.** With angry clients we not only show them what *not* to do when they become angry – interrupt, point, threaten, swear, break things – we offer them a list of positive behaviours that involve self-restraint. That's coaching!

Reward your child – with praise, not sweets – when he asks for something rather than demands it. Teach him how to consider others and then reward him when he shows you that he's learned that lesson. Make clear the importance of apologising when you've acted badly – teaching your child to say 'I'm sorry' is teaching him to take responsibility for his own behaviour.

✔ **Focus on solutions rather than problems.** Children don't need adults to tell them they have problems; what they need (and desperately want) is for someone to tell them what to *do* about those problems. Saying to an angry kid, 'Stop yelling – you're upsetting everybody', doesn't address his problem (whatever caused the outburst). Telling him to stop yelling also doesn't provide him with another option that goes beyond simply showing rage.

Instead, try saying to your son, 'I can tell by how angry you are that you're having a problem. It would help if you could calm down a little so I can understand what the problem is – then maybe I can help you. I'm sure it's something that we can work out if you can turn your anger into energy and words. Now, what were you trying to tell me?'

CASE STUDY

Finding a win–win solution

For years Frank and his daughter would get into angry exchanges as soon as he walked into the house after a long day. He'd ask, 'How are you?' She'd ignore him, or reply irritably, 'What do you think?' Frank would react badly and they'd be arguing again.

One day Frank decided he didn't want to play this game any more, so – as the parent – he took responsibility for finding a way out of this no-win situation. He realised that he and his daughter were both trying to achieve the same end – to have the last word. As she was younger, Frank knew his daughter had more energy to fight her way to the finish, but less wisdom and willingness to change than he had. Neither of them was winning by arguing; instead they were living with constant stress and a tense atmosphere.

From that day forward, Frank decided to let his daughter have the last word (win). He felt in control by deciding when that was (win). He chose to bring the arguing to an end as soon as he saw the conversation heading down the wrong road. He let his daughter know that he didn't want to fight but was interested in what she wanted to say. Then Frank took a few minutes for himself, before coming back to the conversation. And his daughter stopped picking fights and started to answer him.

In calmer moments Frank made sure his daughter got the coaching lesson by explaining to her that anger only causes anger, whereas cooler heads get better results whenever there's a conflict. They'd found a win–win solution that brought benefits to them both.

Children who start out life more impulsive and excitable are more difficult to coach and need more effort from you (read: tough love) than those whose personalities are more thoughtful and calm. You may have several children and can see the differences in their temperaments.

Starting Early and Talking Back

It's never too early to begin raising a non-angry child. The emotional conversation between parents and children begins when children are around three months of age, when infants start 'speaking out' through emotions about what they want. That's when you need to start talking back. Children are smarter than you think – they respond to comforting words ('You're upset, I know, but it's okay') and a comforting tone, long before they learn to talk. (See Chapter 5 for a discussion of the importance of 'toning it down'.)

Your calm words and calm tone tell your child that you're comfortable with emotion – yours and his. The last thing you want to teach your child is that you're afraid of his anger. That will either cause him to suppress his feelings (in an effort not to upset you) or teach him to misuse anger as a means of controlling you and everyone else around him. Rather than emotional maturity, these lessons teach a passive style of aggression that's unhealthy for your child and for you.

We're not saying that any of this is easy. You may be reading this chapter for your child, or because you can recognise your own anger and don't want to pass the same style on. But the early years, until around seven or eight, are so important. It takes many times more effort and coaching skill to see improvement in an angry teenager. Those first few years are a window of opportunity – they're so valuable.

Creating Educating Moments

Don't wait for situations to come up that anger your child. Take the initiative and create opportunities so that he can learn to cope with negative feelings – we call these *teachable moments*. Here are some possibilities – choose one and give it a try:

- ✔ **Play a game with your child and don't just let him win.** When he loses ask him, 'How do you feel when you lose? How do you think other people feel when they lose? Do you think they might feel the same? What do you think we should do with your angry feelings? What do you think we should do about other people's angry feelings?' No right or wrong answers exist here. The point is just to get a conversation going between you and your child so that you can both start thinking about anger and how to manage it when it happens.

✔ **Talk about a situation with your child that involves the breaking of some moral principle – fair play or honesty.** Ask him how he thinks the person who's being treated unfairly, or lied to, feels. Does he think that person would feel angry? Does he think the other person has a reason to feel angry? Ask the child what he thinks should be done about these feelings. For example, what if your child's older sister took something of his and then lied and said she didn't take it? Could he just let the feeling go and play with something else?

✔ **Ask your child to pretend that a boy his age is angry and tries to hurt someone else's feelings.** What would he say to the other child to hurt him? Ask your child, 'How do you think his angry words would make him feel? How would you feel after you said those angry words? Are you sure you want to hurt someone just because you feel angry?'

Children's books about anger are great coaching aides. Typically, they contain one or two lessons about how to manage anger (for example, you'll get over being angry when you find something to enjoy or you'll stop being angry when you find something to do that parents can say yes to, rather than no).

Being a Positive Role Model

When we work with angry adolescents we ask them, 'Who else in your family is as angry as you are?' Without fail, they immediately identify one or both of their parents – most often their father.

You can't teach what you can't do! If you can't control your own temper, how can you expect you child to? Like it or not, you're your kid's primary role model, good or bad, during his early years. So, when it comes to coaching, you have to start with yourself.

If you're unsure whether you're a good emotional role model, ask yourself the following questions:

✔ Do you get irritated or angry at least once a day?

✔ Would you rate the intensity of your anger 7 or above on a 10-point scale?

✔ When you're angry do you stay that way for more than 30 minutes?

✔ Have you ever pushed, shoved or hit someone in anger?

✔ Have you ever threatened or sworn at someone in anger?

✔ Would you say you're angrier than many people you know?

✔ Do your loved ones seem to worry about your temper?

✔ Have you ever lost a job because of your temper?

✔ Have you ever lost a friend because of your temper?

✔ Have you ever spent money repairing something because of your temper?

If you answered yes to more than one of these questions, you may know that you're not the best role model for how to handle anger well. But look at the positive side: managing anger can be a learning experience for both you *and* your child. You can learn as you teach.

Adults who do *not* have a bad temper tend to remember their parents as being loving, warm, close, easygoing, calm and relaxed. Many of our clients with good anger-management skills also remember their parents and others talking through problems. As well as being listened to, adults taught the child to think of a range of possible ways to deal with irritations and difficulties. If you want your child to grow up to be an adult without a bad temper, aim to be affectionate, listen and stay calm, and you're on the right path.

Psychological research shows that healthy children have had 'good enough' parenting. That is, they have parents who got it right most of the time, enough for their child to understand the best way – and some of the other options – for dealing with anger (and stress). You don't have to be perfect, you just need to be trying to reach your goal.

I heard you

Some years ago a colleague was asked to make a community presentation called 'Dealing with the Angry Child' as part of a larger programme aimed at helping parents cope with their kids' attention deficit-hyperactivity disorder (ADHD), drug use and problems at school. To his surprise, the room was packed with distressed-looking parents, all of whom seemed eager to hear what he had to say.

As he spoke, he paid particular attention to one man who stared at him continuously throughout the presentation with a serious and rather hostile expression on his face. Afterwards, as parents stopped to thank our colleague, the man passed by without comment, his expression unchanged.

Several days later our colleague was in a garage. Another car pulled up and the man he'd seen at the presentation said loudly, 'Doc, I heard what you said – you know, about angry children having angry parents and how we should look at ourselves as well as our children. I went home and thought about that and decided you're right. I'm working on my anger before I can help my son with his. Thanks.'

Who'd have thought he'd get the message?

Putting the 'I' in Emotion

Always correct your child when he says something like, 'He made me angry.' Instead, teach him to say, '*I* got angry when he . . .' This is what self-control is all about – taking responsibility for your own feelings. Until your son learns that no one else can *make* him angry, he won't achieve emotional balance. Children need to understand as early as possible that no one has the power to make them feel anything – not fear, not anger, not sadness, not pride, not even joy. Feelings are your own response to others and to situations – you can't always choose the situation, but you can choose your response.

As your child's coach, try to express your emotions the same way. For example '*I* get frustrated when you don't answer me,' and not 'You make me angry when you ignore me.'

Labelling Feelings Appropriately

Before your child can express his feelings in an appropriate and constructive way he needs an emotional vocabulary. You need to teach him to describe – as clearly as possible – how he feels and then help him find the right label to fit that emotion.

Young children are often unable to differentiate emotions, except to say 'I feel bad' or 'I feel good.' Young children and those with few emotion words or a repressive family approach to anger often complain of tummy ache or headaches instead. Your job is to help your child find plenty of words to describe the different levels of those feelings and to be able to problem solve by coming up with more than one way of dealing with a situation. This way, a way out of unhealthy anger always exists.

Consider the following conversation between a mother and her five-year-old son:

> **Mother:** Darling, is something wrong?
>
> **Five-year-old:** I don't feel good.
>
> **Mother:** Do you mean you're ill? Or are you upset about something?
>
> **Five-year-old:** I don't like it.
>
> **Mother:** Okay, tell Mummy what you don't like?
>
> **Five-year-old:** I don't like this silly puzzle. I can't make it fit.
>
> **Mother:** So, you're annoyed. You feel angry because you can't make the pieces fit.

Five-year-old: Yeah, I don't like that silly puzzle.

Mother: I understand. Sometimes we get angry when we can't make something work. Sometimes I feel the same way you do.

As your child gets a little older, you need to teach him the difference between different levels of anger – mild, moderate and severe. An easy way to do this is to help him draw faces showing rage, anger and irritation, or to use a scale from 1 to 10 (more about this in Chapters 2 and 6). A rating of 1 to 3 equals irritation, 4 to 7 equals anger, and 8 and above equals rage. If your son rates his anger as an 8, you can say, 'Darling, you're not just angry, you're in a rage. Why are you that angry?' You need to really want to know – you aren't trying to tell him off with your tone of voice or expression.

Identifying Causes

Don't be satisfied with having your child identify what he's feeling; ask him *why* he's feeling that way. At first, identifying the cause of their anger can be difficult for children – it's difficult even for adults – because they aren't used to tying their emotional reactions to what's going on around them at the time.

Your child may feel anger because:

✔ **Someone (or something) has hurt his self-esteem.** Children often become angry when someone criticises, puts down or otherwise attacks their self-esteem. If someone – including you – calls your child 'stupid' or 'an idiot', he'll probably feel angry. He may also feel angry when he fails at something (for example, he fails a spelling test at school); he may say something like, 'The teacher thinks I'm thick!'

✔ **He's gone through some kind of physical abuse.** Children get angry when they're physically attacked – hit, shoved, pushed – or even when they're threatened by the possibility of being harmed in some way. (This is their 'fight-or-flight' response.) It doesn't have to be an adult harming your child for it to be abuse. Children spend a lot of time with other children, and bullying in the playground or from siblings is threatening to your child.

✔ **He's not getting something he wants.** All children want things in life, and learning how to handle their feelings when they don't get what they want, or when they want it, is an essential life lesson for them. When they're prevented from achieving or obtaining those things, they become frustrated and often angry. Anger is their way of protesting, their way of saying, 'I'm not getting what I want!' Your child's anger – just as likely to be expressed through sulking as rage – can be especially intense if he feels he has the right to the thing in question or if he's the type of child who has difficulty in waiting ('I want what I want *now*!').

Don't tell me how I feel!

Thirteen-year-old Jennifer was in a bad mood as she sat in the kitchen watching her mother make dinner. Trying to help, her mother said, 'You don't have to be so irritable. I know you're tired and hungry. Supper will be ready shortly.' Jennifer exploded. 'Don't tell me how I feel! *I* know how I feel – *you* don't!' Was she right? Absolutely. Did her mother mean well?

Absolutely. But her mother still should've asked whether Jennifer was upset, and if Jennifer said yes, her mother should've asked why. Then she should've left the rest of the conversation up to Jennifer. As it turned out, Jennifer wasn't tired or hungry – she was angry about something another girl had said to her that morning at school.

✔ **His moral principles (yes, he does have them) have been broken.** Just like adults, children have values and beliefs about how the world should work – the world should be fair, people should tell the truth, people should be kind to someone who's hurt. After all, this is the message adults and the world around them send to teach good behaviour. If the situation doesn't follow those values, children often get angry – saying 'That's not fair!', 'You're fibbing!' or 'Leave him alone – you're being nasty.'

✔ **He feels helpless.** Children are very likely to get angry in situations in which they feel out of control, helpless, frightened and vulnerable. They may, for example, get angry when their parents fight a lot because they're afraid that one parent will hurt the other or the family will break up. Adolescents may become very angry when a fellow student commits suicide or dies of cancer – things over which they have absolutely no control.

You may often *think* you know why your child is angry or upset, but most of the time you're wrong. Don't assume. Ask.

Teaching Problem Solving

Children have trouble coping with emotion. Coping is a skill that your child has to learn – and you can be a huge help to your child when it comes to learning coping skills.

Your child needs help dealing with the *feelings* themselves, as well as the *causes*. You can begin by asking your child 'What do you think we should do when you feel angry?' or 'What is it that you're angry about?'

If you start by focusing on the feeling itself, you can try to help your child choose from a number of strategies that work:

✔ Distracting himself (shifting his focus onto something else, preferably something positive)

✔ Creating some distance from the angry situation (going for a walk or out to play)

✔ Relaxing away the tension he feels (taking deep breaths)

✔ Changing his emotional tone (laughing)

✔ Using his imagination to find a safe place in his mind to get away from his anger

If you decide to focus on what *caused* his anger, help him to consider strategies such as:

✔ Telling the person he's angry with (in a non-aggressive way)

✔ Talking about his feelings about that other person with someone he trusts

✔ Accepting the fact that some things can't be changed

✔ Changing how he looks at the other person's behaviour

✔ Giving in and doing what the other person asks

✔ Asking for help in dealing with the problem

Teaching your child to let out his anger by shouting or hitting something like a punch bag or a pillow might provide some temporary relief, but is really only suitable for extreme situations, such as dealing with the early stages of grief. In the long run, it only leads to more anger and ultimately to an increase in aggressive behaviour (as it becomes a habit).

Choosing the Third Alternative

It's human nature that everyone starts out life – as babies and young children – reacting to their own anger by either fleeing or fighting. The *fight-or-flight response* is part of our biological reaction to all kinds of threat. *Flight* means simply that a child runs away from the source of his anger (and the anger itself) and chooses not to deal with it or actively suppresses it. *Fight* means exactly that – the child attacks the source of his anger directly, either physically or verbally.

In a study of primary school children, 26 per cent said they'd just 'walk away' when confronted with another child's anger and try to avoid the situation altogether. Forty-five per cent fought back – answering anger with anger. And 29 per cent indicated they'd 'walk away initially, but return later to discuss the problem' – that's the third alternative, the one that we recommend.

Understanding the Difference Between Wanting and Getting

It's normal – in fact, it's completely healthy – to want things in life. But children need to be taught as early as possible the difference between *wanting* something and *getting* it. This important distinction is especially hard for young children to grasp and that's where you – the parent – come in. Spoiling a child basically means that you teach the child what he wants, he gets, always. Spoiled children have a fierce sense of deserving things ('I'm special, I'm powerful and no one can tell me no'), which quickly leads to anger when their wants aren't immediately satisfied.

Here's an example from one of the author Gill's clients. Jane, a wife and mother of two, was going out for tea with her family. They arrived at the fast-food restaurant, and her husband and son ordered the food while Jane and her daughter went to get a table. Her daughter went straight to a table by the window, but Jane said, 'Let's sit over here. The sun's too bright there.' Her daughter exploded, angrily shouting, 'I'm sitting here. I want to be in the sun. You can sit where you want!' Without a word, Jane – head down with a look of defeat on her face – moved to the table by the window. When her husband came with the food he asked Jane, 'Why are you sitting here? It's too hot in the sun.' Jane replied – head still down – 'Just sit here. Let's not have an argument.'

Do your child a big favour – say *no* once in a while. Your child is going to school, to play with other children, to compete. Eventually, your child will hear 'no' from someone, and he needs to know how to respond when he doesn't get his way. You can't coach if you're not there! Try to introduce your child to this early. If you don't get a good reaction the first time, stay calm and firm. You're teaching your child skills to last his whole life.

Chapter 22

Ten Anger-Freeing Thoughts

*A*nger management is a case of mind over matter – what you have in your mind matters. It spells the difference between being full of anger versus anger-free. In this chapter we offer you ten thoughts that help you manage anger – yesterday, today and tomorrow.

No One – Absolutely No One – Can Make You Angry Without Your Consent

Every time we hear (and we hear it a lot!) someone say 'She made me angry,' we want to tell the person how completely untrue this is. When people say that, it's their way of trying to make other people responsible for their emotions. No circumstance, person or event has that power over you. You aren't a car that can be started by another person's key. You're the only one who has the control.

What *is* true is that external events can (and do) provide you with chances to become angry. Unfortunately, people take this chance all too readily. But you can, if you want, choose not to lose your temper. The decision is yours.

The next time – and there will be a next time – you find yourself facing an opportunity to become angry, remember this comforting thought: no one can make you angry – no matter how hard she tries – unless you decide to let her.

Anger Comes Back to You – And So Does Love

You've probably heard numerous sayings like 'What goes around comes around' and 'You reap what you sow.' Annoying as those sayings may be, they do serve a purpose: they remind you that life is a two-way street. Human emotion has a certain reciprocity; in other words, anger invites anger, fear brings on fear and one act of kindness is often paid back by another. People respond in kind to whatever you throw out there. Throw out anger and you get back anger. Throw out love and you get back love. Emotions work just like a boomerang.

If you want others to treat you positively, begin each day by asking yourself the following questions:

- ✔ Who can I show I care about?
- ✔ Who needs my understanding, not my judgement?
- ✔ How many kind remarks can I offer others today?
- ✔ Is there someone who needs my sympathy?
- ✔ How many people can I hug before the sun goes down?
- ✔ How often can I say *please* and *thank you*?
- ✔ How much happiness can I bring by smiling?

In this frame of mind, it's very difficult for you to get angry.

It's Only Money

The whole world is one giant, global economy. In the end, whether you realise it or not, most things come down to money – money gained and money lost. Far too often you may find yourself upset – angry – because something goes wrong and it has a financial cost. If the cost is minimal, you get irritated. If the cost is more than you can (or want to) bear, you can fly into a rage.

What you need to consider, however, is that it's only money. It's not the end of the world or civilization as you know it. Your life isn't ruined for ever. It's only money. The underlying reason for your reaction may be about your feelings, of course. Money gives you choice, and control. Losing these can feel like a loss of safety or a threat to your survival. Being deceived or cheated breaks principles of fairness and honesty – threats to your trust or faith in others. Now it's easier to understand why money can trigger rage!

Years ago, when the author Dr Gentry was less successful at managing anger than he is now, he used to get mad when one of his daughters called to say she had been involved in an car accident (yes, the prangs were fairly common occurrences). Dr Gentry's first thought – he's sorry to say – was, 'How much is that going to cost?' And Dr Gentry's first question to his daughter was, 'How's the car? How much damage is there? Is it drivable?' (Interestingly, this is exactly how Dr Gentry's father used to react when one of *his* kids had an accident.) Then one day it hit him: the more important question – the one Dr Gentry should be asking – is 'Are you okay? Are you hurt? How are you?' The rest is only a matter of money and metal!

It's all about priorities. What Dr Gentry discovered was that his love and concern for his children was far more important than the 'cost' of *anything*.

Other People Are Not the Enemy

From the biological survival perspective, anger serves a purpose. It's a means to an end – survival. Emotions are built into your nervous system to help you adapt to life so that you can live long and well. Anger has a single purpose – to protect you from your enemies, those who threaten your existence. But who are these enemies and how many do you have?

If your daughter comes home with a 'D' in her school report, is she your enemy? Is her teacher? If your wife isn't as interested in sex as you'd like her to be, is she your enemy? If someone ahead of you in the express-checkout line at the supermarket has 11 items rather than 10, is she your enemy? Is everyone who gets in your way, inconveniences you or beats you to promotion your enemy? If so then you're going to be angry a lot!

Reserve the status of 'enemy' for those people who truly threaten your physical safety or emotional health. Think of the rest of them as *people* – son, daughter, spouse, stranger, person who doesn't see fit to obey the rules in the queue – not enemies. Unless the lady in the queue pulls out a gun and asks you for your wallet, she's just an annoying person, not an enemy – and not worth getting angry over.

Life Isn't Fair – Not Even at the Top

Sometimes humans are funny creatures. When life goes the way you want it to, you call that fair. When it doesn't, you call that unfair. You decide what's fair and what's unfair. In other words, you're the ultimate judge. How you think about what happens to you is what determines how angry you get. Every time you think 'unfair', there's the anger!

We ask you the question we often ask ourselves: 'Is it fair that a close friend has a healthy daughter while another looks after her chronically ill child?' Our argument: having healthy children is no fairer than having unhealthy children. The difference is in your mind. And no one ever gets angry because life is fair in a way that favours her.

Maybe the answer is to stop thinking about whether what comes your way today is fair or unfair and just deal with it as best you can – without being judgemental, which is where the anger comes in. Try it.

Be grateful even when life doesn't go the way you want it to. You still have a lot to be glad about, other things to aim for. People who make a success of their life – whatever they have – are more likely to think 'As one door closes, another one opens.'

Energy Is a Terrible Thing to Waste

Each day, whatever energy you have is 100 per cent of your total fuel to run everything you need and want to do. It takes energy for you to be angry, it takes energy for you to stay angry and it takes energy for you to do all the things you do to express or get rid of anger. Too much anger can leave you utterly exhausted.

Are you sure you want to devote so much energy to one emotion – or, for that matter, to emotions in general? You don't have an unending supply of energy – you can use it up like any other resource. Where you spend your energy pretty much defines your day. If you put most of it into tasks, at the end of the day you feel productive. If you put most of it into anger, at the end of the day you're likely to feel angry, defeated, exhausted and unproductive. If you feel satisfied, what harm have you done to others?

As long as you're alive, you're spending energy on something. The question is, what are you spending it on? Is your energy working to benefit you – to improve your life – or is it simply wasted? You can choose where to put your energy.

Try to divide up the amount of energy you spend paying attention to your emotions, to doing (activities, jobs, tasks) and to thinking (concentrating, considering ideas, planning). Some days you naturally spend more on one area than another. But sometimes you need to make that choice deliberately, tuning out unhelpful areas that don't achieve what you really need. For example, you can choose not to cry when turned down for a job but instead use that energy to sit straight down and fill out another application form.

We're Only Human

The minute you forget that you're human just like everyone else, you're in trouble. Thinking of yourself as superior to other people is an open invitation to anger. Anger tends to flow downhill towards those you regard as inferior – sillier, less intelligent and less competent than you are. You tell yourself: 'They – the lesser people – deserve what they get when they make me angry.'

Besides anger, the second major cause of damaging behaviour in the workplace – malicious gossip, selfishness, theft – is what psychiatrists call *narcissism* (more about this in Chapter 19). The narcissistic employee is one who has a grandiose view of herself – she sees herself as 'special', someone whose opinions should carry more weight than those of others and feels that all the other employees are just there to cater to her needs.

The same is true in marriage. According to marriage experts, as soon as contempt enters the relationship and respect is lost, the marriage is doomed. Contempt goes along with a feeling of superiority and it goes way beyond ordinary criticism of your partner – the intent behind it is to put down, insult and psychologically hurt your so-called loved one.

Settle for just being ordinary. You're still unique. But being one of the human race means you can just relax. The playing field is level. Even if you have a competitive personality, it's now a competition and not a fight.

This Isn't the Time for War

Just as in war, as you struggle your way through life you have to decide which objectives – hills, goals or issues – are worth putting yourself on the line for, and which ones matter less. The more things matter – the more of an emotional investment you have in something – the angrier you get when things don't go your way. Constant anger does your health, your relationships and your choices no good. It pays to be selective in the battles you choose to fight.

Reserve the right to fight just one major battle a day, and live to fight another day!

There's Nothing You Can Achieve With Anger That You Can't Achieve Without It

You can use anger constructively in some instances (see Chapter 13), but anything you want to achieve in life can be yours without anger.

Somewhere along the line, people made a link between getting angry and getting things done. And now the anger comes automatically, when you're faced with obstacles, challenges, insults and problems. You think showing anger is vital to your day-to-day survival. It's not.

Try to remember the last time you got angry. What was the problem that led to you losing your temper? Could you have dealt with this problem in any other way, without needing to be angry? Be honest. Did your anger help or hinder your ability to resolve the problem? We suspect it was a hindrance.

When You're Dealing With People, You're Not Entitled to Anything!

If you discover one thing from reading this book that helps you manage anger better, we hope it's this: you don't *truly* have a right to anything. We believe that a sense of entitlement, and constant talk about rights, is a significant cause of anger in today's fast-moving, complex world.

According to the dictionary, an *entitlement* is anything you have legal claim to – like the title to a piece of property. Historically, it was something that English kings granted noblemen for their loyal service. And yet today, if you're like us, you apply the idea to just about every aspect of life. Developments in ideas around human rights have, of course, brought huge benefits to many. However, the truth is you're born with no rights to anything. Health, safety, love – these are all goals but are not guaranteed to us.

Here are some common examples of things you may have a false sense of entitlement to:

- A good night's sleep
- A husband, wife or partner who always agrees with you
- A promotion at work
- A stable economy

- A world where everything is fair
- Children who always do as they're told or expected to do
- Consideration from everyone, all the time
- Continuous employment
- Enough money
- Freedom from oppression
- Good health and a long life
- Having your ideas, beliefs and opinions valued by everyone
- Peace of mind
- The respect of others

The problem with a sense of entitlement is that it's full of 'should', 'ought' and 'must' demands. As you don't truly have rights to anything, you can't demand that others do what you want, need or expect. For example, you can't demand that your teenage kids will, without question, always do what you ask of them because *they owe you* that courtesy for bringing them into this world. What happens if they don't see it that way? Do you get angry?

Forget the entitlements and instead look for ways to earn, find or successfully create what you want (not demand) out of life – a pay rise, a promotion, respect, love or recognition. You'll find your way with much less anger.

Chapter 23

Ten Anger-Freeing Actions

*A*nger management is a case of one step at a time. Changing your behaviour may be easy to talk about, but how do you do it? Knowing ways to change your usual patterns of behaviour gives you choices. In this chapter we offer you ten practical ideas that help you manage angry behaviour – leaving behind old habits and creating your own style for life.

Counting to Ten

Many books and classes on anger management offer the advice, 'Just count to ten.' We don't know about you, but when we feel angry, just counting to ten doesn't help much. Your body doesn't feel less tense or geared up if you count to ten. You don't have better ideas about what to say next (you've been thinking about counting!). You don't appear any less angry to others around you because your mind isn't on altering your behaviour.

And yet, counting to ten does help:

✔ **Counting to ten makes you pause.** Just for a few moments, you aren't engaged in angry behaviour – shouting, threatening or storming off – because you're counting! Try to make good use of this pause. You have time to take a step back, now! So often, after an angry outburst, our clients wish they'd 'just taken a moment' or 'not just jumped in with both feet'. Remembering to count to ten can simply mean remembering to pause for long enough to step back.

- ✔ **Counting distracts you from the trigger for your anger.** Whether you're going over and over what you're angry about in your mind, standing up to push someone aside or about to say something you might regret, you have the chance to take a break and focus on something unconnected to anger.

- ✔ **Counting gives you a different focus to concentrate on.** Rather than noticing the pounding of your heart, or thoughts of revenge, you're doing a simple activity that's emotionally neutral – it doesn't make you feel either positive or negative. When you achieve this switch of emotional focus you're more likely to be able to manage what you spend your energy on.

Use this exercise like the pause button on your remote control. Take the count of ten to pay attention to your body. Feel where you're holding the anger, and let it go, and move your body so you move your mind. The following section contains tips you can use to relax and move during this time out.

This is a chance to stop and think, 'Do I want to do, or say, what I was just about to?' You've taken ten seconds out, but you can make it longer. You're free to let the other person know that you'd like to come back and talk about it later, giving you time to let your emotional system return to normal and to think about how you want to resolve the problem.

Coming Down from Anger, Fast

Healthy anger management is about reacting in proportion to the trigger, but it's also about making a quick recovery from your body's fight-or-flight state. Most people who want to find better ways to manage anger need to take steps to 'come down' from being worked up.

Try some of the following:

- ✔ **Change your physical position.** Stand up, move around, open a window to cool down. Sit down if it will relax you (standing over others raises their fight-or-flight reaction in return and makes things worse). Step back: anger often leads you to step into someone's personal space, increasing his anxiety or defences.

- ✔ **Deliberately distract yourself.** Do something that interests you that's unrelated to the reason you got angry. You're trying to steady your emotions.

✔ **Do something that's incompatible with anger.** Make a joke or find a lighter side to the situation (but not to put others down). Go and make a drink and take time out to drink it (though watch your caffeine intake: see Chapter 15). If you're caught up in road rage, change tactics – imagine you're on your driving test and think about *your* driving.

✔ **Do something energetic.** Use the physical arousal in your system to take a walk, a run, go to the gym or walk your dog. You can use the chemicals in your system that are preparing you for action to do something positive.

✔ **Use a relaxation technique.** Notice the signs of anger in your body, like muscle tension and feeling hot (see Chapters 1 and 2 for more), and let the tension in your body go, calming your breathing. Chapter 6 can help here. Try yoga, meditation, prayer or chanting. Practise regularly. Any process that brings your muscle tension, heart rate and breathing under your deliberate control gives you a huge advantage in managing your anger.

Letting Anger Evaporate

One of the most common myths about anger is that it has to escape – somehow! Anger is one of your normal emotions, just like happiness, sadness or excitement. It doesn't build up in the body like steam inside a kettle and need to be 'ventilated' – you aren't a machine! Anger disperses, just as the chemicals it produces in your body do. With time, the levels simply fall again. Unless you're fuelling the anger fire by sulking, being vengeful or keeping your own library of grudges, when anger's over, it's history.

Rather than looking for ways to 'vent' your anger:

✔ **Find something else to talk about.** You may think that you're getting rid of unwanted anger when you rant to your friend about your awful boss or brother-in-law. The truth is, you're just gearing your body back up for a second round.

✔ **Do as you were planning to do before you got angry.** Don't change your routine to bump into your boss again, planning to 'show him' this time. Stop yourself changing plans to continue a grudge. You have a busy life, with more important things to do than fight an old fight or carry a grievance.

✔ **Find a peaceful place.** Being in a situation or surroundings that bring a natural sense of calm to you automatically lowers your body's response to threat, allowing you time to think clearly and to feel as you do without having to manage how others see you. If you struggle to find peace, you need to give some attention to the balance in your life.

Treating Others As You Want to Be Treated

Sayings like 'You reap what you sow' and 'Do as you would be done by' carry an obvious message – people respond to each other in kind. How you treat others affects how they treat you. Go in furious and shouting and your boss will order you back to work without booking the holiday dates you wanted. Sound irritable and sulky with your partner and he's likely to switch off and ignore what you want him to hear.

Treating others as you'd like to be treated means keeping a check on your behaviour, particularly when you can anticipate that you may feel anger. Your body language, behaviour, tone of voice and choice of words all matter. To give yourself a head start, you can increase the number of times you're positive towards others. This builds up your own expectations, and theirs, about how you treat them and like to be treated.

If you're constantly irritated, very angry or in a rage, try to do something the person you're in conflict with will appreciate. Doing something kind, or helpful, or expected of you goes against your angry feelings – helping to steady you – and also sends a co-operative message to that person. You could finish the job you've been disagreeing with your boss about and meet your deadline. You could make your partner a cup of tea rather than choosing to continue the argument.

If you want others to treat you positively, try some of the following:

- Smile and greet your family, workmates and others who you see all the time but maybe don't make an effort with.

- Listen when your friend wants to tell you his troubles, without making your views on the subject obvious, unless you're asked.

- Thank someone who often gives you support, to let him know that you appreciate him.

- Show love to those close to you – don't just assume that they feel loved.

- Bring up something you're angry about calmly and clearly. Explain how you feel and suggest a possible answer. Then listen calmly to the other person and discuss a solution you can both accept.

Controlling Your Voice

We're sure you know people who let you know how they feel without actually saying it. One of the most obvious ways to do this is through the tone of your voice. Vocal tone is partly affected by the body's physical reaction to anger – tightening of the muscles also tightens the voice box and muscles around your ribs, affecting your breathing and speech. You can take control of this, taking time to breathe and listening to the pitch and volume of your voice. (See Chapter 5 for more.)

The way you choose to say things – sounding scornful, mistrustful and dismissive, or interested, accepting and calm – makes a big difference to the outcome of conversations. You may naturally find it difficult to talk about your anger – because you can't find the words, struggle to keep control of your emotions, or can't focus and remember what you want to say – but conversation is the primary way that humans resolve conflict. As anger kept in carries risks to your long-term health, choosing not to discuss anger isn't a positive solution. The efforts you make to manage positive conversation about your anger can turn into health benefits, as well as resolving problems you face.

Try the following tips:

- ✔ **Speak slowly.** The force of your feelings doesn't have to force words out of your mouth before you've thought about what you want to say.

- ✔ **Speak at your normal volume.** If you're in a noisy place, choose to move and find somewhere more suitable – it won't help if you're already shouting to be heard over traffic or the children.

- ✔ **Keep your tone level.** Paying attention to speaking calmly, firmly and without overwhelming emotion gives the other person no choice but to focus on the content (*what* you're saying), rather than on the delivery (*how* you're saying it).

Healthy anger management isn't about never being angry. Clients often tell us how frustrated they are that they can't change 'simple things', like tone of voice, easily and in a few weeks. Why should they? Habits take many years to develop. Each time you find that you slip up and don't manage to use these tips, see that as another opportunity to practise (*positive*), and not as another failure (*negative*). And practice makes perfect!

Minding Your Body Language

Humans make judgements very quickly about each other, based on first impressions and appearances. So you need to be aware of how you look to others, particularly when you feel angry.

Before you even start to speak, you may have spoken volumes! You're probably familiar with the idea of body language. The look on your face, any expressions you pull (such as raising your eyebrows), gestures with your hands (waving someone away, making a rude sign) and the posture of your body (defensively crossing your arms, standing over someone, slouching back and appearing not to care) all send signals to the world around you.

Try to focus on each element of body language in turn. Can you recognise how your body portrays your anger? Perhaps you clench your fists or your teeth? Maybe you find yourself invading others' space or walking off when you're angry? Now try to rewrite your habits by paying attention to your body language when you first feel signs of anger. Giving off signals of positive mood and willingness to listen become second nature with persistence.

Getting the Right Kind of Attention

We're sure that when you lose control of your anger, it's not your real goal. Instead, you may be trying to get someone to listen, to convince him to do as you want, perhaps to win the point or to keep your position of authority. Your anger is a way of demanding attention – to you, your view or your needs. When you're very angry, you *are* getting attention, but is it the kind you really want?

People who are composed when angry, who keep control of their feelings and are able to communicate without others feeling bad, often describe being able to keep a 'bird's-eye view' of the situation they're in. Instead of physical feelings linked to angry emotions taking over, they can also hold on to the point they're trying to make, the feelings and views of others, and their goal. People aren't born with this ability; they develop it as a life skill.

Picture having a video camera on your shoulder. Think of a recent situation in which your anger failed to get you a positive outcome. What would the camera have recorded? How did you react physically, how did you behave and what did you sound like? Did you make a clear point or confuse it with insults, swearing or personal remarks – all of which can be fuel to others' reactions? Did the situation end well (agreement to talk again, acceptance of your point of view) or badly (sulking, insults or physical aggression)? Use what you see as you review the camera footage to make a plan for the future – a blueprint for how you come across. Rerun and edit the tape, considering how you want to behave instead.

Healthy anger management is a life skill you learn, usually from those close to you early on in life. As you learn to manage your anger, you're also providing a better model for those around *you*. If you're going to draw attention, it might as well be the right kind of attention! The gains of managing anger well include the respect others develop for you, and the benefits of this to your reputation. Instead of being judged for what you have, you're respected for who you are – the qualities you have (loyalty, trustworthiness, kindness, co-operation) and how you treat others.

As you're looking for ways to manage your anger well, think of someone you admire (whether you know them personally or admire what they achieve) who manages his emotions well. How does your sporting hero manage his feelings when he wins? And when he loses? Put what you see of him in these situations to good use and adopt his style.

Putting the Brakes on Boozing

You know from the experience of seeing other people drunk that it distorts their view of their own behaviour. Drunk drivers insist that their judgement is fine. Slurred speech, forgetting or repeating conversations, loss of physical control, tearfulness, risk taking and aggression are all obvious to those who are sober, but the drunk person seems not to notice. Alcohol acts to reduce your inhibitions and to lower your guard, and is a natural mood depressant (see Chapter 15).

Make a note to yourself to deal with anything you're angry about when you're sober. Walk away from conflict if you've been drinking. If you forget what you were angry about when you're sober, maybe it wasn't that important!

Also take steps to compare your alcohol intake with the maximum recommended healthy limits (see Chapter 15). If you want further advice, information about alcohol is available from many local councils, pharmacists, charities and organisations such as Alcoholics Anonymous.

It's not just those people with an aggressive style of anger management who suffer the serious and negative effects of too much alcohol on their anger control. If you usually keep your anger hidden, you may find that you act 'out of character' when you've been drinking (although you're acting in tune with your hidden feelings). The disinhibiting effects of alcohol can release old grudges you may be holding, or unhappiness about something entirely different may trigger your anger and lead you to take it out on those around you when you're having a drink.

Accepting Apologies – And Making Them

What makes a difficult situation easier? What action can you take to defuse a situation? To manage anger you need to be able to say 'sorry' and accept apologies from others.

In the heat of the moment, just after you've dropped your friend's favourite mug and broken it, or been reminded of a deadline you've missed at work, your defences are likely to go up. The shock of making a mistake triggers your fight-or-flight response, even though fighting or running away would be an over-reaction to what's just happened. At the same time, your friend or boss is likely to react too – maybe with anger, upset or irritation. Chances are, you're really sorry. You didn't plan to make a mistake – it just happened.

Try saying sorry straight away. Before you explain yourself or defend yourself, make an apology. You may be amazed at how quickly 'sorry' can take the heat out of a situation. If you're the one whose feelings, property or business has been hurt, try accepting the apology – without going on to say all the things you first thought of!

Saying sorry means accepting that:

- ✔ You made a mistake or had an accident that you couldn't have avoided.

- ✔ You didn't think before you acted, were careless or forgetful.

- ✔ If you hadn't been involved in the situation, it would've gone differently.

- ✔ You're not saying sorry for everything you've ever done wrong or been blamed for (or even everything someone's holding you responsible for). You're apologising for what you feel you've done wrong, or the hurt you've caused, in *this* situation. Saying sorry doesn't mean you meant to cause harm; it means you regret that it happened.

To say sorry (and mean it) can be quite a switch from the feelings you had just a few moments earlier, and puts into practice some of the other tips in this chapter. But when you manage it, several positives can come out of it. You focus on your feelings of regret, rather than your shock, irritation or defensiveness (and although understandable, your reaction isn't the main point of the situation). This gives you the chance to accept responsibility, and to offer to put the matter right if that's possible. Being willing to apologise, accepting responsibility and offering to do something to help, along with being able to control your feelings – these are all signs of wisdom, self-control and healthy anger control.

Accepting an apology means stopping and taking in that:

✔ This isn't just a chance to vent anger (some of it stored up from past irritations).

✔ Being angry that the job isn't finished, or your favourite mug is broken (although understandable) doesn't fix the problem.

✔ The other person realises his mistake, wants you to know that he accepts he's in the wrong, and doesn't need to be pressured, shouted at or ignored for you to let him know just how upset you are. Just saying 'thanks' will do fine, if you know that saying more would tune you back into anger at this point.

✔ You're in the right in this situation – but that could change if you're ungracious, ignore the apology or lose control of your own anger. Then you're also in the wrong and need to apologise – a lose–lose, instead of a win–win.

Keeping Control for As Long As It Takes

You can deal with some situations that trigger anger quite quickly (see the example in the previous tip). Others, perhaps with your husband, child, close friend or workmate, may have more history or mean more to you than breaking a mug. Dealing with anger in those situations can mean a long conversation or several talks before everyone involved finds a solution they can live with. Keeping your cool while you turn away from insults, correct mistaken views or put your point across clearly is a skill that takes time to master. Longer conversation (or one in which the other person struggles to control his anger) can be hard, but you *can* manage your anger.

Start off dealing with anger through short conversations. Make a time plan and stick to it. When you want to stop, try suggesting that you come back to the matter when you both feel calmer. Gradually allow yourself to have longer conversations, where you need to keep constant control, even when new triggers occur.

Heading off conflict is a very useful skill in more complex situations and conversations. Try to use a range of ways to manage the situation – these can include:

✔ **Diverting an argument.** If you can see that you're headed for greater anger, return to the situation when you're both calmer, or step in and say sorry if you're in the wrong.

✔ **Not taking offence.** You don't have to react, particularly to personal remarks, insults or aggression. They're signs that the other person is struggling to manage his anger, and aren't an invitation to join in or add in other things to feel hurt about.

✔ **Knowing what you want to say.** Try to be clear about what you feel, but avoid making the other person responsible. Your feelings are yours. Your friend doesn't *make* you angry when he's late for work – you *feel* angry when he's late *because* you have to stay and cover his shift instead of going home to relax. Being clear avoids dragging up old grievances, and reduces the problem rather than enlarging it.

✔ **Accepting compromise.** No one gets his way in life all of the time. When you look for a way forward, it may be an answer or solution that you can live with, even though it's not perfect for you.

✔ **Accepting apologies.** In our experience, if you can't accept an apology politely and move on, you're very unlikely to be able to say sorry yourself. Both of these are equally important, because both defuse conflict.

Co-operation or conflict – it's just as hard for other people to practise healthy anger controls, so don't assume you're alone. If you're behaving badly, in a rage, aggressive or passive-aggressive (see Chapter 10), you've given up control of your anger. Ask yourself: why should you expect better from others? Respect begets respect.

Index

FOR DUMMIES®

Making Everything Easier! ™

UK editions

BUSINESS

978-0-470-74490-1

978-0-470-74381-2

978-0-470-71382-2

FINANCE

978-0-470-99280-7

978-0-470-71432-4

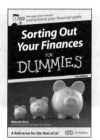

978-0-470-69515-9

HOBBIES

978-0-470-69960-7

978-0-470-74535-9

978-0-470-68178-7

British Sign Language
For Dummies
978-0-470-69477-0

Business NLP For Dummies
978-0-470-69757-3

Cognitive Behavioural Therapy For
Dummies
978-0-470-01838-5

Competitive Strategy For Dummies
978-0-470-77930-9

Cricket For Dummies
978-0-470-03454-5

CVs For Dummies, 2nd Edition
978-0-470-74491-8

Divorce For Dummies, 2nd Edition
978-0-470-74128-3

eBay.co.uk Business All-in-One
For Dummies
978-0-470-72125-4

Emotional Freedom Technique For
Dummies
978-0-470-75876-2

English Grammar For Dummies
978-0-470-05752-0

Flirting For Dummies
978-0-470-74259-4

Golf For Dummies
978-0-470-01811-8

Green Living For Dummies
978-0-470-06038-4

Hypnotherapy For Dummies
978-0-470-01930-6

IBS For Dummies
978-0-470-51737-6

Lean Six Sigma For Dummies
978-0-470-75626-3

FOR DUMMIES®

UK editions

SELF-HELP

978-0-470-74830-5

978-0-470-74764-3

978-0-470-74193-1

Neuro-linguistic Programming For Dummies
978-0-7645-7028-5

Origami Kit For Dummies
978-0-470-75857-1

Overcoming Depression For Dummies
978-0-470-69430-5

Positive Psychology For Dummies
978-0-470-72136-0

PRINCE2 For Dummies
978-0-470-51919-6

Psychometric Tests For Dummies
978-0-470-75366-8

Raising Happy Children
For Dummies
978-0-470-05978-4

Sage 50 Accounts For Dummies
978-0-470-71558-1

Starting a Business For Dummies, 2nd
Edition
978-0-470-51806-9

Study Skills For Dummies
978-0-470-74047-7

Teaching English as a Foreign
Language For Dummies
978-0-470-74576-2

Teaching Skills For Dummies
978-0-470-74084-2

Time Management For Dummies
978-0-470-77765-7

Understanding and Paying Less
Property Tax For Dummies
978-0-470-75872-4

Work-Life Balance For Dummies
978-0-470-71380-8

STUDENTS

978-0-470-74747-6

978-0-470-74711-7

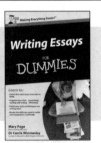

978-0-470-74290-7

HISTORY

978-0-470-99468-9

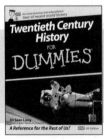

978-0-470-51015-5

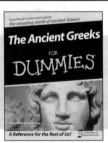

978-0-470-98787-2

13061 p2

FOR DUMMIES®

The easy way to get more done and have more fun

LANGUAGES

978-0-470-51986-8

978-0-7645-5193-2

978-0-471-77270-5

MUSIC

978-0-470-48133-2

978-0-470-03275-6
UK Edition

978-0-470-49644-2

SCIENCE & MATHS

978-0-7645-5326-4

978-0-7645-5430-8

978-0-7645-5325-7

Art For Dummies
978-0-7645-5104-8

Bass Guitar For Dummies, 2nd Edition
978-0-470-53961-3

Brain Games For Dummies
978-0-470-37378-1

Christianity For Dummies
978-0-7645-4482-8

Criminology For Dummies
978-0-470-39696-4

Forensics For Dummies
978-0-7645-5580-0

German For Dummies
978-0-7645-5195-6

Hobby Farming For Dummies
978-0-470-28172-7

Index Investing For Dummies
978-0-470-29406-2

Jewelry Making & Beading
For Dummies
978-0-7645-2571-1

Knitting For Dummies, 2nd Edition
978-0-470-28747-7

Music Composition For Dummies
978-0-470-22421-2

Physics For Dummies
978-0-7645-5433-9

Schizophrenia For Dummies
978-0-470-25927-6

Sex For Dummies, 3rd Edition
978-0-470-04523-7

Sherlock Holmes For Dummies
978-0-470-48444-9

Solar Power Your Home
For Dummies, 2nd Edition
978-0-470-59678-4

The Koran For Dummies
978-0-7645-5581-7

Wine All-in-One For Dummies
978-0-470-47626-0

FOR DUMMIES®

Helping you expand your horizons and achieve your potential

COMPUTER BASICS

978-0-470-57829-2

978-0-470-46542-4

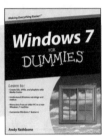

978-0-470-49743-2

DIGITAL PHOTOGRAPHY

978-0-470-25074-7

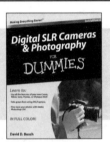

978-0-470-46606-3

978-0-470-45772-6

MAC BASICS

978-0-470-27817-8

978-0-470-46661-2

978-0-470-43543-4

Access 2007 For Dummies
978-0-470-04612-8

Adobe Creative Suite 4 Design
Premium All-in-One Desk Reference
For Dummies
978-0-470-33186-6

AutoCAD 2010 For Dummies
978-0-470-43345-4

C++ For Dummies, 6th Edition
978-0-470-31726-6

Computers For Seniors For Dummies ,
2nd Edition
978-0-470-53483-0

Dreamweaver CS4 For Dummies
978-0-470-34502-3

Excel 2007 All-In-One Desk Reference
For Dummies
978-0-470-03738-6

Green IT For Dummies
978-0-470-38688-0

Networking All-in-One Desk Reference
For Dummies, 3rd Edition
978-0-470-17915-4

Office 2007 All-in-One Desk Reference
For Dummies
978-0-471-78279-7

Photoshop CS4 For Dummies
978-0-470-32725-8

Photoshop Elements 7 For Dummies
978-0-470-39700-8

Search Engine Optimization
For Dummies, 3rd Edition
978-0-470-26270-2

The Internet For Dummies,
12th Edition
978-0-470-56095-2

Visual Studio 2008 All-In-One Desk
Reference For Dummies
978-0-470-19108-8

Web Analytics For Dummies
978-0-470-09824-0

Windows Vista For Dummies
978-0-471-75421-3

**Available wherever books are sold. For more information or to order direct go to www.wiley.com
or call +44 (0) 1243 843291**

13061 p4